Balanced Sourcing

BALANCED

A *Strategy & Business* Book
Booz·Allen & Hamilton

SOURCING

Cooperation and Competition in Supplier Relationships

Timothy M. Laseter

Foreword by William F. Stasior

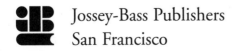
Jossey-Bass Publishers
San Francisco

Jossey-Bass books and products are available through most bookstores. To contact Jossey-Bass directly, call (888) 378–2537, fax to (800) 605–2665, or visit our website at www.josseybass.com.

Substantial discounts on bulk quantities of Jossey-Bass books are available to corporations, professional associations, and other organizations. For details and discount information, contact the special sales department at Jossey-Bass.

For sales outside the United States, please contact your local Simon & Schuster International Office.

 Manufactured in the United States of America on Lyons Falls Turin Book. This paper is acid-free and 100 percent totally chlorine-free.

Library of Congress Cataloging-in-Publication Data

Laseter, Timothy M.
Balanced sourcing : cooperation and competition in supplier relationships / Timothy M. Laseter ; foreword by William F. Stasior.
p.   cm. — (The Jossey-Bass business & management series)
(A Strategy & Business book)
Includes bibliographical references and index.
ISBN 0-7879-4443-2
1. Industrial procurement.   2. Strategic alliances (Business)
I. title.   II. Series.   III. Series: A Strategy & Business book.
HD39.5.L37   1998
658.7'2—dc21   98-29691

FIRST EDITION
HB Printing   10 9 8 7 6 5 4 3 2 1

The Jossey-Bass
Business & Management Series

For Jody, Josh, and Cecilia

Contents

Foreword

For most of this century, Booz·Allen & Hamilton has been working with the world's largest companies and the teams that lead them. Although this period of history has been as furious as it has been fruitful, the topics that now occupy the busy calendars of CEOs and their leadership groups have not changed much from two or more decades ago. Today, as in the past, business leaders are concerned with how to make their companies more competitive while keeping costs in line and competitors at bay. Business leaders today, as in the past, want to create shareholder value, gain market share, and extend their company's capabilities and reach. While the issues confronting today's leaders are the same as in the past, the context in which those issues must be addressed has changed.

Today's business context is more complex than the environment of the past. That is not to say that previous eras were easier than this one. Success in the past—just as now—has never been easy to achieve. But unlike before, businesses today are confronted with a higher level of complexity brought about by globalization, new technologies, rapidly shifting conditions in the marketplace, and competition arising from the most unexpected places. Entire industries—the minicomputer industry, for example—have come into being, reached their apex, and fallen into the abyss of decline in little more than a decade. Others, like the computer mainframe business, which was once almost written off, have come roaring back.

In some industries, focusing on a company's core capabilities and primary business interest is the route to renewed vigor and prolonged health. Other businesses require the ability to be continuously innovative. Some companies, to prosper and grow, have had to reinvent themselves completely. Monsanto, for example, shed itself of its decades-old chemical business to become a bioengineering concern, while Westinghouse, one of America's oldest companies, transformed itself from a company known mostly for its power-generating equipment, including nuclear powerplants, into a media company that renamed itself CBS.

To survive and prosper, some companies have formed linkages with their chief rivals while others have severed linkages with their closest friends. Seen one way, this has been a period of mergers, alliances, and outright acquisitions. Seen another, it has been a period of divestitures, uncouplings, and recouplings. Seen all ways, it has been an era of complexity.

Today's perennial problems, unlike yesterday's, require a host of new, highly individualized solutions. Since the level of complexity is so high, the ability to create cookie-cutter solutions is at an all-time low. As a result, what matters is the ability to analyze problems carefully, quickly, and creatively. What matters is solving problems in fresh and disciplined ways. What matters is the ability to think about a subject while keeping the market in mind. What matters most is creativity.

The aim of *Strategy & Business* books is not to tell business leaders what to think. That would be both presumptuous—even foolhardy—given the rapid rate of change, the diversity of companies' situations, and the personalities of today's business leaders. Rather, the aim is to tell business leaders what to think *about*. The difference between *what to think* and *what to think about* is the difference between a rigid list of thoughts dictated by some font of wisdom, and an agenda set out for discussion. In the current period, the ability to discuss, reason, and argue scenarios and points-of-view beats rigid dictation every time.

Over the last several years, Booz·Allen has spent a lot of time mulling over the corporate agenda. It has done so by interviewing leaders, surveying firms, reviewing its own assignments, and consulting with academics. The contents of this book series—and this book—reflect the contents of the business agenda.

What we have found in our research is that the big concerns over defining values and vision, managing people and risk, adapting to changed markets and new technology, and assessing performance and portfolio mix have only become more important as competition intensifies, the speed of computers multiplies, companies become more complex, and the economy becomes increasingly global.

At the same time, because of external pressures and changing management approaches, new ways of thinking about those concerns have swept through boardrooms and across factory floors with remarkable synchronicity. Some of these shifts reflect radically different orientations; others are wholly pragmatic in nature.

In our own work, we have recently seen the focus of the CEO agenda shift toward growing the top line rather than cutting costs and toward managing the new corporation instead of restructuring the old one. As we see it, three variations on these themes reflect the new agenda for CEOs and their top teams:

Managing for growth
Business process redesign, the next generation
The new organization

It seems clear what has caused CEOs to shift their focus. Many major companies, though not all, have completed the first wave of business process reengineering (BPR) and have thus achieved the first 80 percent or so of cost restructuring. They must now look to revenue growth for the next quantum leap in performance improvement. This situation puts managers in an expansive frame of mind that the rebound in corporate profits over the past several years undoubtedly reinforces.

At the same time, the wave of delayering, restructuring, and reengineering has left many companies in a twilight world between the old and the new. Traditional management processes have been discarded and dismantled; new ones are not always comfortably in place. Learning to manage in the post-restructured world has become a life-and-death priority, which has implications for the CEO's role in shaping a company's core capabilities and critical priorities and in determining which functions to outsource and which to leave in-house.

• *Emerging markets.* Even with Asia's current economic problems, most CEOs look to the emerging markets there and in Latin America (and to a much lesser and potentially myopic extent, eastern Europe) as the keys to future growth. On the one hand, there is the infrastructure boom ($1 trillion by 2000, according to some estimates); on the other, there is an almost infinite potential consumer market as more and more segments of these huge populations enter the market economy. Already, there are about 300 million "consumers" who can purchase power parity in the world's emerging markets. And that number represents only 10 percent or so of the total population of those areas.

• *New products and services.* The ability to sustain innovation in products and services is becoming a principal source of competitive advantage across a broad range of industries.

• *Acquisitions, mergers, alliances, and post-merger integration.* As balance sheets have improved, the number of corporate acquisitions has started to rebound dramatically. In fact, there is even evidence that part of the value liberated by recent acquisitions is being captured by the acquirer's shareholders and not just by those of the acquiree, which has overwhelmingly been the outcome historically. This trend is consistent with our observation that today's acquisitions appear to have a greater fit with the acquirers' core strategies and capabilities than was true in the past.

• *Strengthened "blocking and tackling."* Our clients are placing increased emphasis on the basics in their businesses: enhanced customer care; better marketing and sales force management; and improved, tactical pricing. Much of this change is overdue. Despite the claims of many analysts of BPR, recent rounds of reengineering and restructuring have left many of these basic processes weaker than before.

Relative emphasis among these growth channels necessarily varies. Our own analysis of one hundred companies with an above-average increase in shareholder wealth over the past two decades suggests that expansion in emerging markets is the greatest source of growth; break-out strategies that redefine the basis of competition in mature industries come second; and continuous product innovation and brand building come third. Acquisitions worked less well, with a few notable exceptions.

To capture differentiated growth, CEOs need to foster new and enhanced competencies and attitudes within their organizations. Innovation, for example, has long been viewed as being as much the product of lucky breaks as of a business capability that one can design, upgrade, and manage. As a result, many organizations avoid managing their innovation capability for fear of tampering with creative forces that they do not wholly understand. In fact, as companies such as the Chrysler Corporation and the Sony Corporation have shown, companies can design and manage innovation capability in a number of ways. These include strengthening the business processes associated with understanding markets, planning product lines, managing technology, and developing products or processes; improving measurement systems that track innovation; and developing systematic processes to capture and deploy organizational learning and best practices.

Similarly, to capture the full long-term potential of emerging markets, CEOs will have to move the center of gravity of their organizations, their managerial brain trusts, and their own mind-sets toward these markets—and there is a long way to go. Winning in emerging markets also requires a different type of decision-making process. The pace of change is so fast that traditional planning processes simply do not work. For example, markets that took a decade to develop in the United States and six years in Japan are evolving in less than two years in some parts of China.

What is needed is strategic entrepreneurship, a relatively clear view of long-term objectives, and a strong set of strategic boundaries that can be used to screen opportunities. CEOs also require a highly entrepreneurial approach to creating and exploiting opportunities and shifting between scenarios as they unfold.

Growth also brings uncertainty and more complexity, however, which has implications for how companies must think about risk management. Among the "perennials" on the CEO agenda, we have found that risk management is the issue demanding the most attention.

As CEOs think about growth, their time frames are lengthening. We love to ask clients to estimate their time horizon. Answers vary, depending on the near-term health of their businesses, but strategic focus has moved out to about seven years. On earlier occasions, eighteen months was not unusual. During the last couple of years, our firm has experienced a surge of engagements focused on modeling the relatively distant future and on leading management teams through strategic simulations or sophisticated war games for their industries.

Changing demographics, technology advances, and global shifts have far-reaching implications for competitive boundaries and patterns of demand in virtually every industry. CEOs increasingly view one of their core roles as stimulating their companies' perspectives on what the future will bring. The boldest among them will select a scenario and remold their businesses accordingly.

CEOs have long understood their role in building the corporate vision. Today, this focus is being complemented by a drive to establish and entrench clear corporate values. These are not simply a means to edify the spirit but are vehicles to communicate strategic focus and operating boundaries to all employees. This represents a shift from the focus of most strategists ten year ago.

The breakthrough implies a focus on both vision and communication. The entire organization must understand the company's strategic direction and feel empowered to reach that goal.

A related trend in organizations is renewed interest in the role of the corporate center or core. At a recent symposium at which Booz·Allen partners discussed the most important business issues on the agendas of the firm's clients, we discovered that thirteen of the twenty-five participating partners were working with major companies to retune and redefine the role of the corporate center.

To some degree, that reassessment relates to the need to change management processes to fit the post-restructured corporation. It is also driven by external, competitive pressures, however; the same market pressures that compelled companies to lower costs are forcing them to rethink the integrative logic of their business portfolios.

Much of the thinking in this field comes back to address which businesses belong in the corporate portfolio and how the parent can add value rather than subtract it, as is too frequently the case. In addition to the traditional debate over the most appropriate forms of strategic and financial performance systems, this wave of reexamination is focused on building truly global organizations (in many cases, with traditional "center" functions being distributed geographically), on conceiving and managing strategic alliances and other extended enterprise relationships, and on some of the "softer" forms of added value.

The latter include the inculcation of shared corporate values and identity and the capture and deployment of organizational learning and best practices. Increasingly, corporate added value is more a matter of applying intellectual capital than of sponsoring scale economies in unit costs.

We are also seeing greater top-level attention focused on managing through processes. The wave of restructuring, reengineering, and delayering demands different management approaches than those used in the past. Yet the new approaches have been slow to develop. In a recent analysis that we conducted of twenty-eight "post-reengineered" companies, we found that in most cases, the CEOs and their top management teams were continuing to manage essentially as before. They used the same decision, planning, and control processes and the same management information and reporting systems. Most recognized the disconnection but were uncertain about how to resolve it. The answer lies in taking the following actions:

- Reorienting top executives to manage and enable "processes" rather than organization units
- Explicit reengineering of the decision-making processes involving top management itself, with related changes in authority delegation and style
- Creating new performance management systems that complement the reengineered world and incorporate an ability to learn

In beginning to address these issues, CEOs are also beginning to take more seriously some of the concepts that they nominally embraced over the past several years. The horizontal organization, team-based management, the learning organization, empowerment, and similar concepts have had their place in the executive lexicon for several years. The body language of most CEOs continued to reinforce older, more hierarchical traditions, however. This is now beginning to change as CEOs gain a greater understanding of these ideas and become more sincere in their desire to practice them.

The final element of the new organization relates to the players themselves. Building the management team is always a CEO agenda item. Today, virtually all CEOs with whom we talk say that creating greater entrepreneurship and teamwork among their top one hundred managers is their Number 1 challenge.

There are several drivers behind this renewed focus on the top team. Above all, the pace and volume of change that most corporations face demand that the load be shared; the CEO cannot typically expect to shoulder it alone. Then, too, there is a need to rebuild the social contract between managers and the company. One consequence of restructuring and downsizing has been a unilateral revocation of implied loyalties.

CEOs are exploring various approaches to reengineering their teams, including explicit team-building exercises, adjustments to measurement and rewards systems, and experimentation with such devices as internal "venture funds" designed to stimulate entrepreneurship. We are also seeing a renewed focus on selection, including a willingness to reach outside the home team to enlist the best athletes.

As CEO agendas evolve, the natural question is whether the current focus is correct. In our view, the new agenda is properly directed. Nevertheless, it is almost certain that the next decade will see a sorting of winners from losers at least as significant as the one that occurred during the last two decades. Fewer than half of the Fortune 500 listed twenty years ago are still on the list today, and a fair number of the survivors owe their position to their leviathan scale rather than to stellar performance.

Companies that lost their position failed because they had insufficient insight into their customers' needs and the implications of technology and other trends. In addition, they allowed service bottlenecks and excess costs to accumulate in their delivery systems. As a result, overseas and greenfield competitors were able to outdeliver and undercut them.

In theory, the new CEO agenda will help business leaders avoid similar missteps in the future. It will do this in a number of ways: the concentration on growth and innovation implies improved customer understanding and strengthened value propositions; the second wave of BPR will improve value while keeping costs lean; and the new organization will focus on shared learning, continual improvement, and greater entrepreneurship. Overall, we observe a more concerted attempt by CEOs to understand and position their companies for the future.

In practice, of course, some companies and some CEOs will do better than others. That is the nature of competition. From our vantage point, though, it is clear that the winners will be those CEOs who can integrate the new agenda with their own clear vision while simplifying the execution challenge and inspiring their organizations to perform beyond all expectations.

New York, New York
July 1998

William F. Stasior
Chairman and Chief Executive
Booz·Allen & Hamilton

Preface

My greatest strength as a consultant is to be ignorant and to ask a few questions.
—PETER DRUCKER

During the last decade, chief executive officers in major corporations around the globe have recognized the strategic importance of managing outside purchases and supplier relationships. Thanks to the reputation that Booz·Allen & Hamilton has established among the world's leading corporations, I have been fortunate enough to work with many of them as they have struggled with these strategic issues. This book attempts to capture some of what I have learned in my ten years of consulting at Booz·Allen. Thanks to the foresight of my partners, I have had the opportunity to supplement this base of experience with extensive field research for the book.

Like Peter Drucker, I believe that a consultant's value derives not from having all the right answers but from asking the right questions. As a result, the content of this book reflects not only my own experience, but the synthesis of many experiences shared with me by executives and frontline professionals working in some of the best companies in the world. Those companies provided exposure to an incredibly wide range of industries—aerospace, automotive, building products, consumer goods, communications, electronics, industrial equipment, natural resources, and textiles—across the United States, Europe, Asia, and the Pacific.

Additionally, I have learned from interactions with my colleagues at Booz·Allen, from the most senior partner to the newest consultant. Of course, if I have failed to capture the full sense of the issues, the responsibility lies with me.

Contents

Because purchasing has become a strategic, cross-functional issue, this book is written for an executive audience. It consists of three sections. Section One, encompassing the first two chapters, describes a newly emerging model, which we at Booz·Allen & Hamilton have dubbed *Balanced Sourcing*. Chapter One describes the logic behind the new model and provides an overview of the organizational capabilities that allow a company to effectively balance a commitment to cooperative supplier relationships with an equally important commitment to competitive pricing in those relationships. Although many companies have evolved toward this new model through efforts led by the purchasing function, we argue that achieving rapid transformation requires commitment and leadership from the top. Chapter Two offers guidance to the executive on how to lead a successful transformation to Balanced Sourcing.

The second section, Chapters Three through Eight, addresses the six organizational capabilities for Balanced Sourcing. Each chapter highlights key concepts and principles but, more important, provides practical advice on how to deliver near-term results while building the capability. Accordingly, Section Two is more detailed than Section One but is still written for the generalist. This section draws heavily on examples from the automotive and electronics industries—partly because my own experience is skewed toward those industries, but more significantly because those industries have tended to lead others in innovative purchasing practices.

The third section, Chapters Nine through Twelve, demonstrates the broad applicability of Balanced Sourcing. These chapters provide case studies of companies that represent a wide range of industries, each of which faces a very different competitive environment. Each in its own way, however, has developed many of the key capabilities of the Balanced

Sourcing model. The breadth of these examples should convince individual readers that Balanced Sourcing can also apply in their own companies.

Acknowledgments

Finally, I would like to briefly acknowledge the many collaborators and supporters of this book. As I mentioned, the primary contribution to the book has been from the many clients who have engaged Booz·Allen to help them grapple with the strategic challenges of purchasing and organizational change. Client confidentiality prevents me from listing them by name, but you know who you are.

The direct collaborators from Booz·Allen are referenced in each chapter, but obviously many other colleagues have supported this effort indirectly through our joint client work over the years. Two additional people, not directly employed by Booz·Allen but a part of our "extended enterprise," deserve special mention. Joel Kurtzman, editor of *Strategy & Business,* created this book series along with Jossey-Bass, the publisher. He has provided valuable counsel both in our initial articles on this subject for the journal and in extending that base into the fully developed ideas presented in this book. Max Russell, of the Arc Group, joined me in most of the field interviews and invested many hours and several weekends in capturing the essence of the company case studies in the participants' own words. Further, his critical eye and friendly counsel improved the grammar, flow, and writing style of the entire book.

Most important, I would like to acknowledge the support of my family, not only in writing this book but in allowing me the freedom to pursue a career in consulting. The long hours and torturous travel schedules can wreak havoc on a traditional home life. But my wife, Jody, and my children, Joshua and Cecilia, have always been supportive and understanding, even after a delayed flight and a 2:00 A.M. arrival home. Though it is often hard to comprehend, my family recognize that working with the outstanding people of Booz·Allen on tough strategic issues for some of the best corporations in the world is worth the tradeoffs. I thank them for indulging me.

Charlottesville, Virginia   Timothy M. Laseter
July 1998

Balanced Sourcing

Section One

A New Model for Purchasing

A great wind is blowing, and that gives you either imagination
or a headache.
— CATHERINE THE GREAT

During the 1990s, purchasing has emerged as a business area worthy of
executive-level attention. With outside purchases of materials and services accounting for so much of a typical company's cost, the surprise
may be that it took so long for purchasing to reach the CEOs' agendas.
After all, as far back as 1982 Peter Drucker identified the opportunity:
"Nowhere in business is there greater potential for benefiting from . . .
interdependence than between customer firms and their suppliers. This
is the largest remaining frontier for gaining competitive advantage—
and nowhere has such a frontier been more neglected."[1]

Coincident with the increasing attention on purchasing, the trend
of reengineering business processes shifted attention to cross-functional
processes rather than traditional functional hierarchies. Accordingly, the
new attention paid to purchasing focuses on the process, not the function. Executives are now struggling to improve the purchasing process
to capture the maximum value from their external suppliers of materials and services.

1

Much of the current literature remains tactical and somewhat traditional in concept. The best examples suggest extending to the supply base the concepts of total quality control or lean production. Though generally valuable, such efforts fall short of providing a strategic perspective on how to revamp purchasing into a core business process.

The other category of advice extols the value of supplier partnerships but provides limited practical guidance other than the vague suggestion to build trusting relationships. Such advice can be dangerous: poorly thought-out supplier partnerships can be more detrimental than beneficial.

The first two chapters of this book provide an overview of a new model for balancing cooperation, the mantra of most current purchasing literature, with the more traditional model of pure competition. Dubbed *Balanced Sourcing,* the new model recognizes that effective purchasing requires a set of *organizational capabilities,* not simply a set of skills embedded in a single functional group. Suppliers touch key elements of virtually every business process, so purchasing must also be viewed from a broad process perspective.

Given the organization-wide implications of the Balanced Sourcing model and the criticality of the purchasing process, the first chapter presents an executive-level summary of the model and the organizational capabilities it requires. The second chapter provides guidance on how an executive can lead a transformation to the new model through changes in processes, organization, and the supporting infrastructure. In combination, these first two chapters provide a basic blueprint for executives who want to elevate purchasing to a truly strategic level within their organizations.

Chapter 1
The Emergence of Balanced Sourcing

Man's mind, stretched to a new idea, never goes back to its original
dimensions.
—OLIVER WENDELL HOLMES

Despite the rhetoric around supplier partnerships and the increasing
importance of a company's extended enterprise, few executives feel confident that they are getting maximum value from suppliers. Many worry
that efforts to rationalize the supply base and create long-term partnerships might ultimately come back to haunt them. In many cases, the
worriers are right.

On the other hand, a policy of reverting to traditional adversarial
relationships with suppliers appears obviously flawed: the Japanese have
long cited the value of supplier collaboration to their business success.
Furthermore, in industries where the power base has shifted up the supply chain, the idea of getting results through table-banging negotiations
seems laughable. Even the largest personal-computer manufacturers
must cooperate with Intel Corporation and Microsoft Corporation if
they expect to compete in the mainstream.

Booz·Allen & Hamilton, through research and client work, has
identified an emerging model for finding the right balance between cooperative relationships and a commitment to competitive pricing. The

model, which we have dubbed *Balanced Sourcing,* moves beyond the religion of trust that is so popular today without reverting to an adversarial approach. Unfortunately, Balanced Sourcing is difficult to achieve—far more so than any of the one-dimensional approaches also shown in Exhibit 1.1.

While he was at General Motors Corporation in the early 1990s, Ignatio Lopez set the benchmark for the "Darwinian rivalry" approach (lower right quadrant of Exhibit 1.1). Though he took the art of competitive quoting to new heights, his approach was one-dimensional, incorporating the techniques taught for over three decades by Chester Karass. Karass has trained hundreds of thousands of purchasing professionals and is best known for his airline magazine advertisements that stress: "In business, you don't get what you deserve, you get what you negotiate." Clearly, Darwinian rivalry and the decades-old negotiation techniques it applies epitomize the adversarial approach traditionally

Exhibit 1.1   Purchasing Approaches

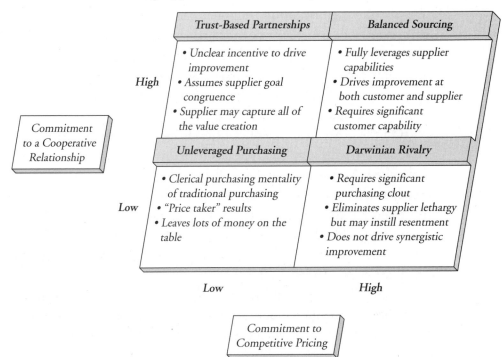

used by professional purchasers. And engaging in such rivalry, even if it requires the global reach and coordination that Lopez initiated, is not as difficult as a balanced approach.

Focusing on cooperation through "trust-based partnerships" (upper left quadrant) is even easier. Increasingly, presumably modern purchasing organizations are preaching the importance of maintaining trusting relationships with suppliers. They ask senior managers to have faith, because the benefits are qualitative and the results will come only in the long run. Avoiding being put on the hook for near-term results has real appeal, and cooperating with suppliers, in fact, comes naturally for many buyers. Though others lambaste them for being overly price-focused, the reality is that most buyers worry more about the prospect of shutting down an internal plant as a result of supplier delivery or quality problems than about the reality of absorbing a higher price from a supplier.

Fortunately, few large companies are operating with "unleveraged purchasing" (lower left corner of Exhibit 1.1). This quadrant reflects the old days when buyers were clerks or expediters relegated to processing purchase orders. In this quadrant no real attempts are made to leverage purchasing processes and supplier capabilities. Unfortunately, people in many organizations still view buyers as clerks who spend their careers shuffling paper. Accordingly, many people question whether the purchasing function is adequately equipped to lead a transformation of the entire organization to a new model. In most cases, these doubters are right.

Organizational Capabilities for Balanced Sourcing

Balanced Sourcing (upper right quadrant of Exhibit 1.1) requires a broad, organization-wide perspective on purchasing and is far more difficult to achieve than any other model. Leading practitioners demonstrate that the key to Balanced Sourcing is not a set of *purchasing skills,* but a broader set of six *organizational capabilities.* As indicated in Exhibit 1.2, Booz·Allen's field research has demonstrated that some capabilities appear universally applicable in any industry, while others are only critical for certain companies or industries. In fact, no single company has fully developed all six capabilities; the very best performer in one of the capabilities may be only average in another.

Exhibit 1.2   Organizational Capabilities for Balanced Sourcing

Universal Capabilities	*Differential Capabilities*
• Modeling total cost	• Integrating the supply web
• Creating sourcing strategies	• Leveraging supplier innovation
• Building and sustaining relationships	• Evolving a global supply base

The first three capabilities are the core processes for defining and developing the supply base; as such, they are universally applicable to any type of company. The first, *modeling total cost,* provides the underpinnings for the entire purchasing process. *Creating sourcing strategies* drives the critical shift from a tactical purchasing perspective to a strategic one. *Building and sustaining supplier relationships* focuses on the cooperative dimension of the Balanced Sourcing model.

The second three capabilities highlight different ways to leverage the supply base for competitive advantage. Most companies tend to focus on one of these three at most; only the largest and most sophisticated can afford to build superior capabilities in all three areas. *Integrating the supply web* ensures rapid delivery of goods and services with minimal waste and has received the most attention over the past decade. However, many companies, particularly those producing highly engineered products, are now focusing on *leveraging supplier innovation.* Finally, as companies increasingly compete in a global marketplace, they are *evolving a global supply base* to support their worldwide needs.

The remainder of this chapter describes the six capabilities and explains why they are important to Balanced Sourcing, using examples from a wide variety of leading companies to illustrate the points.

Modeling Total Cost

Understanding the economics and the cost drivers of purchased items and services through cost modeling is the most fundamental capability. It provides focus to cooperative efforts and ensures that prices reflect underlying economics. For example, over the years McDonald's Corporation has worked with suppliers to develop a sophisticated model for optimizing the cost of chicken. The model captures expected mortality rates and weight gains to determine the optimal breed mix under various conditions such as humidity and space allocation. Also, by modeling how feed mix affects weight gain and mortality, suppliers are able to adjust feeding programs to optimize chicken weight gain in response to changing feed prices.

Such cost models are merely the output of a sophisticated modeling capability; the knowledge developed through cost modeling produces the real value. Take the case of Honda of America. As Honda invested in manufacturing and engineering expertise in Marysville, Ohio, the purchasing function systematically built its cost-modeling capability by creating a central group called Cost Research. Over the years, buyers have rotated into the department and back out to direct-buying positions. By doing so, the cost research function tapped the buyers' specific commodity knowledge and in return taught the buyers Honda's cost table methodology. Now, a department that initially employed twenty to thirty people is down to half a dozen, because the capability is deployed throughout the purchasing organization. Furthermore, Honda's buyers have also rotated out into other parts of the business, spreading their knowledge of cost drivers across the organization.

Cost modeling need not be complicated. In fact, Sara Lee Corporation's experience has shown that simple models that can be developed in about a week offer the right level of sophistication initially. Unduly complicated models are less transferable to the business units, and unless usable tools get into the hands of the businesses, they are unlikely to have much impact.

Without a clear understanding of costs, supplier partnerships, at best, will not focus on the largest opportunities for cooperative value creation. At worst, a customer who does not understand total costs may choose the wrong suppliers—and leave money on the table.

Creating Sourcing Strategies

A sourcing strategy is analogous to a business strategy. Done well, both present a compelling case for creating a competitive advantage that will deliver superior returns. Clearly, an executive would dismiss a proposition to invest in the Internet if the only justification was that "everyone else is doing it." Unfortunately, many organizations approach sourcing strategies with little more than a plan to "rationalize the supply base" and "form long-term supplier partnerships."

Just like a business plan, a well-done sourcing strategy reflects a deep understanding of industry economics and dynamics and, by quantifying the potential returns, presents a compelling case for investment. Good business plans and commodity plans also tap into a broad range of expertise to capture the best thinking and build buy-in.

Whirlpool Corporation prepares commodity business plans, using multifunctional commodity business teams (CBTs). The plans follow a standard outline that includes both internally oriented perspectives, such as the current business issues in each of five regions, and documentation of Whirlpool's global spend, including internal acquisition costs. The plans also document the external environment with an overview of the supply base, an examination of global demand and market share, and an assessment of competitors and their sourcing patterns.

The specific recommendations of the CBTs go beyond supplier selection and incorporate input from commodity value teams (CVTs) that are charged with continuous improvement of cost in a specific area of the buy. For example, the CVTs—which consist of a full-time design engineer, a quality engineer, and one or two buyers—provide input to the plan through technology road maps for the commodity. The CVTs also help to implement the nonsourcing recommendations in the business plans.

A formal structure with dedicated multifunctional teams is only one approach to creating sourcing strategies. Balanced Sourcing requires effective organizational capabilities; the purchasing function need not be the primary driver behind every activity. For example, Florida Power & Light Company uses teams to develop sourcing strategies in a variety of ways. The Power Transformers Commodity Team, which saved over $6 million, operated under the guidance of a Procurement Strategy Board. Other teams have been just as successful under the umbrella of Florida Power & Light's total quality management process. One quality improvement team reduced the cost of in-house repair and maintenance of lift trucks by 56 percent by standardizing to fewer suppliers of more reliable equipment and redefining supplier responsibility for maintaining equipment.

Companies don't have to form special teams to develop commodity strategies either. Some companies embed the process in their organizational structure. At Chrysler Corporation, "platform teams" focused on a single classification of vehicles, like minivans, have become the dominant organizational form. These cross-functional teams possess the full mix of resources needed to design, develop, and continually refresh Chrysler's portfolio of car models. Since most of Chrysler's purchasing resources are deployed into the platform teams, development of effective sourcing strategies requires coordination across the teams. Rather than creating a unique, complicated structure or process, purchasing leverages the Tech Clubs that have formed throughout the company.

The Tech Clubs began as informal meetings among engineers from different platform teams that shared a common system focus, such as windshield wiper systems. Senior management has encouraged the formation of the clubs to share best practices and ensure that the platform teams don't turn into new functional silos. Purchasing has followed suit by joining the clubs and then using them to develop sourcing strategies. The clubs, already focused on technology trends, often discuss specific supplier capabilities. Purchasing simply pushes the clubs a bit further to develop the commodity strategy and implementation plans across platforms.

IBM Corporation develops sourcing strategies on an almost continuous basis, rather than as an annual planning process or in response to specific problems. Given the rapid pace of change in the industry, the company is constantly on the alert for changes in technology as well as changes in cost and capacity.

The emphasis on cost and capacity highlights the unique challenges of the electronics industry. Wafer fabrication for integrated circuits, for example, is an extremely capital-intensive business with a constantly improving process technology. New investment in a state-of-the-art wafer fabrication facility can easily exceed $2 billion. As a result, new supplier capacity generally equates to lower cost. Furthermore, the short product life cycles of the industry can cause a manufacturer to miss an entire wave of demand if the supply base cannot support sales. IBM applies such thinking in examining commodity families: it maps suppliers on a matrix to highlight both emerging technology and planned capacity investments in order to predict which suppliers will become the next industry leaders.

As these examples indicate, different organizations apply different approaches—and focus on different issues—in creating sourcing strategies. However, two main factors distinguish the best firms from the rest. Leading companies demand multifunctional involvement to ensure a broad perspective and buy-in. The best companies also display a depth of analytic rigor. Their plans reflect a level of understanding that often exceeds the suppliers'. Furthermore, they present a clear, well-supported case for building a competitive advantage through sourcing—not a simple list of "silver-bullet" solutions extracted from reading the current literature.

Building and Sustaining Relationships

How a company approaches the challenge of building and sustaining supplier relationships sets the tone for long-term cooperation. Setting improvement targets, structuring incentives, and investing in supplier development all play a role in finding the right balance. An overly soft approach without aggressive targets leads to stagnation in the supply base as well as to trust-based partnerships that don't deliver results. Targets that appear unreasonable or indicate a lack of concern for supplier profitability can leave suppliers in a Darwinian rivalry.

The difficulty of equitably sharing the benefits of collaboration is one of the main obstacles in building and sustaining supplier relationships. SUPERVALU Inc., one of the country's largest food distributors, has eliminated that potential point of conflict with its "dead net sell" pricing to retail grocer customers. Previously, SUPERVALU derived most of its profits by anticipatory buying, a common practice among most wholesalers. For example, wholesalers would buy products from suppliers when prices were low and then resell them later at a higher price, or they would simply retain for themselves the cash discounts suppliers offered as part of their gross profit. Now, SUPERVALU customers are beginning to understand what the products actually cost and pay only a markup that reflects the direct value-added services SUPERVALU provides as the middleman. Consequently, supplier cooperation has increased, because all price reductions are passed along to the retail grocer—a mutual benefit to SUPERVALU, its suppliers, and the retailers.

Chrysler's SCORE (Supplier COst REduction) program is another example of building balanced supplier relationships. Each year, suppliers are challenged to submit cost savings ideas worth 5 percent of their annual sales to Chrysler. In 1994, a third of Chrysler's suppliers chose not to participate in this voluntary program, but by 1996 over 90 percent were involved—and 26 percent of them had met or exceeded the goal. As a result, Chrysler reported savings ideas worth $1.23 billion in 1997—$320 million of which hit the bottom line that year.

Though other companies have supplier suggestion programs, few can claim the level of results achieved by Chrysler. The difference with SCORE is that the reductions must be based on removing *cost,* not simply reducing margins. Furthermore, Chrysler only requires suppliers to pass on 50 percent of the savings from any particular improvement (though suppliers sometimes pass on more). The program builds a balanced relationship with suppliers by using aggressive targets while focusing on win-win opportunities and jointly managing the implementation.

Supplier development can be another element in building and sustaining supplier relationships. For example, Honda of America's purchasing philosophy embodies a commitment to supplier development. One example of that philosophy in action has become a piece of Honda folklore. In the early 1990s, Honda discovered that one of its long-term suppliers was having tremendous quality problems. Honda concluded that the supplier—a small independent—had simply expanded beyond its organizational limits in trying to support Honda's growth.

Rather than drop the supplier and switch to a more sophisticated one that could meet Honda's needs with no problems, purchasing deployed four people to help the troubled supplier. The Honda team rented apartments, moved into the factory, and spent the next ten months helping the supplier develop the business practices necessary to support its expanded size. The supplier now has the ability to support

Honda over the long term. Although Honda did not charge the supplier for the extensive help, Dave Nelson, then Senior Vice President, Administration and Purchasing, noted that it was not an act of charity, but an investment to keep Honda's plants running.

Such a paternal approach may not be applicable in all circumstances. For example, IBM expends few resources on supplier development because a few giant suppliers dominate the global electronics market, each quite capable of self-development. Though supplier start-ups are common, most suppliers have to fend for themselves, because no one customer wants to invest the resources to develop a supplier that also sells to competitors. (Exclusivity is rarely appropriate given the industry's desire for standardization.) IBM's primary relationship challenge is to deal with the same company—for example Toshiba—in a variety of roles: competitor, customer, supplier, and even joint venture partner.

Although the specific methods of relationship building vary across companies, a few common themes stand out. First, trust is an inadequate basis for a relationship, but a lack of trust will surely prevent the type of collaboration that produces an advantage. Effective relationships are built on goal congruence, mutual dependence, and knowledge of the supplier's competency and are sustained through extensive two-way communications about performance expectations.

For example, most companies assess the performance of the supply base, but Sara Lee also allows the suppliers to assess Sara Lee as a customer. Its Supplier Perception Survey, conducted each summer by interns in corporate purchasing, examines suppliers' views on Sara Lee's quality philosophy, approach to purchasing agreements, delivery and inventory methods, commitment to the relationship, and willingness to buy based on value rather than cost.

The single greatest challenge remains finding ways to share value creation appropriately between customer and supplier. Businesses have a responsibility to maximize returns for their own shareholders, and they rightfully strive to capture as much of the value as possible. The solution is to create value for all parties by continuously increasing the size of the future pie, which reduces the pressure to fight over ways to divide the current one.

The second three capabilities focus on different "recipes" for making the value pie even larger.

Integrating the Supply Web

Businesses clearly recognize that the roles their suppliers play in delivering goods to consumers have always been critical to success. The process of making sure that sales forecasts, production plans, and inventory targets are in alignment has traditionally been called *supply chain management.*

Many companies today, however, can easily identify a supplier that functions simultaneously as a customer, a competitor, or possibly even a joint venture collaborator. And as companies' relationships with such suppliers grow even more sophisticated and complex, they will certainly begin to appear much more web-like than chain-like. Managing the flow of goods among companies in such a complex network becomes all the more critical because the cost of an inefficient supply web can be dramatic.

Most companies focus their attention on better integration of the supply web on a day-to-day basis. Many continue to sustain a competitive advantage by shortening lead times and reducing waste in the delivery activities. For example, the heart of SUPERVALU's supplier strategy has been to optimize the shared distribution network with its suppliers and to ensure that pricing reflects the true cost of different channels. The process began with sophisticated modeling of the suppliers' and SUPERVALU's distribution costs to determine the optimal approach. SUPERVALU, however, continues to invest in upgrading its distribution capability and, accordingly, in changing the optimal tradeoffs.

Chrysler considers the supply function to be so critical to effective purchasing that it has considered eliminating the term *procurement* and replacing it with *supply management.* The procurement and supply function, which includes production schedulers, logistics professionals, and even plant forklift operators, manages the flow of materials from the suppliers through the plants all the way to the dealers. Chrysler extends its view beyond direct suppliers as well, explicitly mapping the entire supply network supporting a tier-one supplier as a critical step in identifying opportunities for improvement.

McDonald's tightly manages its chicken supply web from hatchery to processor and into the restaurants. McDonald's explicitly orders hatcheries to place eggs in anticipation of the sales forecast for chicken products. Product movement through the supply base is so well orchestrated that a supplier can confidently place the eggs in the hatcheries seventy-five days before McDonald's expects to sell the chickens as McNuggets.

Though opportunities for improvement through integrating the supply web have been a focal point for many years, they are far from tapped out. The combination of electronic information exchange, flexible manufacturing, and express air delivery is redefining product distribution in industry after industry. Music is delivered over the Internet while blue jeans are custom-fitted with computer-aided design and manufacturing—all to meet the consumer's seemingly insatiable desire for instant gratification.

Leveraging Supplier Innovation

Companies employ a variety of techniques to manage technology development with suppliers. Setting aggressive but valid supplier cost targets (price-based, cost-based, or value-based), for example, drives cost improvement without ruining a cooperative relationship. Obviously, this capability is most critical for companies that sell highly engineered products, but it can be applied in many more settings than is often assumed.

Chrysler's platform teams rely heavily on suppliers in the product development process. Chrysler President Tom Stallkamp uses a motion picture industry analogy to explain his vision. In the 1920s and 1930s, motion picture companies "owned" everything: actors, theaters, movie sets, and so on. Today, a complex extended enterprise of specialists collaborate to create and distribute a motion picture. Chrysler doesn't want to own the extended enterprise, but it believes in managing it. In one case, Chrysler's supply web map highlighted that its three brake suppliers used fifty-two different fasteners, while the rest of Chrysler only had seventy-four. Chrysler actively engaged suppliers to eliminate such low value complexity and drive out the cost.

IBM also relies heavily on purchasing to help manage technology development with its suppliers. IBM's Technology & Qualification group is made up of more than sixty technically oriented staff members who report to the chief procurement officer. Collocated with product development teams, these technologists are linked with IBM's worldwide commodity councils, connecting the company's long-term technology needs with its commercial requirements.

Motorola uses another technique for leveraging supplier technology. Its annual technical symposium, held in a mammoth tent in a company parking lot, typically attracts around 180 suppliers, who use the event to introduce emerging technology to Motorola's engineering and sourcing staff. Motorola also combines total-cost modeling and information sharing to drive supplier technology efforts. For example, battery suppliers currently receive end-consumer warranty data to focus improvement efforts.

Florida Power & Light, which does not sell engineered products, is nonetheless developing the capability to produce them. The company's combustion turbines commodity manager describes his job as reducing the "dollars per service hour" for turbines. A current project involves developing new replacement parts rather than continuing to buy from the original equipment manufacturer. To accomplish this, Florida Power & Light has developed a small extended enterprise that includes an independent team of designers recently retired from a large jet engine producer and a small specialty manufacturer to machine the parts. Even with a significant investment in development costs, the new parts will represent a substantial savings over the high-priced aftermarket parts from the original equipment manufacturer.

In the last few years many companies, shifting their attention from cost reduction to growth, have begun to enhance their ability to innovate. Tapping the broader expertise of a company's extended enterprise by leveraging supplier innovation can increase the applied brainpower exponentially. Companies that do it well have an opportunity to build a sustainable competitive advantage.

Evolving a Global Supply Base

Expansion of the supply base outside of a home market may be prompted by a desire to find low-cost suppliers or to support global expansion of the company's operations. Whatever the motivation, facing the challenges of local content, currency exposure, and cross-cultural communication requires a substantial upgrade in capabilities for most organizations.

Whirlpool has pursued aggressive global expansion for more than a decade along four dimensions: operations, organizational structure, product design, and supply base. The first efforts focused on expanding the operation's footprint with joint ventures outside the United States, particularly in developing regions. Simultaneously, Whirlpool set up an international procurement organization to manage foreign sourcing. Initial successes came from tapping low-cost suppliers in developing areas like Mexico and Eastern Europe to manufacture material for import to major plants in more developed regions. This globalization has accelerated significantly as Whirlpool has launched global product design.

Key suppliers in developed regions have also supported globalization. Some of Whirlpool's largest domestic suppliers followed the company into China and India. Having experienced, capable suppliers in each country allowed Whirlpool to outsource inefficient internal operations. To build on such key relationships, Whirlpool instituted formal strategic partnership discussions to cover global, multicomponent relationship challenges.

Honda Motor Company operates a global company through four regional organizations. A key purchasing philosophy is "Make where you sell and buy where you make." Therefore, Honda of America, which is recognized by most purchasing executives as having one of the best purchasing groups in the United States, does very little global sourcing. Instead of shopping worldwide for low-cost suppliers, Honda of America focuses on developing and nurturing its American supply base.

By contrast, IBM's purchasing organization views global sourcing as a critical capability. IBM employs 150 procurement people worldwide who don't buy anything. They provide research for global commodity management by gathering industry intelligence, preparing competitive evaluations, conducting market analysis, and lending logistics support. Given the importance of the Asian supply base to electronics, the majority—but not all—of these resources are based in Asia.

For some, global expansion presents even more challenges. McDonald's often brings key suppliers along to support expansion into new regions. In doing so, McDonald's works with the supplier to define the risk-and-reward model on a project-by-project basis and in some cases underwrites the risk for the supplier in opening an operation in a new country. At other times, when the supplier has adequate resources, McDonald's may determine that the project bears normal commercial risk for the supplier and will offer no protection.

Since local regulations and customs vary dramatically, Motorola depends on regional organizations to take the lead in most issues. A local organization has a better chance of gaining short-term relief from the local government if targets are not being met. In one example, Motorola negotiated government funding for supplier training and development when local supplier capabilities were lacking. Furthermore, when Motorola has manufactured outside of its home market, it has found that for most commodities, local suppliers are preferred because global companies lack the responsiveness to help fix the day-to-day problems at the local factory.

As Thomas Jefferson noted, "Merchants have no country." And so a global supply base evolves over time, as sales expand in a particular region or exchange and wage rates become noncompetitive in another. Managing such an evolution requires constant, worldwide vigilance and a broad-based organizational capability to capture and synthesize the trends and respond proactively. Few organizations have fully developed such a capability, but truly global firms are clearly striving toward that end.

Conclusion

Balancing competition and cooperation appeals to most executives but appears inherently difficult. Conventional wisdom recommends building trusting relationships with suppliers, though most executives can't help but agree with Agatha Christie's admonition, "Where large sums of money are concerned, trust nobody."

Balanced Sourcing addresses the executive concern by applying a set of basic principles:

- Fact-based decision making
- Long-term, strategic thinking
- Adaptable solutions, not silver bullets
- Collaborative value creation and sharing
- Pragmatic execution

The challenge isn't to understand the capabilities or the principles. Building the capabilities across an organization is the difficult task. Much like the cooperation-competition matrix shown in Exhibit 1.1, the six organizational capabilities are intuitively appealing and rather straightforward in concept. However, Booz·Allen's field research underscores the fact that even the best firms do not feel that they have fully developed all of the capabilities.

The next chapter provides executive-level overview and guidance on driving an organizational transformation to Balanced Sourcing.

Chapter 2
Transforming the Organization

> There is nothing more difficult to take in hand, more perilous to
> conduct, or more uncertain in its success than to take the lead in
> the introduction of a new order of things.
> —JEAN-JACQUES ROUSSEAU

Transforming an organization to the Balanced Sourcing model requires
leadership from the top. Suppliers interact across virtually every facet
of a business, and the capability to balance supplier relationships successfully spans the organization. Without senior support, the already
difficult task of finding the appropriate balance will fail, as the efforts
in one area contradict the efforts in another.

The Imperative of Change

Adopting the new model requires widespread change—in processes,
the organization, and even the supporting infrastructure. First, the
focus of purchasing processes must shift from transactions to strategic

Note: This chapter was developed in collaboration with Chris Shephard of Booz·Allen's Cleveland, Ohio, office and Suzanne Mancus of Booz·Allen's McLean, Virginia, office.

management. Next, organizational changes to upgrade and elevate the purchasing function help to reinforce the shift. Finally, investment in information technology provides the necessary tools to support the new corporation-wide, strategic point of view required for Balanced Sourcing.

Impact on Business Processes

A business consists of three primary processes: innovation, delivery, and control. The innovation stream identifies new ideas and converts them into competitively advantaged products and services, while the delivery stream focuses on consistent execution of the defined products and services. Control includes the activities involved in managing the business to ensure profitability. Suppliers are involved in all three processes, and purchasing activities can be found in each. Unfortunately, in many organizations purchasing activities operate at a predominantly transactional level. Balanced Sourcing demands a broad, long-term view, so the purchasing processes must be elevated from transactional to strategic management.

For example, the traditional quotation process—often referred to as "three quotes in a cloud of dust"—changes dramatically. A request for quote (RFQ) no longer simply asks for prices for a part. Instead, an RFQ may become a "request for information" to capture an understanding of the cost-competitiveness of a new supplier facility. Alternatively, the request may be for the supplier's estimate of activity levels for a particular part—such as the number of strikes required for a stamping—for use in a cost model that already documents world-class cost standards.

Supplier selection provides another example. Although sourcing decisions may still be made on a program-by-program basis, the process becomes more strategic under Balanced Sourcing. A well-defined sourcing strategy provides clear focus and possibly a shortlist of qualified suppliers. Furthermore, targets are provided to the supplier that reflect a detailed understanding of cost and market dynamics.

Also, rather than expediting parts—a major time sink in a traditional organization—Balanced Sourcing addresses the root cause by building the organizational capability to integrate the supply web. Will all expediting be eliminated in a company employing Balanced Sourcing? Of course not. But the allocation of time will shift dramatically away from fire-fighting activities like expediting to strategic activities that build and extend organizational capabilities. Results from a cross-industry survey sponsored by *Strategy & Business* capture the magnitude of change expected.[1] (See Exhibit 2.1.)

Exhibit 2.1   Purchasing Function Time Allocation

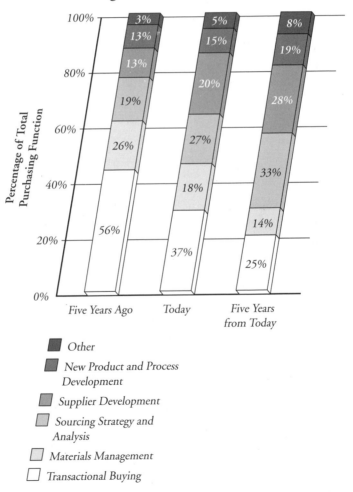

Source: Strategy & Business survey.

Changing Organizational Requirements

Such dramatic shifts in purchasing activities demand very different skills from those traditionally expected in purchasing staff. Employing staff with the requisite training in strategic thinking, like MBAs, may be the fastest way to make the shift, but it isn't the only way. In fact, a survey of purchasing practices conducted by Booz·Allen found no correlation between the educational mix of the purchasing function and the results achieved. Performance variation was explained by the practices employed; educational mix was simply a function of the industry.

IBM employs a number of techniques to raise the skill set in the purchasing function. First, it has aggressively hired outsiders from leading companies to infuse new approaches. It also invests in existing staff through its "shadow executive" program, which assigns high-potential middle managers to shadow senior executives for three or four months to broaden their exposure to the critical strategic issues of the business. Finally, IBM has recently instituted a management development program that rotates new MBAs through a variety of business units and purchasing functions over a two-year period before placing them in permanent positions.

Since Balanced Sourcing requires change across the organization, the purchasing function is not the only area affected. For example, one of Balanced Sourcing's six critical capabilities—leveraging supplier innovation—redefines how product development works and accordingly redefines the role of the design engineer. Instead of developing a detailed knowledge of a particular part or component, designers need a systems engineering mindset to concentrate on the interfaces among systems. Suppliers take responsibility for addressing the details, such as part tolerances, and often work from broad performance specifications.

In many companies the impetus for the shift to Balanced Sourcing has come from the purchasing function, with the support of senior management. Honda of America, for one, places a heavy emphasis on the impact that individuals can have. Honda locates "purchasing alumni" in other functions within the company to create widely placed purchasing disciples. Honda also tracks and regularly communicates with alumni who have moved to other companies and industries in order to stay in touch with advancements elsewhere—and possibly to recruit the former employees back when it is appropriate and advantageous.

Role of Information Technology

Companies all over the world are installing enterprise resource planning (ERP) systems to link purchasing transactions with other enterprise systems such as manufacturing, financial, and resource planning. Often potential purchasing savings are used to justify the multimillion-dollar investments. A recent *Strategy & Business* survey of Fortune 1000 companies found that only 3 percent of the respondents had fully implemented an ERP system, but another 70 percent were in the process of installing one or were at least planning to do so.

Although an ERP system certainly enables a shift to Balanced Sourcing, such systems are not a prerequisite for most companies. An ERP system streamlines transaction processing, freeing up time for strategic thinking, and it also improves the quality of data for planning purposes. However, ERP is still predominantly focused on transactional, not strategic, management.

Booz·Allen's client experience and research suggest that four types of information technology (IT) applications support the evolution to Balanced Sourcing:

1. Transactional management systems
2. Electronic commerce
3. Purchasing information management
4. Decision support tools

Transactional management systems streamline transactions through the use of integrated software solutions and standardized policies and procedures. Transactional management is at the core of ERP systems. However, the predefined procedures mandated by such software may not always match a particular company's processes, forcing the company to extensively modify the system or its practices. As a result, new transactional systems may not be the optimal solution, since current systems can usually manage the transactional details with some simple upgrades.

But as common transactional systems or interface standards such as SAP or the Internet become widely deployed, they enable *electronic commerce,* the second type of IT application that supports Balanced Sourcing. Electronic commerce streamlines transactional management across the extended enterprise to issue purchase orders, track material flows, and transfer funds. Until the advent of the Internet, extensive implementation of electronic commerce was limited to industries with a highly concentrated customer and supply base where common technology standards could more easily be applied. For example, according to a study by the Center for Advanced Purchasing Studies at Arizona State University, the automotive industry processes nearly 80 percent of its purchase dollars through electronic commerce, while the appliance industry processes less than 2 percent.

Purchasing information management, the third IT application that supports Balanced Sourcing, encompasses the data warehousing of purchasing information as well as the procedures for gathering and maintaining the data. Key information includes internally generated data, such as historical trends of purchases summarized from the transactional systems, and supplier performance metrics covering material quality and delivery reliability. Increasingly—again thanks to the Internet—purchasing information management now includes externally derived data, such as economic indicators reported by government agencies or capacity figures reported by supplier industry associations.

Leading companies are demonstrating that *decision support tools,* the fourth category of IT applications, generate the greatest returns from IT investments. These analytic tools convert data into useful information and, in the hands of a skilled analyst, convert information into knowledge. According to Joe Sandor, Director of Corporate Purchasing & Logistics for Sara Lee, Sara Lee has "avoided building major transactional systems." With its fairly diverse mix of premium, branded consumer goods businesses, Sara Lee has focused its IT investments to support cost modeling of standard materials, such as corrugated cartons, flexible film, and industrial-use carbon dioxide. But the real investment is in knowledge, not hardware and software. Sara Lee views IT simply as an important enabler.

Pragmatic Steps for Driving the Change

To date, most of the movement toward Balanced Sourcing has been driven by charismatic purchasing executives. These executives have captured the imagination of their direct reports, as well as that of the rest of the organization, to force recognition of the fact that effective purchasing is critical to corporate success.

Though he did not practice Balanced Sourcing, Ignatio Lopez clearly stimulated an organizational transformation at General Motors in the early 1990s. His "purchasing warriors" wore watches on their right wrist and adopted a host of other practices that indicated their membership in an elite function that had previously been viewed as an organizational backwater. Over the course of two years, Lopez and his warriors added a desperately needed billion dollars to General Motors' bottom line.

Lopez's antics—and results—put him on the front page of the *Wall Street Journal* and put purchasing on the agenda of all car company CEOs. Since then, dynamic leaders have emerged at other vehicle manufacturers to drive an industry-wide shift in the role of purchasing. The trend quickly spread beyond automobile manufacturers to high-technology companies and is still expanding across a wide variety of industries and companies.

Although successful transformations are under way across a wide range of companies, in our view, purchasing-led change programs are unlikely to be adequate. The organizational capabilities and the necessary ingredients for transformation are simply too rare at most companies unless the CEO takes a visible role in driving the change. Booz·Allen's experience and research on current change efforts suggest four actions that a CEO should take to trigger a transformation to Balanced Sourcing:

1. Upgrade the skills and visibility of the purchasing function.
2. Set aggressive near-term and long-term improvement goals.
3. Launch pilot efforts to demonstrate that the goals are achievable.
4. Make selective investments in IT.

The following sections expand on each of these actions and illustrate the lessons learned with a variety of case examples.

Upgrade the Purchasing Function

The CEO is uniquely positioned to start the transformation by ensuring that the purchasing function has the appropriate leadership. For example, IBM hired Gene Richter as its Chief Procurement Officer to drive its transformation in purchasing. Richter draws upon his extensive experience beginning with Ford Motor Company, followed by Black & Decker Corporation and then Hewlett-Packard Company—all leading-edge companies with extensive organizational capabilities for Balanced Sourcing.

In cases where the required expertise already resides internally, the CEO may want to signal the strategic role of purchasing by elevating the status of the purchasing function in the company. In the early 1990s, Ford signaled the increasing importance of purchasing as part of its global reorganization. Carlos Mazzorin, the new Vice President of Purchasing, was charged with responsibility for all of Ford's production and indirect purchases worldwide. He reported directly to the company president, as did the vice presidents of the five vehicle centers, which are the heart of any car company.

A recent trend, seen at Honda and Chrysler, has been the expansion of the responsibilities and upward mobility of the purchasing executive. Dave Nelson's title at Honda of America—Executive Vice President, Purchasing and Administrative Services—reflected the expanding role of purchasing, as did his position as the only American on the four-member management board for Honda of America. Recently, after ten years at Honda, Nelson was recruited by Deere & Company to extend its purchasing capabilities. When Tom Stallkamp headed purchasing for Chrysler he wore two hats, like other Chrysler senior executives. At that time he was also General Manager of Minivan Operations in addition to his purchasing role. In the fall of 1997, Stallkamp became President of Chrysler.

Of course, one person alone cannot drive change organization-wide. But with the right leadership and visibility, the purchasing executive can attract others to the task. Many high-performing individuals from other functions typically see the opportunities—and challenges—afforded by Balanced Sourcing and jump at the chance to be part of the transformation. Equally important, the purchasing executive operating at an appropriate strategic level can solicit support from his or her colleagues who head other functions. In fact, as noted previously, without broad-based support, the organizational capabilities required for Balanced Sourcing cannot be developed.

The need for enhanced skills does not necessarily lead to a wholesale replacement of the existing purchasing team. The reorganization case study of a global agriculture and construction equipment manufacturer in this chapter illustrates that some purchasing professionals make an easy transition into the key strategic roles. Others can continue to focus on areas that match their traditional skill set, because even companies that are applying Balanced Sourcing still need some traditional buyers in selected areas.

Set Aggressive Goals

Greater visibility and enhanced resources for the purchasing function merely provide a foundation for change. Balanced Sourcing requires building *organizational capabilities,* not just a stronger purchasing function. Unless the full organization embraces the need for change, even the best purchasing executive faces an uphill battle.

Fortunately, nothing stimulates change better than a combination of fear and redemption. Setting aggressive goals for improving purchasing performance, the second pragmatic step for the CEO, provides the initial stimulus. The third action, launching targeted pilot efforts, offers the path to redemption.

To have the desired effect, the goals should

- Be aggressive enough to force major change
- Incorporate both near-term and long-term objectives
- Hold business managers accountable, not the functional managers

Reorganization Case Study

A global agriculture and construction equipment manufacturer decided to enhance the capabilities of its centralized European purchasing department. The company as a whole had adopted a more strategic view of purchasing and recognized the need to upgrade the skill set of its people. A small senior team within purchasing led the process and worked hard to communicate objectives to the organization.

The team began by developing a new set of job specifications that described each position and the skills it required. Circulation of these specifications throughout the department clarified management expectations to the staff. The company then employed an external organization to interview and test the skill levels of all existing employees. Again, the process was clearly explained, and any concerns raised by the staff were directly addressed by the project team. Once it had completed the staff assessments, the team set about matching the skills of the existing workforce with those required by the new positions.

The results were quite interesting. First, the company discovered only a few people who could not be placed in the new organization, and it helped them to find other positions within the company that suited their particular skill set. Second, the company identified a group of people who had been underutilized and who had the potential to grow substantially in the

Instilling Balanced Sourcing in an organization requires a fundamental change—a paradigm shift—for most companies. The required breadth and depth of the organizational capabilities greatly surpass the practices at most companies, even large ones. Forcing such a shift requires the CEO to challenge the organization to reach new heights, well beyond past experience. Otherwise, the organization will not engage in a critical rethinking of its current approach to purchasing.

The most successful change programs deliver both near-term and long-term results. Near-term results build momentum for change by harvesting the "low-hanging fruit." The organization must understand, new organization. These people were happy to accept the increased responsibilities of their new positions.

A third group of staff revealed through the review were those whose talents were mismatched with their current roles. They were moved to different positions within the department to better utilize their talents. Those involved saw this as a very positive move. The final group identified included staff who had potential, but who required further training before they would be ready to assume their positions in the new organization. This led to the launch of a significant training program to help the staff learn those needed skills.

Ultimately, several positions could not be filled from the existing workforce. These were subsequently filled through internal transfers from other parts of the corporation, as well as through external hires.

Rather than becoming a major demotivator, like most restructurings, this exercise ultimately provided a real motivational lift to the staff. The employees developed a clear understanding of their individual strengths and weaknesses. More important, thanks to the new training program, the staff had the opportunity to enhance their skills so they could progress within the organization. The entire process took about six months but ultimately paid huge dividends in employee morale and productivity.

however, that the next harvest will need to reach higher, requiring more resources and increased cross-functional involvement.

IBM provides a good example. During his first eighteen months at the helm, Gene Richter delivered substantial savings for IBM. Now his organization focuses on the longer-term goals. Cost improvement receives only a 50 percent weighting in performance objectives; new measures like availability and customer satisfaction make up the remainder.

Finally, material productivity should be incorporated directly into business unit and/or program budgets to ensure cross-functional ownership. Though purchasing should lead the charge and measure the performance, it should not have independent accountability. Purchasing should, however, have new longer-term process measures that track the rate of change to the new model—measures such as the percentage of spend managed by purchasing or the number of active commodity teams.

Launch Pilot Efforts

Pilot efforts demonstrate that aggressive goals can be achieved; this is the path to redemption. Different types of pilot efforts can be employed depending on the capabilities that a company is targeting. But any pilot should be a cross-functional effort, not a purchasing program that lacks senior management sponsorship.

For example, a pilot effort for creating sourcing strategies, one of the six Balanced Sourcing capabilities, should focus on a few high-opportunity spend categories. Booz·Allen's client experience indicates that a three-month pilot with a full-time, multifunctional team of three to five people provides the time and resources to develop a sufficiently rigorous commodity business plan. Two to three commodities should be addressed simultaneously in this initial effort to demonstrate the breadth of strategic challenges offered by different commodities. Pilots on a single commodity may be quite successful for that specific commodity, but companies have a tendency to extrapolate the strategy to a "one size fits all" approach. Concurrent examination of several commodities highlights the fact that strategies must address a specific commodity's cost drivers and dynamics. Additionally, such a commitment of resources underscores the importance of building this capability.

Pilots to build and sustain supplier relationships, another of the Balanced Sourcing capabilities, could take on many forms. Implementation of commodity strategies offers one opportunity to structure new supplier relationships. Alternatively, a focused effort to restructure the relationship with a particular key supplier offers the opportunity to enhance this capability. Finally, a supplier development program could focus on a particular improvement area like transferring lean manufacturing techniques to the supply base. Honda's "BP" program, discussed in Chapter Eleven, provides an excellent example.

Integrating the supply web more effectively may start with a pilot focused on a particular plant or business unit. A goal to improve service levels while simultaneously reducing inventory investment could be an initial target. Such a pilot would examine material flow along a particular supply line, looking for opportunities to remove time and uncertainty. The pilot should be cross-functional, perhaps even cross-company, directly involving suppliers and distributors.

The most effective approach for leveraging supplier innovation focuses on a particular development project. Rather than trying to reengineer the development process to ensure early supplier involvement, a pilot effort should focus on tangible results on a real product.

For example, ITT Automotive's Electrical Systems group recently launched a pilot effort to develop a new, lower-cost global windshield wiper motor by leveraging suppliers in the process. The company started with a set of market-driven cost and performance targets. Next, the team identified broader subsystems that could be assigned to technically sophisticated suppliers and allocated the market-driven targets to the subsystems. Suppliers were then selected based on their technical competence and willingness to commit to the aggressive improvement targets. The resulting new design will serve as the foundation for ITT Automotive's wiper system product line for the coming decade. And the process, which required far less elapsed time, provided the foundation for a new approach to product development for other product lines.

Pilot efforts for evolving a global supply base could focus on a particular region. For example, a major automotive company launched an effort to dramatically increase sourcing from Eastern Europe, to capture the advantage of low-cost labor in the region and in anticipation of future growth in car sales. Similarly, Whirlpool conducted a focused effort to build its Asian supply base, even deploying one of its senior purchasing executives to Singapore for nearly a year to lead the effort.

All of these pilot efforts share two common features: multifunctional involvement and measurable results. None of them were internally focused process improvement programs with unclear goals or an overly narrow functional scope. Such pilots allow a company to begin to build the organizational capabilities with an action-oriented "learn by doing" approach. Furthermore, by delivering results, the pilots create the momentum to institutionalize the organizational capabilities for Balanced Sourcing.

Modeling total cost requires a different approach from the other five Balanced Sourcing capabilities. Pilot efforts to build cost models would not deliver direct results, but understanding cost is fundamental to each of the other capabilities. Incorporating cost modeling as a part of each of the other pilot efforts is one option for stimulating the development of this capability. Another is to begin to institutionalize the capability immediately by creating a group to build—and more important, to deploy—cost models throughout the organization. Honda formed its Cost Research department for just this purpose, and Sara Lee's small corporate purchasing group views cost modeling as a key activity in supporting the business units. Regardless of the approach employed, it is worth noting once more that without a solid understanding of the drivers of total material cost, none of the other capability-building pilots will truly succeed.

Invest in Information Technology

Selective investments in IT provide the infrastructure to institutionalize the Balanced Sourcing capabilities. The examination of leading-edge companies consistently uncovered targeted investments in IT tools, most often decision support tools and Internet-based systems for sharing information.

Florida Power & Light focused on information systems as the first step in transforming its purchasing organization from a tactical function to a strategic one. Thanks to a custom on-line ordering system for low-dollar, high-volume purchases like office supplies, users buy directly from key suppliers without any purchasing department intervention. Florida Power & Light has recently created a decision support tool to help buyers choose the best freight terms. An on-line screen lets the buyers quickly compare the rates Florida Power & Light would pay for transporting a particular product using its own carrier and route with the cost of having the supplier deliver it.

SCORE, Chrysler's highly successful supplier suggestion system, now receives and tracks suggestions on-line. Chrysler attributes much of the recent increase in supplier participation to this user-friendliness.

Black & Decker also uses information systems to manage improvement ideas. Its Value Improvement Project Electronic Reporting system enhances the sharing of ideas across facilities and avoids duplicative efforts by centralizing the information in a common format.

SUPERVALU made significant investments in IT to support its ADVANTAGE program for suppliers. For example, a major element of the program is the flow-path tool that examines shipping patterns at the stock-keeping-unit (SKU) level to determine the optimal distribution path. The tool assesses the tradeoff between direct shipments in smaller quantities and consolidated shipments through a distribution center. By comparing the transportation, warehouse handling, and inventory costs for both SUPERVALU and the supplier, the least-cost flow path can be selected.

Each commodity team at Lucent Technologies maintains a home page describing information, such as industry trends and key cost drivers, drawn from the commodity business plan. Cisco System's Internet-based planning and scheduling systems provide real-time information to suppliers. Cisco is reluctant to provide a detailed explanation of the system but claims that it provides a competitive advantage in response time and flexibility. Given that Cisco has managed to offer two-week order lead times on its wide range of custom-made products, while increasing sales at a rate of up to 100 percent per year, the company's claims are easy to believe.

Conclusion

Henry Mintzberg, a widely published management educator, once wrote, "Leadership, like swimming, cannot be learned by reading about it." This book does not profess to have all of the answers for driving an organizational transformation to Balanced Sourcing. Like *Strategy & Business,* the journal that sponsors this series of books, the objective here is to challenge the thinking of senior executives and provide some useful ideas worth further pursuit.

If you are intrigued by the entire concept of Balanced Sourcing, read the next section, which expands upon each of the six organizational capabilities. If a particular capability seems more relevant to your organization than the others, skip ahead to that chapter. Although the chapters are presented in a logical sequence, each of them can be examined independently. If Balanced Sourcing does not appear to be relevant to your organization because your company is somehow different, at least scan the case studies in the third section. The four companies represent a broad spectrum of industries and company cultures, but each employs many critical elements of the Balanced Sourcing model.

Though it is not a silver-bullet solution, Balanced Sourcing addresses an increasingly critical challenge for most companies: how to maintain productive, cooperative relationships with suppliers while simultaneously ensuring competitive pricing. No single company has fully mastered the capabilities, but the best are fast evolving toward the ideal. No company can afford to ignore the trend.

Section Two

Building the Capabilities

Even if you're on the right track, you'll get run over if you just sit there.
—WILL ROGERS

The first section of this book described six organizational capabilities for Balanced Sourcing and suggested that pilot programs help a company to build the capabilities. The six chapters in Section Two elaborate on the key concepts of each capability and offer some pragmatic advice to CEOs and purchasing executives alike on how to begin building them.

Chapter Three describes the key principles for modeling total cost, extracted from the real-life experiences of a large number of companies. It also describes a framework for thinking about what drives cost, which adds structure to cost-modeling efforts. Finally, the chapter describes, through a case example, an approach to building cost models using a top-down approach with progressively deeper analysis at the commodity level, the supplier level, and finally the part level.

Chapter Four presents seven principles that should guide a pilot effort to create sourcing strategies. The chapter also describes the key elements of an effective commodity business plan—the output of a pilot sourcing strategy effort. Extracts from an actual report on discrete semiconductors demonstrate not only the elements of a commodity business plan but also the appropriate level of analytic rigor required.

Chapter Five addresses the "softer" issue of building and sustaining relationships between companies and their suppliers. First, it explores the benefits of long-term relationships. Next, it describes three key ingredients for making trust tangible, using examples drawn from a variety of companies. Though it is less analytic than some of the other capability chapters, the advice offered on ways to build and sustain relationships is pragmatic. The chapter concludes with a discussion of three different types of pilot efforts that can help build this capability: relationship structuring and renewal, supplier development, and supplier suggestions.

Recent trends in integrating the supply web provide a context for the discussion in Chapter Six. The key principles for effectively integrating the web of suppliers are presented and illustrated with real-life examples. The chapter concludes with a brief review of important issues to consider in developing a pilot program.

Chapter Seven explores the capability of leveraging suppliers in innovation, beginning with three critical concepts: sharing technology plans, defining scope boundaries, and setting target costs. It also describes a methodology for building the capability though a specific product development pilot effort.

The final chapter in Section Two addresses the increasing importance of the Balanced Sourcing capability of evolving a global supply base. Two quite different strategic imperatives for global sourcing form the framework for a discussion of the inherent complexity of purchasing on a global scale. A case study offers insight into the practical challenges of global sourcing and suggests ways to meet them.

Chapter 3
Modeling Total Cost

It is a capital mistake to theorize before one has data.
—Sir Arthur Conan Doyle

In a recent survey of leading purchasing organizations sponsored by *Strategy & Business*, cost modeling tied for first in a ranking of the most critical purchasing skills. More significantly, the difference between cost modeling's importance ranking and the respondents' self-assessed level of skill—the "development gap"—was among the largest of the seventeen items (see Exhibit 3.1).

Recent research also sponsored by *Strategy & Business* found that 25 percent of companies surveyed had no cost models. Moreover, of those companies that did build models, many elements of the total cost of ownership were not included or even tracked systematically. Furthermore, two-thirds of the respondents were not confident that the cost information provided by suppliers gave more than a general sense of the true costs. Firsthand experience in Booz·Allen's work with many companies paints an even worse picture. Only the most sophisticated companies truly understand the total cost of materials with

Note: This chapter drew heavily upon a *Strategy & Business* article coauthored with Julie Ask of Booz·Allen & Hamilton's Cleveland office.

Exhibit 3.1   *Strategy & Business* Purchasing Survey

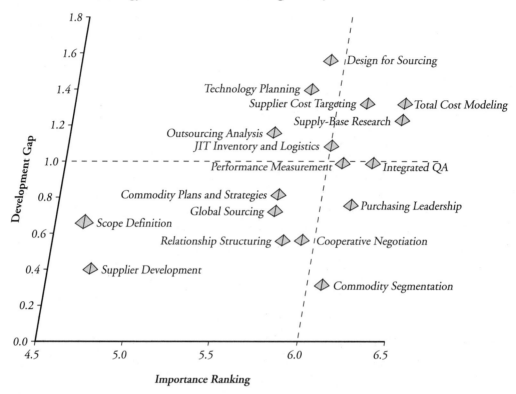

Source: *Strategy & Business* survey.

an adequate level of rigor. In fact, many don't understand their own costs, let alone their suppliers'.

The best companies don't think of cost modeling as a purchasing skill, but rather as a critical organizational capability led by purchasing. Purchasing plays a lead role because cost models developed in cooperation with suppliers are the most effective. Collaborative development improves the quality of the cost model by capturing supplier insight. More important, a jointly developed model has a greater probability of being fully applied in joint improvement efforts.

This chapter explains the key principles of cost modeling for Balanced Sourcing. It also describes a process for developing purchasing cost models even with limited information and uncooperative suppliers—the norm, unfortunately, for most organizations.

Key Principles for Cost Modeling

Cost modeling generates a lot of interest in most organizations—and a lot of confusion, too. Cost models mean different things to different people, in part because they can have many different purposes. For example, knowing the direct labor content and shipping economics of a product could lead to a strategic decision to develop suppliers in a low-wage country like China. At a tactical level, a more detailed cost model could be used to choose between two suppliers of the same materials. Or a cost model that documents setup cost could be used at an executional level to determine optimal order quantities.

Regardless of the cost model's immediate purpose, five key principles apply to developing cost models for purchased goods and services. Following them creates more accurate *and* more robust cost models.

1. Capture cost drivers, not just cost elements.
2. Build commodity-specific models to highlight the key drivers.
3. Consider the impact of total cost of ownership.
4. Start simply and add complexity only as needed.
5. Triangulate around data to improve accuracy and confidence.

Capture Cost Drivers, Not Just Cost Elements

The most basic components of a cost model are the cost elements captured by accounting: direct labor, materials, and overhead. But documenting cost elements is only a start; a cost model should also capture the drivers of cost, such as labor productivity or hourly wage rates.

Capturing the drivers produces a model that answers the question "What if?" not just "What is?" It also highlights tradeoffs, since the same driver can affect different cost elements in different ways. For example, increasing production lot sizes can lower production cost because fewer setups are needed, but it increases inventory cost because more inventory is held on average. As a result, models that consider cost drivers provide far more insight for decision making.

Build Commodity-Specific Models to Highlight the Key Drivers

Inherent differences in products will cause different cost drivers to emerge among commodities; therefore, models should be commodity-specific. Exhibit 3.2 illustrates this point through a comparison between semiconductors and wiring harnesses.

The largest cost element for semiconductors is facility overhead, while material and labor costs dominate the harness cost structure. Such differences in the relative magnitude of cost elements indicate that different cost drivers will dominate the models. For example, design considerations, such as the number of cut leads, breakouts, and connector types, should be captured in a cost model for wiring harnesses. A model for a semiconductor manufacturer, on the other hand, should focus on the scale and utilization of the facility, because spreading capital cost is so critical.

Consider the Impact of Total Cost of Ownership

Common among all commodities is the importance of modeling the total cost of ownership. Few purchasing decisions should be based solely on the product's purchase price. Cost models to support such decision making should include factors beyond mere price, such as shipping expenses, quality costs, and inventory-carrying costs. In fact, in some purchased products, the cost of acquisition and use can be a multiple of the purchase price and/or the supplier's cost. Exhibit 3.3 demonstrates the range of ownership costs across various cost models drawn from a variety of companies.

Start Simply and Add Complexity Only as Needed

The first three principles for developing cost models encourage a broad approach to cost modeling that includes the drivers of total cost of ownership. Although these principles are critical to developing robust cost

Exhibit 3.2 Comparison of Two Commodity Cost Structures

Semiconductors

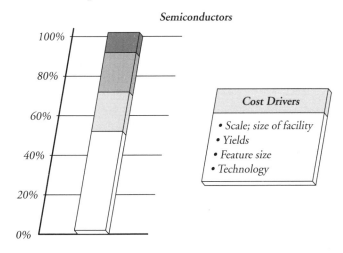

Cost Drivers

• *Scale; size of facility*
• *Yields*
• *Feature size*
• *Technology*

Wiring Harnesses

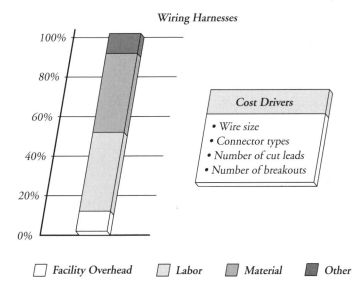

Cost Drivers

• *Wire size*
• *Connector types*
• *Number of cut leads*
• *Number of breakouts*

☐ *Facility Overhead*   ☐ *Labor*   ▨ *Material*   ■ *Other*

Source: Simplified case examples.

Exhibit 3.3   Cost of Ownership

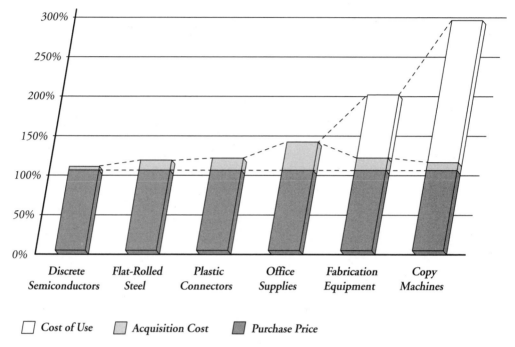

Cost of Use   Acquisition Cost   Purchase Price

Source: Booz·Allen client case examples.

models, experience has shown that initial efforts should focus on simple models that include only the most important cost elements and drivers.

Many efforts stall because overly complex cost models may lack good-quality information. No matter how conceptually sophisticated the model, the old adage applies: "Garbage in, garbage out." The most effective models ultimately achieve the "simplicity on the other side of complexity" that Oliver Wendell Holmes Jr. valued so highly. Such models strip out unnecessary "noise" by focusing only on the most critical drivers.

Triangulate Around Data to Improve Accuracy and Confidence

Another trick of the trade is to use multiple data points to bracket the numbers and improve accuracy. For example, even though the magnitude of cost elements differs among suppliers, their values generally fall into a small range. At the initial stage of cost modeling, using cost structures from multiple suppliers helps to zero in on the actual value, even if some suppliers are less willing to share data. Alternative indirect sources of information also help in triangulation, for example, observations from facility tours, internal experts, capital equipment suppliers, industry literature, and published statistics, to name a few.

Applying the five key principles ensures maximum benefit from a cost-modeling effort. The best models meet Einstein's test for his own theories: they should be as simple as they can be, but no simpler. The following section describes a typical approach for building cost models by starting at a high level and then drilling down to greater detail and complexity.

A Top-Down Modeling Methodology

A top-down methodology, using the five principles described earlier, provides a systematic approach to modeling a company's outside purchases. This approach builds a broad baseline of the total spend across all categories, allowing a deep analysis of a few select commodities. The ultimate objective in modeling is to transfer knowledge throughout the organization while ensuring that everyone working with the commodity understands the important cost drivers. This is far more important than having an exact model for determining costs at the part level.

The evolution of the cost research function at Honda of America illustrates this concept well. Initially, Honda employed a group of twenty to thirty experts in a central purchasing function. Working cooperatively with suppliers, this group developed sophisticated cost models. Over the past decade, Honda has systematically codified its expertise into cost tables that anyone, not just a commodity expert, can use to cost out a part quickly based upon key drivers. Now that cost modeling has become an *organizational capability,* not just an individual skill, the central function needs only a half-dozen individuals.

Unfortunately, the typical purchasing organization has not achieved Honda's level of sophistication. The following methodology describes a process for developing the capability by beginning simply and adding complexity over time. By concentrating resources and approaching the problem systematically, a company can begin to develop sophisticated models quite quickly.

Step 1: Baseline and Segment the Spend

By developing a baseline and segmenting the spend, a company can combine individually purchased items and services into logical groupings or commodity families. Baselining the spend, however, can appear deceptively straightforward. Few companies have good commodity-coding systems, and those that do often find the codes inconsistently applied. Large companies also often find that each business unit has completely different purchasing systems and incompatible data formats.

Even in companies with standardized company-wide purchasing systems, a significant number of outside purchases, such as advertising and travel expenses, are often not processed through purchasing. This phenomenon is so pervasive that Daryl Skaar, Chief Procurement Officer at Lucent Technologies (and formerly head of 3M Company's purchasing organization), considers the percentage of total outside purchases managed through the purchasing function to be a key performance measure. A recent survey sponsored by *Strategy & Business* determined that on average fewer than 75 percent of a company's outside purchases are managed by the purchasing function. Even leading companies seldom exceed 90 percent.

Once the total spend has been baselined, purchases should be aggregated into logical groupings that are conducive to cost modeling. As an example, consider the simple pie chart in Exhibit 3.4, which illustrates a baseline of the total spend of a hypothetical industrial equipment manufacturer. In segmenting the spend, this company could either define all castings as a commodity or separate them into ferrous and nonferrous materials. Another segmentation might be process and/or type of mold. Sand casting and permanent mold casting could be considered separate categories regardless of the material, as could horizontal and vertical molding.

Generally, the best segmentation will group the items by "supply industries" and/or "process technology," because understanding supplier

Exhibit 3.4   Purchases by Commodity

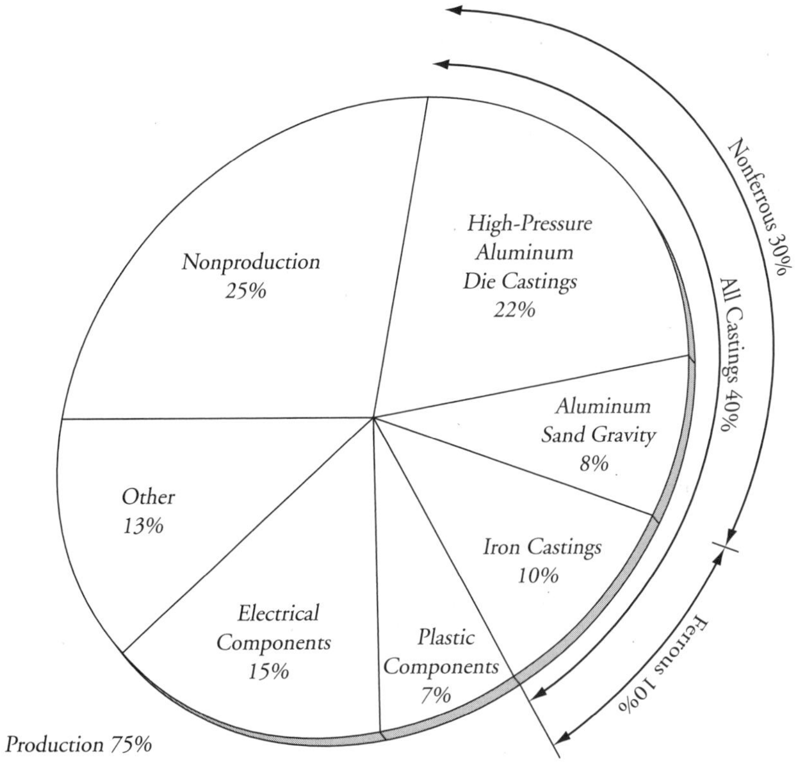

Source: Modified case example.

economics provides the foundation for the initial cost models. The least effective segmentation scheme—one used by many companies—groups parts by the end-product application. For example, castings used for a compressor are grouped separately from castings used in a motor, even though both could come from the same supplier and be manufactured on the same type of casting equipment.

Step 2: Quantify Significant Elements of the Cost of Ownership

Once the overall spend is documented and segmented into logical groupings, a general total cost of ownership model should be developed. Some cost elements that are not obvious may be significant—and typically difficult to quantify. For example, many companies capture the cost of ordering, expediting, managing returns, and qualifying suppliers. The materials-related costs of downtime, warranty, and disposal are less obvious, however, and sometimes go uncaptured. The findings of the *Strategy & Business* purchasing survey shown in Exhibit 3.5 bear this out.

At this stage the total cost of ownership model may exist only at the company-wide level. For example, an organization may only be able to measure the fact that inbound transportation costs average 2 percent of material purchases, or that the materials-related warranty cost is about 60 percent of total warranty costs. Though not particularly accurate, such estimates broaden the organization's thinking about the purchasing process and materials costs by highlighting their magnitude.

Step 3: Use Cost Drivers to Build a Total Cost of Ownership Model at the Commodity Level

Although capturing absolute cost values helps, the analysis should not stop there. An effective model captures cost drivers, not just elements. For example, an obvious cost driver for supplier certification is the number of suppliers. For transportation, part weight, travel distance, and transportation mode are the critical drivers. With such insight, the overall total-cost model can be refined to allocate cost differently across commodities. As Exhibit 3.3 showed, the relative size of the total cost of ownership components can differ significantly across commodities.

To demonstrate how an understanding of the cost drivers and the elements of total cost of ownership are combined, return to the die-casting example for the industrial products company. In Exhibit 3.6, the cost of ownership model highlights several interesting issues around castings. First, for this company, the total cost adds 30 percent to the piece price, well worth considering when developing buying strategies. Also, given that tooling is such a significant cost, an examination of policies such as capacity buffers, dual sourcing, and dual tooling is critical. A look at transportation costs could also lead to questions about whether a lower-cost mode of transportation could reduce the transport cost without unduly affecting inventory.

Exhibit 3.5   Modeling Cost: Elements of Total Cost Tracked by Supplier

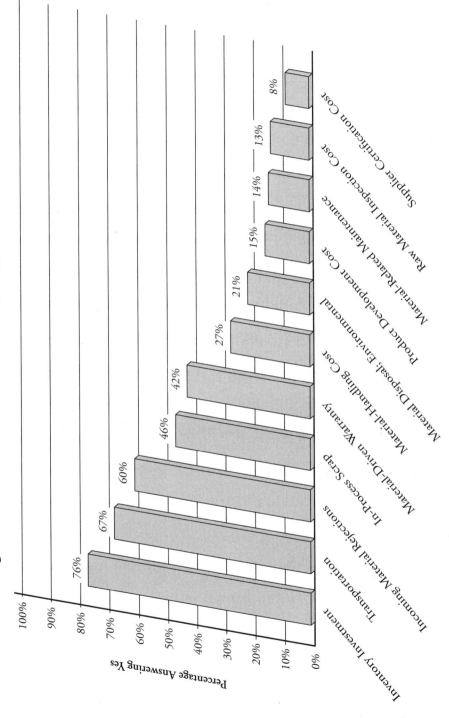

Percentage Answering Yes

Inventory Investment
Transportation — 76%
Incoming Material Rejections — 67%
In-Process Scrap — 60%
Material-Driven Warranty — 46%
Material-Handling Cost — 42%
Material Disposal, Environmental — 27%
Product Development Cost — 21%
Material-Related Maintenance — 15%
Raw Material Inspection Cost — 14%
Supplier Certification Cost — 13%
— 8%

Source: Strategy & Business survey.

Exhibit 3.6   High-Pressure Aluminum Die Casting: Total Cost of Ownership

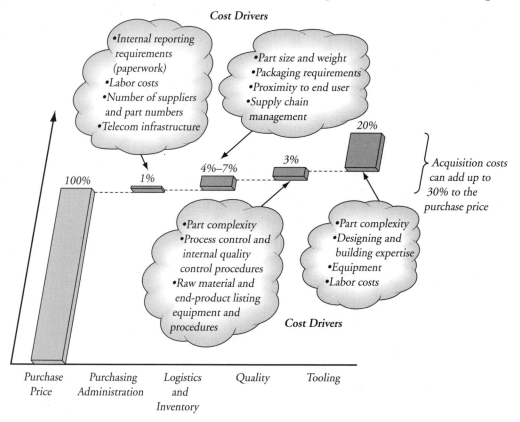

Source: Disguised electronics industry case example.

The total-acquisition-cost model encourages us to think about the sourcing strategy for a commodity. At this stage, however, the modeling has only opened our eyes to the broader set of issues beyond purchase price. To move further in our strategic thinking, we need to understand the drivers of cost *within the suppliers' operations,* as purchase price is still likely to be the largest component of our total cost.

Step 4: Build a Supplier-Level Total-Cost Model Based on Key Drivers

The cost model resulting from Step 3 is actually a compilation of costs from a mix of suppliers. Accurate ownership cost models reflect the fact that the suppliers are not all the same; for example, shipping makes up a higher percentage of the cost for a supplier that is located further away. The commodity-level model also does not capture the differences in production costs among different suppliers. For example, one supplier might have lower labor rates; another might have lower overhead costs due to economies of scale. Even fairly similar suppliers might have different costs as a result of differences in capacity utilization and the resulting overhead absorption rate.

Building the supplier cost model is similar to building the cost model at the commodity level. First, break the supplier's overall cost structure into key components: direct labor; materials; manufacturing overhead; selling, general, and administrative costs; and profit. With the exception of profit, most suppliers are willing to provide such details as part of a site visit, even if the relationship is adversarial.

Individual supplier cost structures will vary somewhat; understanding the variances provides the initial insight into cost drivers. For example, if one company has lower direct labor costs but higher manufacturing overhead compared to another, there is probably a difference in their degree of automation. Or one may pay higher wage rates—possibly because it is unionized and the other is not. Wage rate differences can also be an important consideration when comparing suppliers internationally. If material costs are significantly lower, the supplier is probably more vertically integrated, buying raw materials and performing the basic transformation processes in-house instead of simply doing final assembly.

The next task in building a solid supplier cost model at the facility level is to quantify the key drivers for each major cost element. For example, an initial facility model will capture the number of hourly employees and their annual wage rates. For a more sophisticated model, it may be appropriate to separate direct labor from indirect hourly labor and capture the different wage rates. Though documenting the mix between direct and indirect labor may provide more detailed information than necessary at this stage, such information can provide insight into the manufacturing practices of different suppliers. Lean manufacturers tend to have proportionately fewer indirect laborers compared to direct laborers, because much of the material handling and off-line inspection is eliminated.

By adding complexity only as needed, a facility-level model can be simple but powerful. For example, a comparison between a supplier with high labor costs and a similar one with the same facilities but low labor costs requires us to know only the differences in wage rates between the suppliers—or maybe simply the differences in average wage rates between countries. This analysis alone might convince senior management to support sourcing from emerging markets.

Most sourcing decisions are more complicated: suppliers with identical facilities across countries are rare. For example, suppliers with high labor costs typically offset their disadvantage by investing in automation and have larger facilities that provide economies of scale. Also, productivity levels, duties, and transportation costs can often offset low labor costs, reconfirming the need to model total cost and not just supplier price.

For more information about a structure for capturing cost drivers to build a facility-level model, see "A Framework for Thinking About Cost Drivers."

Step 5: Build Cost Tables at the Item Level

Creating cost models at the item level takes the process to even greater detail. Facility-level models identify world-class standards and are adequate for developing sourcing strategies and joint improvement efforts. But cost estimating and target setting for a specific part demand a more detailed model that adds additional variables to the supplier-level model or uses specific part-number estimates rather than facility averages.

Returning to the die-casting model, several of the key components of a detailed cost model are facility-specific, for example, wage rates, equipment up-time, and material cost. Estimates at a part-number level require additional part-specific information, such as finished weight, machine cycle times, and material yield. A more complicated model might take into account drivers of part complexity, such as wall thickness or number of inserts, to calculate a complexity factor to be applied to the cost estimated from the tables. Such information can be organized into a simple spreadsheet application with input screens for the primary variables.

Cost tables are created by calculating a range of scenarios using the model and organizing the results in tabular form. A table for a given

A Framework for Thinking About Cost Drivers

Even when the net cost differential among suppliers is relatively small, the effects of different cost drivers can be dramatic. Determining cause and effect can be complex but is well worth the effort. A useful framework groups cost drivers into four categories, as indicated in Exhibit A.

Design

Design-related costs are typically addressed first to ensure "apples-to-apples" comparisons. Often, different suppliers will use different designs to meet the same functional requirement. In die-casting, for example, a company's cost-modeling effort revealed that two suppliers used different mixes of scrap to ore in their foundries. One used high-grade scrap, such as old railroad rails, with a low percentage of new ore. Another used lower-grade scrap with a higher mix of fresh ore. Though both met the same end-product quality standards, the material costs were quite different.

Exhibit A   Cost Driver Framework

Category	Description	Examples
Design	Costs attributable to product design tradeoffs	■ Material specifications ■ Product-line complexity
Facility	Costs related to the size of the facility, equipment, and process technology employed	■ Facility scale ■ Degree of vertical integration ■ Use of automation
Geography	Cost associated with the location of the facility relative to the customer	■ Location-related wage rate difference ■ Transportation cost to customer
Operations	Costs that differentiate a well-run facility from a poorly run facility	■ Labor productivity ■ Facility utilization ■ Rejection rates

Another cost driver could be product-line complexity and the resulting impact on operations. One foundry might make lower-volume parts in shorter-length runs, causing more plant down-time due to changeovers. In an automotive company example, a comparison of engine valves revealed that one had a highly complex single-piece design that was very expensive to cast, whereas another used a two-piece assembly that allowed simpler, lower-cost castings. Although the cost to cast one design was significantly lower than that of the other design, the differential was much less when assembly costs were considered.

Design-related costs can be the most significant. For example, changing fundamental choices, such as using plastic instead of casting, has a huge impact on the final design. Many companies, therefore, are moving toward "black-box" specifications to avoid locking a supplier into a technology that may not be appropriate.

Facility

Scale effect is typically the most important facility-related cost factor, because unit cost generally decreases as total capacity increases. For example, both a 200-employee plant and a 400-employee plant require only one plant manager, and the size of other overhead functions such as human resources and finance is less than double at the larger plant. Scale is also observable in the factory operations: a building designed to hold 400 people need not be twice the size of one for 200 people—and even if it were, the cost of the building could well be lower on a per-square-foot basis.

Other facility-related cost drivers include the degree of vertical integration and automation. A company that produces sub-assemblies in-house may or may not have lower costs, but the costs will probably be different from those of a supplier that buys subassemblies from an outside supplier. The degree of automation typically varies between low-labor-cost countries and high-labor-cost countries, where automation is critical for survival.

Geography

Geography-related cost drivers are associated with the location of a facility; they include wages, local taxes, utilities, and import and export taxes. In die casting, the labor and transportation components are heavily influenced by location-related factors. Die castings can be heavy and costly to transport: both the distance from the foundry to the final assembly location and the proximity to transportation, such as major roadways, rail, and water, are important. In this case, the advantage of the low wage rate of an emerging market must also be weighed against the transport costs to minimize total cost. Since most suppliers already have made significant investments in their manufacturing footprint, changes to geography-related costs are often best achieved by identifying suppliers in developing markets rather than by encouraging suppliers to relocate there.

Operations

Operations-related costs are those affected by *how well* a facility is operated, and as a result they can be changed in the shorter term. The drivers of operations-related costs include the day-to-day dimensions of operations such as plant productivity, number of shifts, efficiency, and scrap rates. Going back to the die-casting example, the key operational driver of material costs for the supplier would be scrap rates, while labor costs would be driven by the efficiency and productivity of the workforce.

Operations-related cost drivers are among the easiest to influence in the near term. For example, driving a supplier to adopt best-practice worker-machine ratios can create a significant bottom-line impact quickly. Exhibit B illustrates the cost drivers for die casting using this framework.

A Framework for Thinking About Cost Drivers (continued)

Exhibit B   High-Pressure Aluminum Die Casting: Cost Drivers

	Design	Facility
14%–32% Tooling	•Part complexity •Tolerances •Number of design changes	•Manual/automated equipment •Computer-Aided Design/Computer Numeric Control •Testing equipment
1%–8% Quality	•Complexity •Tolerances •Porosity standards	•Machine and die condition •Built-in quality-control mechanisms on casting machines •Testing equipment
4%–7% Logistics	•Part shape and weight •End-user packaging requirements	•Internal raw material and finished products transport infrastructure (overheads, forklifts)
1%–2% Purchasing Administration	•Number of design changes •Number of prototypes	•Administrative paperwork requirements •Reporting requirements •Organizational structure •Electronic Data Interchange
5%–10% Scrap	•Tool design •Part complexity	•Melting and casting equipment •Process flow efficiency •Temperature management
1% Supplier's Inventory		•Capacity availability
5%–6.5% Fixed Cost		•Foundry scale
16%–20% Indirect Labor	•Part complexity •Testing and quality requirements	•State-owned/layoff restrictions •Facility layout
10%–15% Direct Labor, Trimming 10%–15% Direct Labor, Casting	•Number of cavities per tool •Tool design—amount of trimming required •Part complexity—visual inspection	•Equipment type for melting, holding, filling, casting, trimming, machining—level of automation •Die heating and cooling mechanisms •Computer-controlled settings for machine
2%–3% Consumables		
4%–5% Energy	•Part design; yield	•Gas vs. electricity vs. oil
30%–40% Material	•Material specifications •Tool design	•Melting equipment •Casting equipment •Material inspection equipment •Quality of purchased material •Scale

Source: Booz·Allen client case example.

		Operations	Geography
14%–32%	Tooling	•Experience with tool making •Tool design expertise •Die maintenance routine	•Labor costs
1%–8%	Quality	•Machine and die maintenance •Disciplined use of Statistical Process Control •Personnel qualifications •Skill set of operators	•Transport distance, road conditions
4%–7%	Logistics	•Production planning and scheduling •Supply web management techniques	•Proximity to end user
1%–2%	Purchasing Administration	•Buyer experience •Workload; frequency of transactions •Number of suppliers/Number of part numbers	•Factor costs •Telecommunications infrastructure
5%–10%	Scrap	•Material loss rate from melting •Poor quality of end product due to casting process out of spec or operator	
1%	Supplier's Inventory	•Scheduling	•Distance to end user
5%–6.5%	Fixed Cost	•Utilization	
16%–20%	Indirect Labor	•Waste •Level of automation—quality checks, measuring of prototypes—done by computer or manually •Parent companies •Utilization	•Local labor rates
10%–15%	Direct Labor, Trimming	•Operator skill and experience •Cycle times •Die maintenance	•Local labor rates
10%–15%	Direct Labor, Casting		
2%–3%	Consumables	•Scrap rate	
4%–5%	Energy	•Scrap rate and yield	•Local utility rates
30%–40%	Material	•Loss in melting, holding, transport, and so on •Net weight vs. gross weight •End-user rejection rate and external scrap •Internal scrap •Incoming raw material storage and inspection practices	•Proximity to foundry •Material source

supplier (or simply for a best-practice compendium) could show a range of part weights across the columns and machine cycle times across the rows. A set of these tables could show the effect of different yield assumptions, since part design often affects yield. The output of such analysis is a simple lookup table that allows even an inexperienced buyer (or better still, a designer) to estimate the cost of a part using only three variables—weight, cycle time, and yield—as shown in Exhibit 3.7.

Combining cost tables produces an overall total cost of ownership model at the part-number level. For example, another set of cost tables could provide part-number estimates for transporting the casting. It could use part weight as the column heading (as was done in the original die-casting model) and the various shipping distances for the rows. Separate tables could be used for each of a variety of "modes": normal full-truckload delivery, less-than-truckload delivery, and expedited air freight.

Cost tables are simplified extractions from a model that make costing information available to everyone, which can be very powerful. However, a deeper understanding of cost drivers—and use of that knowledge to drive cost out—is far more powerful. Rather than simply estimating the cost of a casting, a greater advantage is gained when the design engineer understands that increasing wall thickness by two millimeters raises weight by an extra half-pound, which in turn adds fifty cents to the cost.

Conclusion

Modeling total cost is one of the most critical organizational capabilities for Balanced Sourcing. A complete understanding of cost provides the foundation for virtually everything in the purchasing process, from setting strategy to simplifying designs to improving supplier operations and negotiating piece prices.

Research also highlights the fact that few organizations have evolved this total-cost modeling capability to the desired level. This chapter provides a road map to help organizations close the development gap. Experience has shown that useful models can be developed surprisingly quickly using a focused effort and applying the principles and methodology described.

Exhibit 3.7   Cost Tables: High-Pressure Aluminum Die Casting

95% Yield

Cycle Time (Seconds)	Part Weight (in Kilos)								
	0.05	0.06	0.07	0.08	0.09	0.10	0.11	0.12	0.13
50	$0.45	$0.49	$0.53	$0.57	$0.61	$0.65	$0.69	$0.72	$0.76
52	0.46	0.50	0.54	0.58	0.62	0.66	0.70	0.73	0.77
54	0.47	0.51	0.55	0.59	0.63	0.67	0.71	0.74	0.78
56	0.48	0.52	0.56	0.60	0.64	0.68	0.72	0.75	0.79
58	0.49	0.53	0.57	0.61	0.65	0.69	0.73	0.76	0.80
60	0.50	0.54	0.58	0.62	0.66	0.70	0.74	0.77	0.81
62	0.51	0.55	0.59	0.63	0.67	0.71	0.75	0.78	0.82
64	0.52	0.56	0.60	0.64	0.68	0.72	0.76	0.79	0.83
66	0.53	0.57	0.61	0.65	0.69	0.73	0.77	0.81	0.84
68	0.54	0.58	0.62	0.66	0.70	0.74	0.78	0.82	0.85
70	0.55	0.59	0.63	0.67	0.71	0.75	0.79	0.83	0.86

90% Yield

Cycle Time (Seconds)	Part Weight (in Kilos)								
	0.05	0.06	0.07	0.08	0.09	0.10	0.11	0.12	0.13
50	$0.47	$0.51	$0.55	$0.59	$0.64	$0.68	$0.72	$0.76	$0.81
52	0.48	0.52	0.56	0.60	0.65	0.69	0.73	0.77	0.82
54	0.49	0.53	0.57	0.62	0.63	0.70	0.74	0.78	0.83
56	0.50	0.54	0.58	0.63	0.67	0.71	0.75	0.79	0.84
58	0.51	0.55	0.59	0.64	0.68	0.72	0.76	0.80	0.85
60	0.52	0.56	0.61	0.65	0.69	0.73	0.77	0.81	0.86
62	0.53	0.57	0.62	0.66	0.70	0.74	0.78	0.82	0.87
64	0.54	0.59	0.63	0.67	0.71	0.75	0.79	0.83	0.88
66	0.55	0.60	0.64	0.68	0.72	0.76	0.80	0.84	0.89
68	0.56	0.61	0.65	0.69	0.73	0.77	0.81	0.85	0.90
70	0.57	0.62	0.66	0.70	0.74	0.78	0.82	0.86	0.91

Source: Adapted from automotive company case example.

Chapter 4
Creating Sourcing Strategies

Plans are nothing; planning is everything.
—Dwight D. Eisenhower

Most companies develop some form of sourcing strategies and/or commodity business plans. But the degree of organization-wide involvement, level of analytic rigor, and thoroughness of documentation vary widely across companies. In fact, few companies create sourcing strategies as well as they would like. From the *Strategy & Business* survey of a wide range of companies, this capability has the greatest development gap between the average "criticality" rating and the average "competency" rating.

As is true of most tools and techniques—particularly ones that include the word *strategy*—the output of the process is useful, but the process itself can provide the greatest value. When commodity plans are done well, multifunctional teams are forced to step back and make a rigorous examination of the current supply base and take a long-term view of purchasing-related decisions. Most important, effective sourcing strategy development builds cross-functional buy-in to the priorities for each commodity and supplier.

Note: This chapter was developed in collaboration with Cosmo Takamatsu of Booz·Allen & Hamilton's Tokyo office and Anne Chung of Booz·Allen & Hamilton's Cleveland office.

This chapter provides a number of principles for creating effective sourcing strategies. It also elaborates on some of the key concepts and presents a case example of a commodity business plan to illustrate the techniques and to show the level of rigor that leading firms apply.

Strategic Sourcing Principles

Over the years we have developed the following principles for creating effective sourcing strategies:

1. View supply-base rationalization as a result, not the objective.
2. Use multifunctional teams.
3. Coordinate across regions and business units where necessary.
4. Conduct rigorous global research.
5. Examine total cost of ownership.
6. Segment the spend for focus and to break compromises.
7. Quantify the benefits.

Principle 1: View Supply-Base Rationalization as a Result, Not the Objective

Most executives like to have progress measures, and supply-base reduction numbers seem to be natural ones. Given all of the hype over the small, close-knit supply base of Japanese companies, the broad supply bases for most Western companies are probably too large. Companies often proudly report reductions in their supply base in an attempt to mimic the Japanese. Many companies publicize their progress in setting up long-term sole-source relationships. Despite the rhetoric, the Japanese typically single-source at the part-number level but dual-source at the commodity level to drive competition in their supply base. At best, supply-base reduction is an indirect measure for improving purchasing. At worst, it can drive perverse behavior.

One company consolidated all of its purchases under a single distributor that would source from the original suppliers but add a 30 percent premium as compensation for its role as a first-tier supplier. Fifteen suppliers were now replaced by one—at least in the tracking records. Clearly, the customer company reduced some transaction costs, but probably not enough to offset the 30 percent premium. But no matter, the performance records showed a significant reduction in the supply base and senior management was happy.

It is true that Western manufacturers generally use too many suppliers. Furthermore, a shift to the Balanced Sourcing model will shrink the supply base. Reducing the supply base, however, should be the result of optimizing the number of suppliers for a commodity, not an end in itself. Optimization should start with a broad look at the supply-base options and only later winnow them down.

One test of whether a strategy employs the optimal number of suppliers is to examine the supplier roles. Unless each supplier has a unique role, the supply base is still too large. On the other hand, unless you can show that adding another supplier with a somewhat different scope—for example, one that supports a different business unit—demonstrably increases total cost, the supply base may have been overrationalized.

Principle 2: Use Multifunctional Teams

The creation of sourcing strategies should be viewed as an organizational capability, not a purchasing task. Effective sourcing strategies result from cross-functional collaboration. Multifunctional teams provide two key benefits. First, broader involvement ensures a greater diversity of opinion, which produces more creative solutions. More important, multifunctional involvement builds organizational buy-in, and no matter how comprehensive and elaborate a plan may be, its real value is captured only if it is implemented.

According to our survey, unfortunately, most companies still have inadequate multifunctional involvement. As Exhibit 4.1 shows, most companies use multifunctional teams for developing sourcing strategies, but many important groups are not consistently involved. Unilaterally developed plans may be effective in addressing the competition-based opportunities that typically occur in the domain of purchasing: source selection and price negotiation. Without the support of other functions such as manufacturing and engineering, however, cooperation-based opportunities may not be realized.

**Exhibit 4.1   Creating Sourcing Strategies:
Functions Participating in Developing Sourcing Strategies**

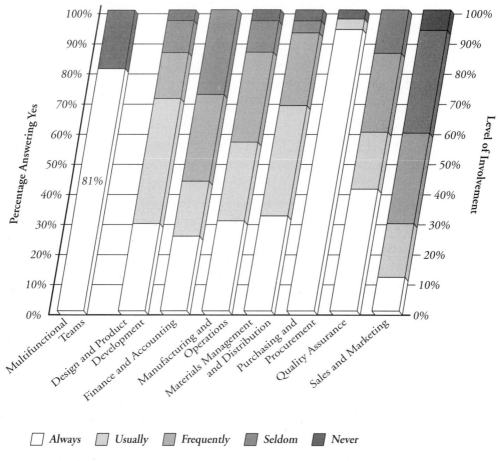

Source: *Strategy & Business* survey.

Principle 3: Coordinate Across Regions and Business Units Where Necessary

Senior managers frequently question what the appropriate degree of co-ordination is in developing sourcing strategies. The unsophisticated ex-ecutive often mandates global coordination across all business units to ensure maximum negotiating leverage. Unfortunately, such mandates are misguided, since few supply industries are truly global and negoti-ating leverage is only one of several opportunity levers in Balanced

Sourcing. Many of these opportunities, such as improving supply chain management or better leveraging of supplier innovation, may require strong involvement at the business-unit level to be effective. Process efficiency provides a more sophisticated argument for centralized strategy development: why have each business unit reinvent the wheel in developing an understanding of the drivers of value in a particular commodity? Unfortunately, aggregating demands across business units or geographies also complicates the effort and can ultimately slow down the process.

Balancing this tradeoff requires recognition of the fact that there is no generic best answer. The balance between centralized and decentralized control varies by commodity. For example, one company resolved the problem by first creating a standard commodity-planning process to gain "expertise scale" through information sharing. Next, the company defined three possible models for managing individual technology families:

1. Centrally controlled and managed for the benefit of the company
2. Managed by the lead division to ensure corporate coverage but with ownership by the primary-user business unit that is the key buyer
3. Business-unit-specific to allow businesses to develop strategies independently (but according to the appropriate process)

Finally the team analyzed each technology family along six dimensions, three that tended to argue for centralized, corporate control and three that argued for decentralized, business-unit control. Based on the ratings for each of the six factors, each technology family was assigned the appropriate responsibility model (see Exhibit 4.2).

Principle 4: Conduct Rigorous Global Research

Far too many sourcing strategies start with the current supply base and try to rationalize from there (see Principle 1). Effective strategy development, however, requires a global view. Admittedly, global sourcing does not make sense for many sourced products; global research almost always does. The first, most obvious reason is that global research may uncover an advantaged supplier that previously was not known. Second,

Exhibit 4.2   Responsibility Assignment

Technology Family	Corporate Perspective			Business-Unit Perspective			Recommended Responsibility Model
	Commonality of Requirements	Process-Modeling Complexity	Corporate Leverage	Business Criticality	Logistics Integration	Design Integration	
Steel Flat Rolled	●	●	●	●	●	●	Lead
Steel Bar Stock	●	●	●	●	●	◐	Lead
Plastic Molded Parts	○	●	◐	◐	◐	●	Business Unit
Stampings	○	◐	●	◐	●	●	Business Unit
Stainless	◐	◐	●	○	◐	◐	Central
Springs	◐	◐	◐	◐	○	○	Central
Maintenance, Repair, and Operating Supplies	●	○	●	○	●	○	Central
Lumber	●	○	●	◐	●	○	Lead
Outside Tooling	○	◐	●	●	◐	●	Business Unit
Castings	○	●	○	◐	◐	●	Business Unit
Outside Processing	◐	○	◐	●	●	◐	Business Unit

● High —— ○ Low

Source: Automotive supplier case example.

the research provides potential benchmarks of world-class performance in a supply industry.

For example, one company recently sent a multifunctional team on a world tour of suppliers of connectors. Through interviews and careful observation, the team identified each supplier's key practices and created a composite of best practices (see Exhibit 4.3). The team was most surprised to discover the higher operator-to-machine ratios of the Japanese supplier. Although the ultimate strategy for this U.S. company focused on the domestic supply base, the world-class benchmarks were used to drive improvement by the U.S. suppliers.

Principle 5: Examine Total Cost of Ownership

An effective sourcing strategy does not focus on price reduction. Instead, the strategy identifies ways to improve performance in the full set of supplier-related costs and opportunities. Most strategic decisions require tradeoffs—usually between the price of materials and some other material-related cost. For example, a decision to source from a low-cost supplier in a developing country may offer immediate price reductions. But once the incremental costs of acquisition such as shipping, duties, and inventory-carrying cost are considered, the company may achieve no savings. Worse, the decision could increase costs, even though the price-to-price savings appear tremendous.

Examining total cost of ownership also offers the opportunity to identify areas for collaboration. In fact, much of the benefit of collaborative relationships comes in the form of reduced acquisition costs. For example, a cooperative program that decreases inspection through supplier certification may have no immediate effect on purchase prices, but it could substantially reduce the customer's internal quality costs.

Principle 6: Segment the Spend
for Focus and to Break Compromises

Inexperienced strategy development team members often question why purchasing is so complicated. Having read the typical book on the subject, they quickly jump to the answer: "Buy complete systems from

Exhibit 4.3 Connector Manufacturing Practices

Key Parameters	Supplier 1 (Germany)	Supplier 2 (Germany)	Supplier 3 (U.S.)	Supplier 4 (U.S.)	Supplier 5 (Taiwan)	Supplier 6 (Japan)	Best Practices
Stamping							
• Strokes per minute	400–1,000	300–600	600–1,500	1,200–1,450	420–1,200	500–700	1,500
• Machines per operator	5	3	4.5	2.5	2.5	10	10
• Utilization	60%	55%	30%	40%	50%	70%	70%
• Tooling sets	2	2	2–4	1	2–5	2–3	3–4
Plating							
• Environment	Proprietary	Outsource	Average	Outsource on Header Pins	Below Average	Outsource	?
• Line speed (feet per minute)	?		30		20		?
Molding							
• Machines per operator	7	4	8	12	3	14	14
• Shift number × hours × days	3 × 8 × 5.5	3 × 8 × 6	3 × 8 × 5	2 × 12 × 7	3 × 8 × 6	1 × 8 × 5	168 hours per week
• Changeover (minutes)	180	30–120	30–60	45	30–60	30	30
• Utilization	75%	70%	80%	95%	90%	90%	95%
Assembly							
• Machines per operator	2.5	1	1	1	1	5	7
• Rejection rate (in parts per million)	900	2,500	4,400	5,000	3,000	100	100
• Utilization	40%	35%	45%	30–45%	50%	45%	50%
• Line speed (cycles per minute)	40	30	12	30	15	60	60

Source: Supplier visits and team analysis.

full-service, world-class suppliers that are the low-cost producers on a global scale using JIT, TQM, CAD/CAM, MRP, TPM, and other TLAs." ("TLAs?" you ask? "Three-letter acronyms," of course.)

The reality is that you can't have everything—this is the fundamental challenge in strategy development. The power of segmentation comes from the fact that it forces recognition of key drivers and helps break compromises. Consider the earlier example of tapping into low-cost suppliers in developing regions, which can increase inventory-carrying costs and obsolescence. Segmentation offers a way to have one's cake and eat it too. Tradeoffs are broken through segmentation: one segment chooses one side of the tradeoff equation while another selects the other side. Using the previous example, a strategy team should recognize that some of the purchased parts may have very predictable demand patterns, whereas others pose a high risk of obsolescence. The predictable parts, therefore, could be purchased from a low-cost global supplier with significant savings while the parts with a greater degree of risk are sourced locally. Exhibit 4.4 provides an example of such a segmented strategy for purchasing bar stock. In addition to segmenting the parts, the company also segmented the supplier roles.

Principle 7: Quantify the Benefits

Sourcing strategies seek to maximize the value in material purchases, but from a pragmatic perspective, value can be hard to define and measure. Strategy teams, therefore, should quantify costs whenever possible. Qualitative decisions regarding value then can be judged relative to the hard quantification of costs.

For example, suppliers often argue that their high levels of responsiveness create value for customers. Though it clearly is valuable, responsiveness should be evaluated against its cost. The first step is to quantify the value as much as possible—for example, as lower inventory-carrying costs for the customer and savings from fewer stock-outs. Such an analysis may not capture all of the benefits of a high-service supplier, but a rigorous comparison ensures that tradeoffs are made with an adequate understanding of the cost implications.

In practice, all too often the hard savings do not justify the incremental cost of suppliers who tout their "service orientation." Unfortunately,

Exhibit 4.4   Bar Stock Segmentation

Supplier	Role	Rationale	Strategic Imperatives
U.S. Minimill	Serve as key low-cost supplier with strong goal congruence and mutual dependence	• Low-cost continuous caster • Minimill leanness • Freight advantage	• Concentrate volume long term for mutual dependence • Jointly work size rationalization • Jointly optimize scheduling • Drive direct reduction of iron capability as needed
U.S. Integrated Mill 1	Additional low-cost "partner" for wider range and provides a hedge in scrap cost	• Basic oxygen furnace steel making • Wide grade and size capability • Coil quality and size • Willingness to partner	• Source for products outside the range of minimill • Commit to long-term volume to ensure that they keep a wide product range • Ensure that basic oxygen furnace investments are made as needed
U.S. Integrated Mill 2	Strong technical relationship to support aggressive transition from ingot to bloom	• Technical service • Highest-quality steel • Large reduction ratio of Ingot today; Bloom next year	• Key focus for grade rationalization • Long-term commitment to be supplier of key "families" of products • Transfer families of products (such as spindles) as design rationalization is completed • Demand high technical support
Russian Mill	Low-cost developmental source in a non-partnership relation	• Labor cost at 7% of domestic • Energy and materials at 56%	• Segment the buy into lead-time, critical and noncritical • Source noncritical, predictable demand from Russia

Source: Forging company case example.

suppliers who focus on service often do so because they are unable to compete on cost. Fortunately, the most cost-competitive companies, once they're found, often provide superior service as well as low cost because they have adopted the lean manufacturing principles that eliminate waste and enhance responsiveness.

Components of a Commodity Business Plan

Commodity business plan is the most common term for a documented sourcing strategy; these plans have become quite common. But few companies employ an appropriate level of rigor in developing the strategy or in documenting the plans. Leading companies recognize that the commodity business plan is part of the institutional memory for the company. The plans serve to educate a wide audience, from the new buyer just out of school to the senior manager preparing for supplier visits or negotiations.

Though each company has its own format, a comprehensive commodity business plan should include at least the following seven elements:

1. Documentation of the spend
2. Industry analysis
3. Explanation of cost and performance drivers
4. Segmentation of supplier roles
5. Business process priorities
6. Quantification of opportunity
7. Action plan for implementation

The first three elements document facts, providing the basis for decision making. As Charles F. Knight, Chairman of Emerson Electric Company, once said, "Getting the facts is the key to good decision making. Every mistake that I made—and we all make mistakes—came because I didn't take the time. I didn't drive hard enough to get the facts."

In developing a sourcing strategy, these three elements are often presented as an intermediate work product. Doing so grounds the team, and the management committee that typically oversees the work, in a common knowledge base. Often members of the team—and especially members of the management group, which is not as close to the supply market—tend to rely on their own set of "facts," which may be out-of-date or based on too narrow a point of view. Unless the group shares a common understanding of the real facts, members are unlikely to reach a consensus about the correct strategy.

The second three elements of a comprehensive business plan represent the core of a sourcing strategy. Through segmentation of supplier roles, the company determines the type of suppliers needed and the roles the suppliers should play. A typical strategy does not, however, name specific suppliers or make decisions about which parts or programs should be assigned to a given supplier. Selection decisions to craft the supply base are best handled at a tactical level within the boundaries of the strategy.

Business process priorities capture the key reason for the cooperative dimension of Balanced Sourcing: longer-term, collaborative supplier relationships make investing in joint processes possible. Companies that are able to integrate supplier business processes more effectively can create a competitive advantage, even though they may be using the same suppliers as their competitors.

Quantification of the opportunity, although it is often missing from commodity business plans, is an absolutely critical element. Quantification ensures that the strategy makes the optimal tradeoffs and "sells" the plan within a company by setting a stake for achieving results.

An action plan, the last element, is not actually part of the strategy—nor even strategic. Instead, the plan is a translation of the strategy into a set of tactical initiatives to capture the opportunity. Obviously, unless the strategy is implemented it is of no value, regardless of how well it was researched and documented.

The following case example demonstrates the kinds of information considered in each element and the level of analytic rigor used by a large automotive electronics company. The example is extracted from two reports issued by a discrete semiconductor commodity team during a twelve-week effort to develop a sourcing strategy. The first report marked the end of the research phase of the work and covered analyses of the spend, the supply industry, and the cost drivers. The final strategy report drew upon this baseline, as well as on additional research, to create a strategy and action plan.

Documentation of the Spend

One of the first challenges in developing a commodity business plan is to define the scope. In many organizations, particularly those that span multiple business units or geographies, the total outside purchases for a given commodity cannot be ascertained from any single source. As a result, most commodity business plans include an analysis of the spend along several dimensions:

- By business unit or product lines
- By buying location
- By supplier
- By subcommodity

Exhibit 4.5 shows an analysis from the discrete semiconductor team's report that shows usage by subcommodity and business unit. The analysis highlights the fact that power field-effect transistors (FETs), Zener diodes, and rectifiers account for 85 percent of the purchase dollars. Also, the powertrain and antilock braking system (ABS) business units were the major users. The analysis of the business units within the subcommodity shows that the two business units have different usage patterns.

The ABS business unit purchases little more than power FETs and, with the powertrain business unit, it dominates 95 percent of that subcommodity. The purchases in the powertrain unit are skewed much more toward the diodes, but other groups use a significant percentage as well. Also, the air controls and audio controls business units—though not major groups—account for most of the "miscellaneous categories." Understanding this distribution of the spend focused the company's efforts on understanding the needs of the key business units and subcommodities.

Such analysis is only a start and can sometimes even be misleading, because it examines historic usage patterns. Analysis that examines *future*

Exhibit 4.5 Discrete Semiconductor Usage

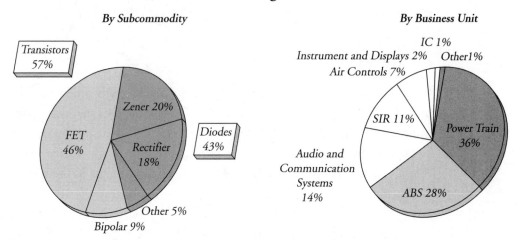

By Subcommodity

By Business Unit

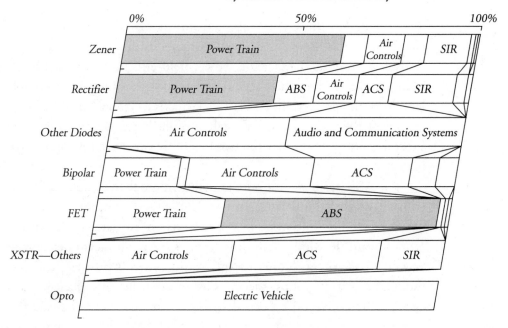

By Business Within Subcommodity

Note: ABS = Antilock Brake System
ACS = Audio and Communications
SIR = Safety, Integrated Restraints
Source: Automotive electronics supplier commodity business plan.

usage patterns can be even more important. For example, a dramatic growth in the electric vehicle business unit might lead to a significant shift in the purchases of optoelectronics. In this case the analysis showed fairly even rates of growth and less dramatic shifts in mix.

Proper spend documentation should also capture the total acquisition cost for the commodity. Such analysis reinforces the principle that a proper strategy should address total cost, not just price. As noted in Chapter Three, in some commodities the acquisition-cost elements can even exceed the direct cost of purchases.

The discrete semiconductor team initially identified incremental costs that amounted to just under 8 percent of the outside spend, as shown in Exhibit 4.6. Most of this cost was in transportation, some of which involved premium rates for expedited delivery. All in all, this company operated a fairly lean supply chain in the typical areas of total acquisition cost. But, as shown later in this chapter, the second report by the team uncovered some additional internal costs that were not adding value.

Exhibit 4.6   Total Cost of Ownership of Discrete Semiconductors

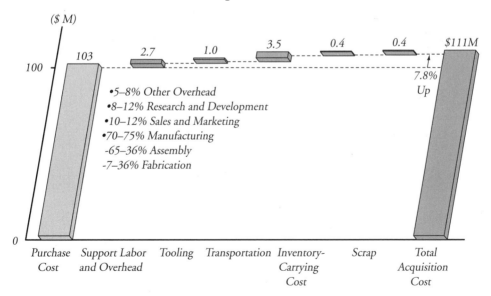

($ M)

| 103 | 2.7 | 1.0 | 3.5 | 0.4 | 0.4 | $111M |

•5–8% Other Overhead
•8–12% Research and Development
•10–12% Sales and Marketing
•70–75% Manufacturing
-65–36% Assembly
-7–36% Fabrication

7.8%
Up

| Purchase Cost | Support Labor and Overhead | Tooling | Transportation | Inventory-Carrying Cost | Scrap | Total Acquisition Cost |

Source: Automotive electronics supplier commodity business plan.

Industry Analysis

A thoughtful examination of the supply industry broadens the perspective of a commodity team. As noted in Principle 4, the analysis should take a global view as well. Effective industry analyses explore a variety of questions such as these:

- Who are the major suppliers by county or region? What are their market shares?
- Does the industry compete on a global basis? Why?
- Who are the major customers and customer industries?
- What are the basic strategies (cost, quality, time) employed by suppliers?
- How fast is the industry growing? Why?
- How common are new entrants?
- What is the level of merger and acquisitions activity? Why?
- What new technologies are on the horizon?

It should be noted, however, that there is no single list of questions that apply in all cases. Each industry is different and only the relevant issues should be documented.

For example, the discrete semiconductor team identified the top semiconductor manufacturers around the globe, noting that their current sourcing pattern was highly focused in the United States even though the industry operated on a global scale (see Exhibit 4.7).

The team also noted that different companies employed different degrees of vertical integration (see Exhibit 4.8). All did fabrication and assembly, but many relied on a second-tier supplier for wafer fabrication. Such findings raised questions about potential individual suppliers' responsiveness, cost, quality, and innovativeness. As the team began to understand its own strategic supply-base priorities, this issue reemerged as a consideration in supplier selection in certain segments.

For teams struggling to figure out the right questions to explore, an industry map and Michael Porter's "5 Forces" analysis, described in his classic book, *Competitive Strategy: Techniques for Analyzing Industries and Competitors,* provide a good starting point.[1] An industry map is a

Exhibit 4.7 Discrete Semiconductor Manufacturers in the World

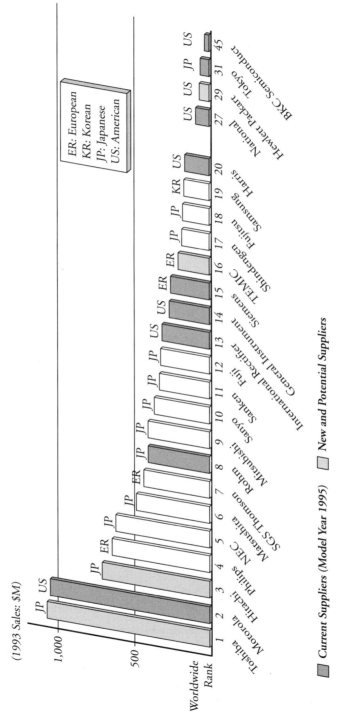

(1993 Sales: $M)

ER: European
KR: Korean
JP: Japanese
US: American

■ Current Suppliers (Model Year 1995)   □ New and Potential Suppliers

Source: Dataquest and team analysis.

Exhibit 4.8 Vertical Integration in the Semiconductor Industry

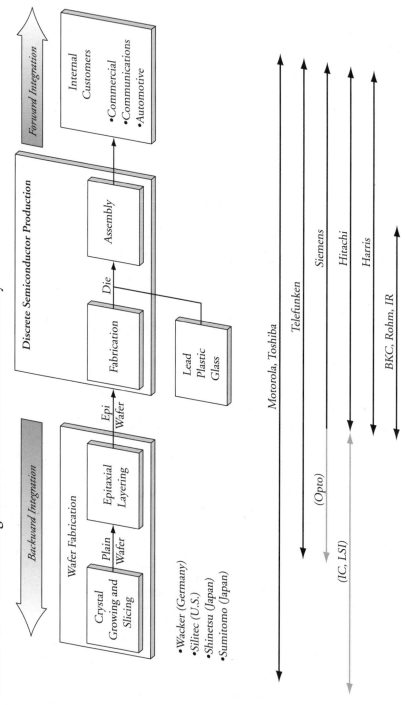

Source: Commodity team research.

simple one-page diagram of the supply industry. The map highlights the flow of product from key supply industries to major customer industries. It also shows the different roles that companies may play: assembler, manufacturer, or distributor. A sophisticated map might even show the percentage of sales in various channels. Constructing such a map is particularly important when a team is examining the option of shifting sourcing from distributors to upstream manufacturers or when an industry is undergoing restructuring.

The map provides the initial information needed to examine the basic competitive dynamics in the industry using the Porter "5 Forces" model:

1. Customer power
2. Supplier power
3. Intercompany competition
4. Threat of substitution
5. New entrants

Explanation of Cost and Performance Drivers

Chapter Three examined cost modeling in detail and highlighted the importance of building an understanding of cost. An effective commodity business plan should reflect a solid understanding of cost drivers as well as of other important performance metrics such as quality and flexibility.

The typical starting point in documenting cost and performance drivers is to map the manufacturing process. Documenting technology options at each stage provides further insight into the optimal approach. For example, Exhibit 4.9 illustrates a flowchart of the fabrication process for discrete semiconductor production. The chart highlights the multiple iterations of layering, photolithography, and doping. Such an understanding begs the question, What drives the number of iterations required? Furthermore, the chart notes that a wide range of options is available for photolithography. A number of logical questions flow from such a finding: Which technologies are most cost-effective? Which provide the best quality? Which have the greatest flexibility?

Exhibit 4.9   Fabrication Process Flowchart

Generic Process Steps

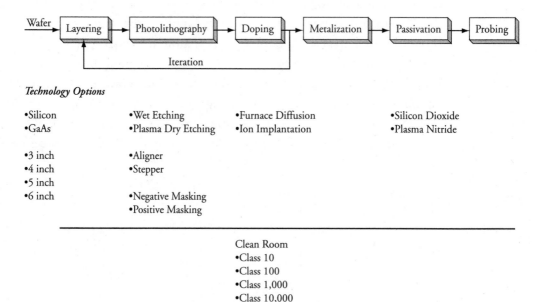

Technology Options

•Silicon	•Wet Etching	•Furnace Diffusion	•Silicon Dioxide
•GaAs	•Plasma Dry Etching	•Ion Implantation	•Plasma Nitride
•3 inch	•Aligner		
•4 inch	•Stepper		
•5 inch			
•6 inch	•Negative Masking		
	•Positive Masking		

Clean Room
•Class 10
•Class 100
•Class 1,000
•Class 10,000

A cost buildup by process step helps to answer these questions. Generally, strategy development only requires high-level cost models based on an understanding of the major cost drivers. Supplier selection, which follows strategy development, requires more detailed, comparative models of specific suppliers.

For example, the team identified two major cost drivers for discrete semiconductors—unit volume and the learning curve effect—from their examination of the process flow. Unit volume was significant because of the high setup cost of the capital-intensive manufacturing process. The team also learned that process yield was often low in the early phases of a product introduction due to the high number of iterations in a process that is often not yet under control. Accordingly, as a company improved the process with experience, the yields went up and the costs came down. The team developed a simple model, shown in Exhibit 4.10, that illustrated the two effects.

Exhibit 4.10   Volume and Learning Effects

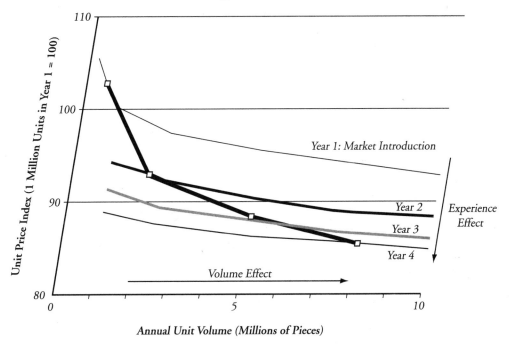

Segmentation of Supplier Roles

Segmentation of supplier roles is the first element of the actual strategy. It focuses on segmenting the purchases across a set of differentiated supplier roles. For example, the team decided that the right way to think about the purchases was not by subcommodity or consuming business units—the traditional ways to segment the buy. Instead, since they understood that volume and learning effects were critical cost drivers, the team decided to classify the parts by stage in the product life cycle, as shown in Exhibit 4.11.

The team also recognized that different drivers were appropriate to each segment and recommended fundamentally different sourcing strategies in each segment. Despite an overall philosophy of cooperation with the supply base, the team concluded that a more traditional strategy of annual competitive bidding was appropriate for the high-volume parts

Exhibit 4.11   Discrete Semiconductor Segmentation

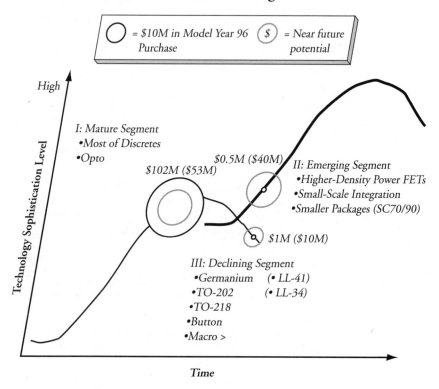

in the mature segment. Field interviews had shown that discrete semiconductor suppliers recognized that pricing was the primary basis of competition, given that most parts were industry-standard designs and interchangeable among suppliers. A bidding approach was not viewed as a lack of commitment to a cooperative relationship, simply as a business reality.

The team noted, however, that annual bidding would cost more than it would save for the lower-volume, mature parts. Therefore, they bundled these parts and bid them on a multiyear basis, with a commitment for annual price reductions based upon further learning-curve cost reductions.

The team concluded that the emerging segment was the most critical, because a more rapid implementation of emerging technologies could provide a competitive advantage. As a result, the team recommended establishing long-term partnership agreements with select suppliers to focus on several high-potential areas. Though the suppliers would not bid on these parts on an annual basis, prices would be driven down continuously by applying the team's knowledge of the learning and volume effects. As the company adopted these new products as standard, the volumes would increase and the supplier could continue on a steep learning curve.

The declining segment was relatively small but was expected to grow as mature products were dropped by suppliers. This segment also demanded a nontraditional approach. Since the products were in the declining phase, few suppliers were available, making competitive bidding impossible. In fact, the company often had to convince a supplier to continue to produce a product even though demand by other customers was dropping off.

Not surprisingly, in such negotiations the supplier has the leverage and can extract premium pricing. The heart of the strategy for this segment, therefore, was internally focused: the team recommended identifying the parts that were shifting into the declining phase so that the company could proactively design the parts out of the end product to reduce risk in pricing and availability. This concept may seem relatively straightforward, but in fact, it is not. Parts shift into the declining phase based on *overall* industry demand, and unless a company is monitoring the market, it may not realize that a part has dropped out of favor in the industry.

Interestingly, the company had previously applied a Pareto (or ABC) segmentation as the basis of its strategy. This approach identified the high-volume and high-value parts for annual competitive bidding. However, it missed the implications of the other segments. The segmentation group put all low-volume items into the C category. These C items were grouped and bid out as a long-term, blanket contract with fixed pricing. Unfortunately, many of the C items were in fact parts that were in the emerging segment, where volumes would be growing dramatically as the technology caught on. The fixed-price contracts did not capture the huge cost reductions available as volumes increased and yields improved. The new segmentation ensured that only the true long-term, low-volume items were bundled into such contracts.

Business Process Priorities

Defining the appropriate supplier roles creates much of the benefit in strategy development, but far from all of it. The Balanced Sourcing model includes a commitment to cooperative relationships for a reason: better integration of business processes. Therefore, a strategy should define the critical areas for supplier integration.

For example, the discrete semiconductor team found several opportunities for changes in business processes. The key benefits came from eliminating low-value activities that the customer demanded of the supplier. Specifically, the team recommended the following:

1. Eliminate bar codes on the leader tape of reels for surface-mount devices (see Exhibit 4.12).
2. Use suppliers' standard labels instead of high-density bar codes.
3. Accept suppliers' standard marking in lieu of unique part marking.
4. Conduct necessary lead-forming internally.

The first three items covered activities that suppliers performed for the customer, which the team—using their understanding of cost drivers—determined were not worth the cost. The fourth item required significant analysis by the team. The team first examined the reasons for lead forming to determine whether it could be eliminated. After all, the best way to save money is to not spend it! The team identified three reasons for lead forming:

1. Stress relief (not removable)
2. Circuit-board space savings (not removable)
3. Error proofing (removable)

The team also discovered that the category of "removable lead forming" provided limited cost savings because 95 percent of the items in question needed to be lead-trimmed, which required the same efforts as lead forming. Accepting that lead forming could not be eliminated, the team next examined whether it could be performed less expensively.

Exhibit 4.12 Leader Tape Bar Code Requirement

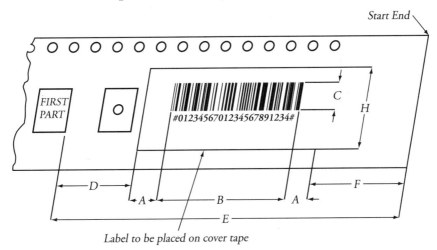

Label to be placed on cover tape

Leader Tape Bar Code Placement Dimensions

A =   5.08 mm (0.200 in) Minimum
B =   83.8 mm (3.30 in for 9.4 CPI Reference (High Density)
B =   121.14 mm (4.77 in) for 6.5 CPI Reference (Standard Density)
C =   4.0mm (0.157 in) Minimum, Leader Tape only
C =   6.35 mm (0.250 in) Minimum, Reel Only
D =   203.2 mm (8.0 in) Minimum
D =   304.8 mm (12.0 in) Maximum
E =   500 mm (19.68 in) Minimum
F =   50.8 mm (2.0 in) Minimum

Source: Case Company's Engineering Specification Book.

Conventional wisdom suggests outsourcing as a solution. Rather than simply following conventional wisdom, the team compared the cost of lead forming in-house with outsourcing it to suppliers and documented a significant savings opportunity. Interestingly, the team found that in some cases the supplier really did not care to provide the service and had done it only at the customer's insistence. Supplier pricing generally reflected the suppliers' desire—or lack thereof—to perform the activity. Not surprisingly, the savings were substantial.

Quantification of Opportunity

Quantification provides the proof of a well-done strategy. As Grace Murray Hopper, a former U.S. Navy admiral, said, "One accurate measurement is worth a thousand expert opinions." Money is the language of management, so measuring in dollars (or yen, pounds, or duetsche marks) produces the best translation.

The discrete semiconductor team documented a savings opportunity of 11 percent to 15 percent on the total acquisition-cost baseline of $111 million, as shown in Exhibit 4.13. The chart shows the four actions that provided the savings, as well as a fifth action—better management of declining parts—that would avoid cost in the future. The team also identified the timing of savings for use in budgeting and setting long-term business plans.

The bulk of the savings identified by the discrete semiconductor team came from enhanced competitive practices, which again seems to go against conventional wisdom. The reasons were threefold. First, using the matrix shown in Exhibit 1.1, the company was probably best classified in the top left quadrant, "Trust-Based Partnerships." Though the clout-based approach to supplier relationships works for the automotive industry, the company recognized that it would not work with gigantic global semiconductor manufacturers. Unfortunately, the company had overcompensated because of a lack of understanding of the appropriate balance between competitive practices and cooperative relationships in the industry.

Second, discrete semiconductors are some of the most commodity-like components produced by semiconductor manufacturers. One company's parts are easily substituted for another's, and though technology has been continuously evolving, it has changed in response to industry demands, not the needs of any individual customer. So cooperation in innovation provides little advantage.

Third, the company already had a relatively lean supply chain, as indicated by the low acquisition-cost increment in the baseline cost model. The team found some savings by eliminating low-value activities such as special marking and external lead forming, but these did not require special cooperative integration activities. In fact, the elimination

Exhibit 4.13 Summary of Savings Opportunities

Opportunity	*Acquisition Cost ($M)*	*Savings Opportunity ($M)*	*Savings % of Acquisition Cost*	*Timing*	*Comments*
1. High-Volume, High-Dollar Mature Parts Competitive Bidding	$77	$6–9.5 M	12	Short to Mid	• Dual approval promoted • Multiyear contracts not preferred
2. Low-Volume, Low-Dollar Mature Parts Bundling	26	1.0	3–5	Short	
3. Migration to Emerging Parts	47	4.0–5.0 + α	8–10	Mid to Long	• α: Small-scale integration, not quantifiable
4. Elimination of Low-Value Work	—	1.0 (plus 0.5)[a]	—	Short to Mid	• Internal lead forming • Standard bar codes and labels • Standard part marking
5. Better Management of Declining Parts	10	(1.0–2.0)	(10–20)	Mid to Long	• Cost avoidance
Total Opportunities:	111	12–16.5	11–15		
• Short term		3–4			
• Medium term		5–7.5			
• Long term		4–5			

[a]Effect of elimination of leader tape bar codes for all the surface mount parts, such as resistors, capacitors, and integrated circuits.

Source: Commodity team analysis.

of low-value activities reduced the need for close supply web integration by returning to industry-standard labeling standards rather than customized requirements.

Action Plan for Implementation

An action plan is the final element of an effective sourcing strategy. A good implementation plan defines the activities, resources, and milestones for achieving the objectives of the strategy.

A key element of any implementation plan is a Gantt chart of the timing of the task. Exhibit 4.14 shows the Gantt chart prepared by the discrete semiconductor team. The first action item for the team is a common one: to communicate the results of the strategy to the supplier base. Despite the fact that much of the opportunity identified by the team came from an increase in competitive practices, the company firmly believed in a Balanced Sourcing model. Living the philosophy for this company included the belief that suppliers deserved to know and understand the reasons for the company's behavior. The company discovered that suppliers are likely to be more cooperative when they understand the rationale behind a set of actions, even if they do not agree with the decisions.

The other action items tie directly back to the quantification chart prepared by the team. Keeping the plans consistent with the quantification helps in setting resource plans. Since resources are often constrained, understanding how the benefits compare with the resources applied ensures solid decision making and accountability.

Conclusion

Sourcing strategy is far more than a simple allocation of business to suppliers by the purchasing function. Instead it is a multifunctional activity that produces a plan of action for several years. Effective plans are built on a rigorous analysis of the buy, the supply industry, and the fundamental drivers of value. Consistently creating and implementing effective sourcing strategies is a key organizational capability for Balanced Sourcing.

Exhibit 4.14 Discrete Semiconductor Implementation Plan

Model Year 97
Business Plan Start

Action Items	Jun	Jul	Aug	Sept	Oct	Nov	Dec
	19 26 3	10 17 24 31	7 14 21 28	4 11 18 25	2 9 16 23 30	6 13 20 27	4 11 18 25

Supplier Feedback Document — Document, Communicate

Mature Segment
- Supplier Base Finalization — Evaluate
- Second Source Evaluation and Approval — Approve
- Bundling Units Determination — Develop, Test and Refine

Emerging Segment
- Partnership Option Evaluation
- Commodity Symposium Setup
- Partner Selection — 1st Symposium in Jan. ◇

Declining Segment
- Macro X Replacement
- Asian Supplier Evaluation
- Industry Trend Monitoring

Little Value-Added Work Elimination
- Lead Forming
- Bar Coding
- Labeling
- Part Marking

Source: Commodity team plan.

Chapter 5
Building and Sustaining Relationships

> Any business arrangement that is not profitable to the other fellow
> will in the end prove unprofitable to you. The bargain that yields
> mutual satisfaction is the only one that is apt to be repeated.
> —B. C. FORBES

One of the fundamental principles of Balanced Sourcing is that a customer and a supplier working together to find savings opportunities will do better than each working independently. Through modeling total cost, the first Balanced Sourcing capability, customers and suppliers can focus their joint effort by identifying the critical elements and drivers of cost. Creating sourcing strategies, the second organizational capability, builds upon the knowledge gained from cost modeling and works toward long-term value creation in customer-supplier relationships. But capturing the long-term value most fully depends upon the customer's capability for building and sustaining relationships with suppliers.

In a recent *Strategy & Business* survey of a diverse group of large corporations, respondents ranked building and sustaining supplier relationships as the most critical of the six Balanced Sourcing capabilities.

Note: This chapter was written in collaboration with Dorian Swerdlow and Beverly Wolfer of Booz·Allen & Hamilton's New York office and draws on an article originally published in *Purchasing* magazine.

Almost all indicated, however, that they had not fully developed this capability. Though a few respondents—about 18 percent—indicated that they have strategic relationships with more than half of their suppliers, most admitted that the numbers were much smaller.

When probed about the techniques they employ in structuring supplier relationships, only a few companies said that they have adopted the most popular techniques cited in the literature. For example, no respondent reported that direct equity investment in suppliers was a standard practice, while 50 percent admitted that it was never used. "Evergreen" or "life of part" contracts were standard with only 13 percent of the respondents, and only 10 percent employed productivity clauses. Even some of the more simple techniques, like supplier councils and recognition programs, were not standard practice. Only 31 percent of respondents indicated that supplier recognition programs were standard, and even fewer—22 percent—employed supplier councils.

Building and sustaining *balanced* relationships with a company's strategic suppliers requires a truly advanced capability, built on and supporting the other five capabilities. This chapter briefly explains why building long-term relationships produces more value than taking a transactional approach. More important, it describes a model for building relationships with the appropriate balance between cooperation and competition. The chapter concludes with suggested pilot programs that business organizations can use to enhance this capability.

Long-Term Supplier Relationships

Game theory suggests that cooperation is a poor tactic unless the participants in the game have repeated opportunities to interact. In the game of business, companies and their suppliers tend to interact over long periods of time, even if they are not explicitly pursuing supplier partnerships. Because it encourages cooperation, Balanced Sourcing implicitly recognizes this need to take a long-term view in relationships. The benefits of long-term cooperative relationships generally fall into two categories: relationship-specific investment and communication.

Relationship-Specific Investment

Increased investment is the most often cited value derived from long-term supplier relationships. Suppliers secure about the future stream of business from a customer are more likely to invest in the relationship. For example, new manufacturing equipment can often reduce a supplier's cost of manufacturing, but only when the capital cost is amortized over many years. Dedicated equipment, assigned exclusively to one customer, can improve responsiveness as well as reduce cost. In the automotive industry, suppliers even build dedicated plants—literally next door to their customer's assembly plant—to enable just-in-time delivery. But once again, such investments appear excessively risky without a long-term point of view.

The opportunity for supplier investments goes well beyond plants and equipment. For example, Nippondenso, a sophisticated producer of automotive subsystems such as radiators and alternators, makes huge investments in developing new technologies for Toyota Motor Corporation well in advance of being awarded a specific vehicle contract. Though often difficult to measure, a supplier's investment in tailoring its business processes, such as its quality or planning systems, can add tremendous value. More specifics about integrating suppliers in manufacturing and product development are addressed in the next two chapters.

Of course, the investment in long-term relationships applies to both sides. Customers also make significant investments in suppliers. For example, 40 to 50 Honda purchasing professionals work full-time on-site with suppliers as part of their unique "BP" supplier development program. Since the company's entire purchasing department consists of only 360 people, this represents a big investment by Honda, which it can justify only if the benefits accrue over the many years of a long-term relationship.

Communication

The number of links and the degree of interaction between customers and suppliers can be mind-boggling. Exhibit 5.1 depicts the results of a survey of a dozen key suppliers for one large manufacturer. The analysis

Exhibit 5.1   Interfaces with People per Supplier (by Process Type)

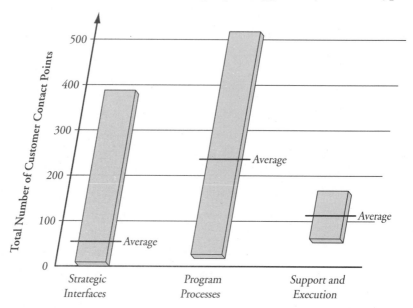

Source: Automotive company example based on survey of suppliers.

revealed that, on average, suppliers dealt with more than four hundred different people in the customer organization—and that some suppliers dealt with twice that number. The types of individuals suppliers contacted covered the full gamut of the customer organization, from senior executives dealing with strategic issues to front-line employees managing the day-to-day execution activities.

These myriad points of contact provide the channels for communication, and many companies spend inordinate resources trying to control the information flow through these channels. Company executives fear that corporate secrets will leak to competitors through the supply base; suppliers share the same fear about their customers. The more common reality, however, is exemplified by the Honda supplier executive who initially resisted working cooperatively with competing suppliers. After touring competitors' plants in an effort to share best practices, he noted, "I now realize that most of what I thought was a secret wasn't so secret after all."

Even where the risk of leaking proprietary information is real, the benefits of open communications typically outweigh the risks. As a customer and supplier work together for a long period of time, their employees get to know each other. They talk regularly and understand the context of the shared business relationship. Just as employee turnover within a company disrupts business and drains productivity, so does supplier turnover. With each change of supplier, a large number of personal contacts are broken and establishing new ones means returning to the top of the learning curve. Long-term commitments not only keep relationships intact; they also allow for continued refinement—replacing disjointed, ad hoc interfaces with efficient, quickly understood transactions.

For example, a team of academics at the University of Michigan recently investigated the frequency of communication among various vehicle manufacturers and their suppliers. To the team's surprise, they discovered that although Toyota leverages suppliers in innovation more extensively than its competitors, it communicates with the suppliers *less* frequently. Follow-up interviews with suppliers indicated that through many years of working with Toyota they had developed a deep understanding of Toyota's processes and expectations, so less frequent communication was required—this despite the broader role suppliers play in product development for Toyota.[1]

Most companies recognize the value of investment and communication in long-term supplier relationships. After all, talk of "supplier partnerships" and "strategic alliances" inundates current business literature. And the popular literature suggests that "trust" is the key to effective customer-supplier relationships. But simply preaching trust as a new gospel is unworkable at best—and definitely naive.

Translating Trust into Action

So how do customers and suppliers build relationships on a more solid footing than that of vague trust in one another? Translating trust into action requires three things: mutual dependence, goal congruence, and knowledge of competency.

Mutual Dependence

Mutual dependence occurs when both parties understand that cooperation is necessary for each company to succeed. A supplier's dependence on a customer obviously increases as its sales to that customer increase. But volume is only one form of supplier dependence, and frankly the less balanced form. Customers that are capable of helping their suppliers improve can be more critical to the success of a supplier than a large, detached customer. Such a recognition led many U.S. automotive suppliers to seek out the Japanese transplants even before their production volumes were significant.

Likewise, a customer that has rationalized its supply base by concentrating its purchasing volume with only a few suppliers for each commodity has increased its dependence on individual suppliers. Exhibit 5.2 shows a list of supplier switching costs developed by a chemical company. It highlights the fact that replacing an existing supplier

Exhibit 5.2   Supplier Switching Costs

- Physical Costs
    Investment by the supplier in new equipment
    Equipment and fixture transfer
    Inventory buildup (to cover transition time)
    Product validation

- Information-Associated Costs
    Supplier engineering investment in production processes
    Product redesign (if a proprietary supplier design)
    Updating engineering drawings and training supplier personnel
    Supply chain linkage

- Transition Management
    Management time
    Legal and contracts
    Travel

- Contract dissolution with the old supplier

can mean huge one-time costs. But customer dependence based on avoiding switching costs is rather tenuous. Suppliers who offer a set of capabilities unmatched by their competitors increase their customers' dependence on them in a far more stable way.

Mutual dependence demands balance, not extremes. Despite the common misconception, Japanese companies illustrate very balanced examples of mutual dependence. Though they single-source at the individual part-number level, Japanese original-equipment manufacturers almost always have two or more suppliers at the commodity level, so one can step in if the other fails. Also, according to one study, though they are generally partially owned by a larger company in a Keiretsu, even small Japanese subcontractors (defined as those with fewer than fifty employees) had an average of three customers. According to the study, across the Japanese manufacturing sector as a whole, only 17 percent of subcontracting firms had only one customer.[2]

Honda of America demonstrates a balanced form of mutual dependence: the company maintains a small supplier network and strives to be each supplier's most important customer. Honda invests in supplier development and continuously value-engineers the products it buys. Such efforts help suppliers to become more competitive overall and enable them to win new customers in addition to Honda. But by continuing to raise the bar on its suppliers' performance while giving them a boost to help them scale it, Honda maintains its position as the most valuable customer.

Because such investments in supplier development are expensive, Honda focuses on a small number of suppliers and depends on long-term relationships with them to generate returns. At the same time, Honda typically has two suppliers with the potential to replace one another, therefore avoiding overdependence. Nonetheless, Honda's associates and suppliers cite multiple examples where the company invested millions of dollars to help suppliers solve problems rather than simply replacing them with new suppliers. After relating one of these examples of supplier support, however, Dave Nelson, then Vice President of Purchasing and Administrative Services for Honda, quickly pointed out that Honda's motives were hardly altruistic. "Of course we didn't charge him for what we did. But it was also self-serving. There was plenty of benefit to be gained on both sides by making sure we kept this supplier for the long term."

Cisco Systems clearly recognizes the importance of mutual dependence. Cisco has only a minimal level of in-house manufacturing, for final assembly and testing, making the company extremely dependent upon outside suppliers. With 65 percent gross margins and very short product life cycles, Cisco can ill afford missed sales resulting from a supplier shortfall. Accordingly, Cisco employees continuously ask suppliers to "bet with us" by adding or reserving capacity to support Cisco's growth. Growth rates that often reach 100 percent per year indicate that Cisco clearly places some good bets. But even when an individual bet doesn't pan out, Cisco works hard to cover the suppliers by awarding them business from other products that are exceeding expectations. Such mutual dependence has stimulated rapid growth for suppliers while driving a hundredfold increase in Cisco's stock price in a mere seven years.

Goal Congruence

Mutual dependence by itself can lead to stagnation. Common, aggressive goals drive both sides to achieve maximum benefit from the relationship. Unfortunately, unbalanced incentives often stymie collaboration. To make goal congruence real—and something beyond an ill-defined strategic imperative—the key business issues of profits and risks must be addressed.

Who Gets the Profits?   Even in cooperative relationships, power in the marketplace—a function of supply and demand—matters. Which company gets the majority share of the value created depends on the uniqueness or scarcity of what each company brings to the table. The first requirement in splitting the pie is that each side gets enough to foster the mutual dependence discussed earlier. The second requirement is to ensure that the pie doesn't shrink as it is being cut.

SUPERVALU, one of North America's largest wholesale grocers, ensures goal congruence with its suppliers by not fighting over the pie at all. Thanks to SUPERVALU's ADVANTAGE program, all supplier price reductions are passed directly on to the retail grocer customers. Before SUPERVALU launched its ADVANTAGE program, the majority of its profits, like those of other wholesalers, were achieved through techniques such as forward/anticipatory buying and reselling at a higher price or retaining discounts from suppliers. Such techniques, though profitable, clearly did not instill a sense of common purpose or trust with suppliers or customers. Now customers see the real cost of the product and pay a markup that reflects the direct value-added services that SUPERVALU has provided. As a result, suppliers now share the common goal of reducing their costs to SUPERVALU, since price reductions are passed on to the retail grocer to stimulate additional sales volume, to the joint benefit of SUPERVALU and the suppliers.

Who Takes the Risks? All business ventures face risks such as uncertain future demand or unproved technology. Achieving goal congruence requires risk as well as profit to be balanced in the relationship. Typically suppliers and customers hold different views on the same element of risk because each has a different amount of control over the situation. Collaborative relationships can reduce the overall risk for the companies by placing the greater burden for the risk on the company best able to bear it.

Contracting for routine construction services—such as painting and minor repair work—illustrates the opportunity to trade off risk. Construction contractors face two primary risks: inefficient utilization of their labor force—the bulk of their cost structure—through the seasonal cycle and the actual-versus-estimated work hours on an individual project. With short-term, fixed-priced contracts, the supplier fully bears both of these risks. A customer that can reasonably predict the level of demand for such services over the year can reduce the supplier's risk through an annual service contract without increasing its own risk.

With a long-term contract, the customer may also choose cost-plus-fee pricing rather than a firm fixed price and thereby mitigate the supplier's second risk. Such a contract, however, could also lessen the supplier's motivation to finish the work in the fewest possible hours, which merely shifts rather than reduces the risk. In this case, the best answer to "Who takes the risk?" depends on who has the most control over the actual hours worked. If the customer is relatively uncertain about what needs to be done—and expects to change the project scope once the work begins—a cost-plus contract would be best. A fixed-price contract would encourage the supplier to price with a large contingency buffer to ensure profitability under the worst-case scenario. Under anything but the worst case, however, the supplier makes excess profits. Alternatively, when the customer has clearly defined the desired output and the supplier has a better understanding of the effort required, a fixed-price contract places the risk burden on the appropriate shoulders.

Cisco Systems provides another example. Cisco has more ready access to cash than many of its suppliers. To take advantage of its lower risk in financing, Cisco employs a payment system that allows suppliers to tap into this lower cost of capital to fund inventory, shifting the investment risk to the party most capable of bearing it.

Knowledge of Competency

Blind trust of even the most committed supplier is misplaced. Mutual dependence and common goals mean nothing if the supplier lacks the capability to meet the customer's requirements: an incompetent but well-intentioned supplier is still incompetent. In order to trust a supplier partner, the customer has to be confident that the supplier is competent.

Testing competency requires a detailed understanding of the supplier's competitive position. Today, most leading companies have halted the historic practice of using "three bids in a cloud of dust" to find out which supplier has the lowest price. Instead, thanks to Xerox Corporation's pioneering work in benchmarking in the 1980s, today most leading companies use benchmarking to test supplier competency in a broader range of areas such as new technology, delivery lead times, and price competitiveness. The most capable suppliers welcome such comparisons as opportunities to prove their prowess.

Assessments of supplier competency typically cover four broad areas: capabilities, cost structure, risk factors, and relationship potential.

Capabilities. The first area to consider in assessing supplier competency is the supplier's technical and business know-how and its processes. For example, does the supplier have sufficient capacity and flexibility to change the product volume and mix quickly? How quickly can product design changes be incorporated? Can the supplier coordinate the supply web to ensure minimum inventory expense and just-in-time delivery? Will the supplier be able to meet future needs in terms of volume and product technology? What services, such as product design, materials purchasing, inspection, and warehousing, can the supplier provide more effectively or economically than the customer? Clearly, evaluating supplier capabilities across such a wide range of topics requires a strong, multifunctional assessment team.

Cost Structure.   The supplier's underlying cost structure determines whether its pricing is sustainable over the long term. Furthermore, the cost structure determines how easily and quickly the supplier will be able to reduce costs—and ultimately prices. For example, two steel mills may quote similar prices based on similar costs. Further examination may indicate that one has a less expensive process technology, such as a continuous caster, whereas the other better utilizes its capital equipment. Demand, and therefore utilization, may change overnight, while process technology changes may require a huge investment. Such cost understanding allows a company to choose the supplier with the best long-term cost structure when establishing a long-term relationship.

Risk Factors.   Even if the capabilities and cost seem in order, the risk of the unexpected needs to be managed. A check of the supplier's financial strength and stability can indicate its ability to meet its commitments and to continue to invest in the relationship. A move toward long-term relationships with fewer suppliers magnifies such risks.

Relationship Potential.   A supplier must be willing and able to "partner" with the customer to tap into the value created by a collaborative relationship. A supplier that is interested in a long-term relationship should also be willing to invest in defining and building the relationship. Requesting a specific proposal from the supplier about how the companies might collaborate provides an excellent indicator. Part of the proposal should address how the customer fits into the supplier's long-term strategy. If the customer's needs don't fit logically, the supplier is not likely to value the relationship in the future.

Exhibit 5.3 provides examples of possible supplier evaluation criteria, adapted from Booz·Allen's client work, grouped under each of the four competency areas. Although the list of criteria to consider is extensive, a proper assessment will focus on the critical few that are relevant for a particular type of purchase and supplier.

A couple of words of caution are warranted concerning supplier assessment. A common trap involves creating an overly simple scoring system for comparing different suppliers along the four dimensions. The tendency is to award scores in all the categories of criteria and then add them up. The first caution is to recognize that on some criteria, capacity, for example, the supplier is either acceptable or unacceptable, because incremental capacity beyond the customer's needs isn't valuable and could even be considered wasteful. The second caution is to recognize that some shortfalls are more easily corrected than others. For example, it may be easier to teach one supplier statistical process control than to convince another supplier to build a new plant in a low-labor-cost area to match the first supplier.

Trust Is Not Enough

Admittedly, mutual dependence, goal congruence, and knowledge of competency lack the appeal of a single philosophical ideal like trust. And translating trust from a philosophy into a workable set of corporate practices may clash with the inspired vision of gurus preaching supplier partnership. It should be pointed out, however, that the leaders of a faith cannot rely on divine revelation for long. Sooner or later, they must resort to such management tools as commandments and doctrine. Long-lasting relationships grow from such a foundation, not from blind trust.

Pilot Programs to Build the Capability

Building and sustaining supplier relationships is a bit more amorphous than either of the first two capabilities discussed here. Relationships are

Exhibit 5.3. Supplier Evaluation Criteria

Capabilities	Cost	Risk	Partnership Potential

• Production capabilities
  Products
  Capacity
  Product quality assurance
  Delivery lead time
  Flexibility for volume and
    mix changes
• Service capabilities
  Purchasing
  Incoming inspection
  Transportation and
    warehousing
  Product development
  Specification and design
    change accommodation
  Financial and operational
    reporting
  Information systems and
    electronic data interchange
  After-sale service
• Service quality and reputation
  Delivery history
  References
  ISO 9000 (or other relevant
    certifications)
  Regulatory compliance
	• Supplier cost structure
	  Product and process
	    technology
	  Scale and utilization
	  Location
	  Labor
	  Other
	• Initial investments and
	  transition costs based on the
	  transition plan
	• Added or eliminated customer
	  costs based on services
	  provided by the supplier
	• Pricing
	  Base pricing
	  Volume discounting
	  Performance incentive or
	    penalty
	  Year-over-year reduction
	    commitments
	  Contract length
		• Financial strength and stability
		  Sales, profitability, and
		    growth
		  Assets
		  Relationship to parent
		    company
		  Investment ability
		  Bond rating
		• Agreements
		  Insurance and indemnification
		  Risk sharing (for example,
		    equipment and inventory
		    ownership)
		  Alliances
		• Quality of transition plan
		  Timing
		  Takeover of equipment and
		    workforce
		  Financing
		  Subcontracting required
		  Contingency plans
		  Quality and experience of
		    implementation team
		  Linking the supply chain
			• Fit of proposed process and
			  infrastructure
			  Completeness of proposed
			    operation
			  Process integration with
			    customer
			  Implementation of customer's
			    vision
			• Compatibility
			  Strategic direction
			  Proposed kind of contract
			  Cultural fit
			  Management stability
			  Willingness to share
			    information

dynamic and continuously evolving—we hope in a positive direction. The output for pilots to build this capability aren't as tangible as a cost model or a commodity business plan, but they are nonetheless measurable.

Three different types of pilots offer opportunities to build supplier relationship capabilities: a relationship structuring and renewal pilot, a supplier development program, or a supplier suggestion system. Each enhances a different element of the capability.

Relationship Structuring and Renewal

Truly strategic relationships are built one supplier at a time, because each supplier offers a different value proposition. Tailoring a relationship with a single key supplier offers the opportunity to demonstrate the value of long-term relationships in a tangible way, rather than simply preaching the need.

Implementation of a sourcing strategy—as described in Chapter Four—offers the opportunity to build relationships with specific suppliers to support the commodity strategy. A good sourcing strategy describes the value-creation levers and the specific roles a supplier might play. Sharing the strategies and then assessing supplier competency against a tailored set of criteria provides the basis for establishing new supplier relationships with the appropriate focus.

Alternatively, some companies have launched pilots to improve this capability by simply selecting a key long-term supplier for a targeted improvement effort. Through facilitated working sessions, the company and the supplier identify and then jointly resolve problems in the current relationship. General Electric Company applies its well-publicized "work out" process with suppliers toward this end. Exhibit 5.4 illustrates an actual example of the type of opportunity that can be discovered through such joint working sessions. In this example, a manufacturer of forged steel parts and its bar stock supplier identified ways to reduce total scrap by optimizing across both operations rather than independently. Implementation required a simple change in order policies—and pricing—based on a better understanding of the total cost across the two companies.

Exhibit 5.4   Working Together to Reduce Scrap Cost

Customer Process for Using Steel Bar

Customer process cannot use 6 inches at each end of bar
Percent scrap = (2 x 6 inches) / bar length
= 6.7% for a 15-foot bar
= 3.3% for a 30-foot bar

Measuring the Cost Savings Requires Communication

The customer specified 30-foot-long steel bars from the supplier to keep the scrap rate to a minimum. However, the length specification increased scrap at the supplier by more than it decreased scrap at the customer. If the customer lowers its length requirement to 15 feet from 30, total scrap at the customer would increase by 3.3% while decreasing at the supplier by 7%. The net improvement would be 3.7%. (Note: The net cost benefit is somewhat less than 3.7% because the steel can be remelted and the customer scrap must be shipped back to the supplier.)

Supplier Process for Rolling Steel Bar

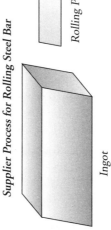

Ingot

Rolling Process

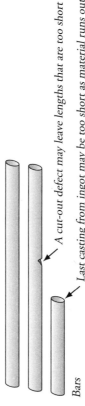

A cut-out defect may leave lengths that are too short

Last casting from ingot may be too short as material runs out

Bars

Supplier process sometimes fails to produce longer bars
Scrap rate increases as required length increases
= 5% for 15-foot bars
= 12% for 30-foot bars

Expanding the Pie: An Oil Industry Case Example

A major oil company developed a set of sourcing strategies reflecting the value-creation opportunities across a wide range of commodities. The negotiations for well services provide an excellent example of an implementation of the sourcing strategy as a relationship-building pilot.

A critical well service, pressure pumping attempts to stimulate wells to increase the rate of oil production. Without some form of stimulation, the output rate of a well follows a fairly predictable decline. Accordingly, the effectiveness of pressure pumping can be measured by examining incremental oil production beyond the expected trend versus the incremental cost of the service.

Traditionally, the oil company negotiated rates for materials, equipment, and labor with the well service provider, employing them as needed on a well-by-well basis. The suppliers faced significant utilization risk because of the unpredictable pattern of demand by the customer. As a result, well service providers set prices based upon pessimistic utilization rates.

On the flip side, the oil company held the performance risk of the actual job scope. Generally, it failed to leverage service providers' expertise and instead independently paid the suppliers on hourly or other unit rates.

The sourcing strategy identified a cost savings opportunity by contracting over a longer time period and allowing the supplier more flexibility in scheduling the work. Recognizing that the suppliers often had superior regional field knowledge, the strategy recommended allowing the suppliers to take more responsibility for job definition as well. Transferring job design responsibility and allowing flexible scheduling, however, placed the oil company at a significant risk of increased job costs and lack of control over production.

A joint customer-supplier team developed a performance-based pricing mechanism with cost and production incentives and penalties (see Exhibit A). Under the new agreement, the service provider will use its expertise to share in production gains—with a strong incentive to create the most cost-effective job designs—while accepting the risks associated with job performance. Reducing the overall cost and risk for both the oil company and the supplier shifts the required returns for stimulating the well. The shift in economics produces an increase in the number of well stimulations per year and increases the size of the pie for both the oil company and the service provider.

Exhibit A   Basic Pricing Structure

Cost Incentives

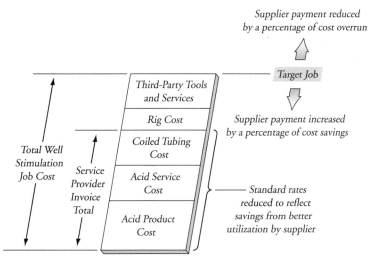

Value Incentives

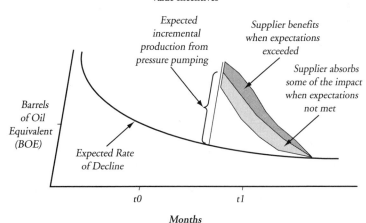

Source: Oil company case example.

Whether a new relationship is created by a commodity strategy or simply a relationship renewal effort, such pilots should apply three key principles:

1. Focus on specific issues relative to the supplied commodity and supplier role, not some generic objectives.
2. Involve cross-functional representation from the customer and supplier organizations.
3. Have measurable and aggressive goals to demonstrate the return on such an investment.

Supplier Development

As discussed previously, investing resources in supplier development offers one of the healthiest ways to build mutual dependence. Such programs are most effective between large, sophisticated customers and smaller, developing suppliers. By sharing its expertise, the customer becomes more than simply a future stream of revenues; it becomes a means for a supplier to improve overall competitiveness.

Honda's "BP" program offers an excellent model of effective supplier development under such conditions. Though Chapter Eleven describes Honda's approach in more detail, the principles employed are worth summarizing here:

- *Set aggressive, measurable goals.* Honda shoots for a 100 percent improvement in productivity.
- *Provide adequate, competent resources.* Honda's specialists work full-time for thirteen weeks on the typical improvement project.
- *Involve the supplier's employees.* Honda implements initial suggestions from the supplier's staff immediately to gain commitment from the supplier's associates whether or not the suggestions improve productivity.

Supplier Suggestions

Supplier suggestion programs offer another way to engage the supply base by building goal congruence. Such programs deliver immediate value for the customer and supplier by eliminating waste, which increases the "profit pie" for both parties.

As mentioned in Chapter One, Chrysler's SCORE program provides an excellent model. Each year, suppliers are challenged to submit cost savings ideas worth 5 percent of their annual sales to Chrysler. Suggestions must remove *cost;* suppliers cannot simply reduce margins to meet the goal. Fifty percent of the savings from a particular suggestion go to Chrysler, while the supplier retains the other half (though suppliers sometimes pass on more). In 1997, Chrysler reported savings ideas worth $1.23 billion from SCORE, $320 million of which hit the bottom line that year.[3]

Chrysler's and other companies' supplier suggestion programs highlight several important principles:

- *Set aggressive, measurable targets.* Chrysler reports supplier performance against the 5 percent target and has continuously increased the pressure for suppliers to participate.
- *Respond rapidly to the suggestions.* SCORE is a company-wide program, with engineers rapidly reviewing and responding to each suggestion as it is logged into an on-line tracking system available to suppliers.
- *Share the benefits.* Chrysler shares the benefits but also ensures that it captures an appropriate share.

Conclusion

Building and sustaining supplier relationships is a critical organizational capability for Balanced Sourcing and one that appears deceptively simple. Improving supplier relationships is, in fact, one of the easier tasks in evolving to the new model, but finding the right balance in relationships can be among the most difficult. The benefits from increased investment and enhanced communication through sustained relationships, however, are well worth the effort.

Simply labeling suppliers strategic partners has no more impact than calling employees associates. The business model and behaviors must support the objectives implied by the term, just as Honda's egalitarian white uniforms and complete absence of executive perks demonstrates its respect for all associates. Building true strategic partnerships requires a careful structuring of the relationships to achieve mutual dependence and goal congruence based on a solid knowledge of supplier competency.

There are no magic formulas for building and sustaining supplier relationships, though there are a variety of techniques that demonstrate the appropriate behaviors. These techniques should be employed, however, only if there is adequate organization-wide commitment to see them through. Halfhearted attempts to build this capability do more damage than good.

Chapter 6
Integrating the Supply Web

You can't sell from an empty wagon.
—WILLIAM DILLARD

Delivering goods to consumers as needed has always been critical to business success. And retailers recognize that suppliers play a critical role in meeting the consumer's needs. The traditional term for these activities was *supply chain management*. However, the increasing sophistication and complication of supply linkages requires a new metaphor: *the supply web*. Just as the world has become wired with myriad links to create the World Wide Web or Internet, many industries have developed complex sets of relationships that appear more web-like than chain-like.

In the electronics industry, for example, a company can easily identify another company that functions simultaneously as a supplier, customer, competitor, and possibly joint venture collaborator. Balancing cooperation and competition in such an environment becomes critical because the cost of an inefficient web can be dramatic.

Note: This chapter was prepared in collaboration with Mark Henneman of Booz·Allen & Hamilton's Chicago office, Marco Kesteloo of Booz·Allen's Amsterdam office, and Mike Goulder of Booz·Allen's Cleveland office.

For example, one consumer goods company recently identified an opportunity to reduce total supply web costs by 13 percent through independent improvements by both retailer-distributors and manufacturer-suppliers. But by jointly optimizing the supply web, the cost reduction opportunity increased to 21 percent (see Exhibit 6.1).

Not surprisingly, in most companies that serve the end consumer, integrating the supply web has been one of the first of the Balanced Sourcing capabilities developed. As mentioned in Chapter One and ex-

Exhibit 6.1   Supply Web Integration Benefits

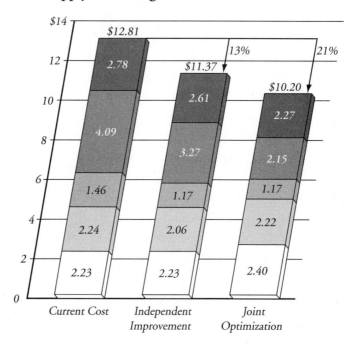

Source: Consumer products industry case example.

amined in detail in Chapter Ten, wholesale grocery giant SUPER-VALU's recent transformation focused primarily on its retail supply web from its suppliers—consumer goods manufacturers—to its customers—retail groceries. But supply web management can be just as critical in industrial settings, as demonstrated by the Cisco Systems case study in Chapter Twelve. Cisco sells products seldom seen by individual consumers, but it works diligently, nonetheless, to build an efficient and responsive supply web.

Given its long-standing importance, many of the concepts of supply web management have been around for decades. Three recent trends, however, are driving further evolution in this organizational capability:

1. Just-in-time (JIT) inventory management
2. Tiering and specialization throughout the web
3. Increasing availability of information

Such trends create new challenges—and new opportunities—for companies throughout the entire supply web. Many companies find themselves in new roles, facing new competitors that set ever higher benchmarks for performance. For most, being awash in real-time information simply brings problems to light faster, instead of helping to address the root causes.

Despite the new trends in supply management, effective integration continues to rely on consistent application of a few simple principles:

- Structure the supply web based on strategic objectives and competencies.
- Employ differentiated supply policies to manage the tradeoffs between customer needs and cost to serve.
- Apply consensus-based forecasts and cross-functional planning processes.
- Plan resources against forecasts, but allow orders to move products through the supply web.
- Rely on simple tools and analytic techniques rather than large, complex system solutions.

This chapter briefly reviews the implications of the three trends on supply web integration and shows how these five principles can be applied to enhance an organization's capability for integrating the supply web.

Trends in Supply Management

Over the last two decades, supply web management has gone through some fundamental paradigm shifts. Many practitioners experience the same feeling as that of the university alumnus who, visiting his economics professor during a reunion weekend, glanced at an exam on the professor's desk and exclaimed, "This is exactly the same exam you gave when I was an economics student thirty years ago!" The professor responded wryly, "I know. But the answers are now different."

Just-in-Time Inventory Management

When Taiichi Ohno first began to form his vision for the now-famous Toyota Production System, he drew on the model of a typical supermarket. The consumer "pulls" the exact item desired from a relatively small stock of physically visible inventory, triggering a response by the stockkeepers to replenish the product. But Ohno didn't stop at the retailer: he envisioned the entire supply base responding rapidly to actual demand rather than forecasts.

As other industry groups have applied the Toyota principle of lean production, retailers have again taken the lead in leveraging suppliers for competitive advantage. Efficient consumer response (ECR) has become widespread in most retail industries, along with a recognition that responding quickly to consumer demand requires changes by both customers and suppliers. For example, a recent analysis at a packaged goods manufacturer indicated that most demand variability was driven not by the end consumer, but by the promotional practices employed along the distribution chain (see Exhibit 6.2).

Wal-Mart Stores' collaboration with the Procter & Gamble Company led both to reduce or eliminate cost-inducing promotions by applying "everyday low pricing." Such focused cooperation has made their

Exhibit 6.2   Shipments Versus Consumer Takeaway (Packaged Goods Example)

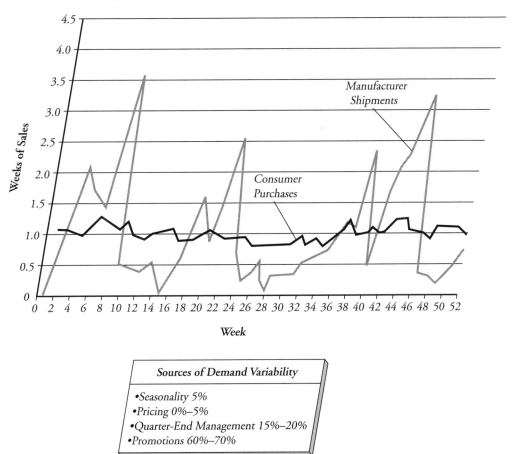

Source: Packaged goods case example.

relationship the benchmark of the retail industry. For example, Procter & Gamble and Wal-Mart hold only three days' worth of inventory from the plant through distribution to the stores—compared to the norm of twenty-five to thirty days.

Maintaining such low inventory required a dramatic increase in volume stability. Before launching the joint program, Wal-Mart would receive up to forty full truckloads of Proctor & Gamble fabric conditioner into its distribution centers on some days and none on other days. After implementation of the program, shipments stabilized at twenty-five to twenty-seven full truckloads every day. Furthermore, the inefficient practice of expediting shipments with partial truckloads at premium rates has been virtually eliminated.

Daily delivery has become increasingly common with suppliers of industrial goods as well, producing superior results for companies all throughout the web. A survey of sourcing practices conducted by Booz·Allen in the early 1990s found a significant difference in purchasing practices across a wide range of manufacturing companies.[1] The research documented materials price reduction, inventory turns, and incoming material rejection rates to segregate top-performing companies from a bottom tier of lower-performing companies. Next, variances in practices between the two groups and the overall sample were examined to test for differences. Exhibit 6.3 displays the delivery patterns of

Exhibit 6.3   Delivery Patterns and Inventory Turns

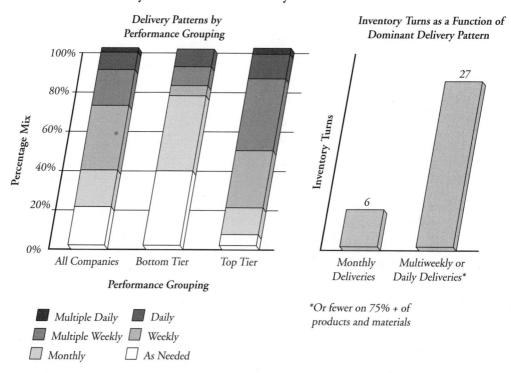

Source: Strategic Sourcing: A Competitive Imperative.

each group and the entire sample of companies. The survey findings demonstrate that top-performing companies employ more frequent deliveries and achieve better inventory turns.

Tiering and Specialization

In the early 1900s, Henry Ford's Model T plant on the River Rouge started with barge-loads of iron ore at one end of the complex and shipped finished automobiles out of the other end. But the world has changed dramatically since then. Introduced in 1993, Chrysler's LH platform, which includes the Dodge Intrepid, Eagle Vision, and Chrysler Concorde, required only about 200 suppliers rather than the typical 600 to 700.[2] Ford followed suit—and even raised the ante—with the 1995 Contour/Mystique. The all-new vehicle used a mere 227 suppliers for worldwide production, compared to more than 700 for the Ford Tempo, which it replaced.[3] Some vehicle manufacturers plan to push even further in their new assembly locations, with as few as 15 to 20 direct suppliers with dedicated plants in a common industrial park. Since the new cars have just as many parts, the other suppliers didn't simply disappear. Instead they were subsumed into the new tiered structure of the automotive supply web.

The increasing complexity of products and the need to tap into cross-industry expertise has led to a continual deintegration of most industries, not just the automotive industry. The pace of deintegration has clearly accelerated over the past two decades, and in the growing computer and electronics industry it has evolved to a new model that would be almost unrecognizable to Henry Ford. For example, Cisco Systems, the leading manufacturer of hardware and software for operating the Internet, has over $6 billion in sales but fewer than a thousand manufacturing employees. Cisco chooses to keep only final assembly and testing in-house while outsourcing everything else to specialists in various types of electronics manufacturing.

Manufacturing provides only one opportunity for specialized supply web roles. Increasingly, third-party logistics service providers play an important role in industrial and retail supply webs. Companies such as TNT, Excel, and GE Capital leverage their expertise and scale in transportation, warehousing, and inventory management to assume

Economic Order Quantity: A Supply Web Anachronism?

In the current era of JIT inventory management and ECR, the economic order quantity (EOQ) concept appears a bit out of place. Is this mathematical formula flawed—or just out of favor?

The EOQ equation calculates the optimal order size by balancing the cost of carrying inventory against the cost of placing an order (or setting up equipment to run an order in a factory). Conventional wisdom in lean production holds that a lot size of one is the ultimate ideal. Clearly the two points of view are at odds. But can they be reconciled?

Reconciliation comes through a recognition that the EOQ mathematics are valid but solve for the wrong variable. EOQ assumes that setup or ordering costs are a given and calculates the lot size that will spread this cost over as large a lot as possible without incurring excessive inventory-carrying costs. JIT practitioners do the reverse: they take a lot size of one to be the ideal and therefore work to reduce setup costs. As setup or ordering costs come down, the optimal lot size as defined by the EOQ formula also comes down.

JIT and ECR proponents also tend to put a little more weight on the cost of carrying inventory. JITers hold that inventory is "evil" because it hides the problems in a production process. Using the analogy of a river, JIT practitioners recommend lowering the water level (inventory) to uncover the rocks (production or delivery problems). Rocks can then be removed to allow for a smoother flow.

ECR proponents have also recognized that the cost of carrying inventory was often understated. Taking their retailer perspective, they place a great deal of value on a lost sale, simultaneously recognizing that an unreasonable amount of inventory is sold at discount because of demand shortfalls. The solution is a shorter, more responsive supply web.

So proponents of ECR and JIT should not reject the EOQ formula as anachronistic. An order size that balances setup and inventory costs is still optimal. Rather than simply plugging in numbers from a traditional mindset, however, leading-edge companies recognize the full cost of carrying too much inventory while simultaneously working to reduce their setup costs. The result is ever smaller lot sizes—and far more responsive supply webs.

responsibility for the entire distribution process for a wide variety of customers.

Such tiering and specialization make supply webs more complex, and vulnerable to a phenomenon called the "Forrester effect." Jay Forrester, professor emeritus at MIT, noted that variability at the end of a supply line is magnified and distorted as it proceeds up the line. In other words, a change in demand for a certain brand of cereal at the grocery store generates a bigger shift at the third-party warehouse operation, triggering a still bigger swing at the cereal manufacturer's plant, which causes an even bigger swing for the cereal box producer. Fortunately, supply lines that respond quickly suffer less "natural" distortion, and the third trend—better information—also reduces the effect.

Increasing Availability of Information

A few decades ago, tracking bar codes were found on the sides of railcars, but not many other places. Today, the ubiquitous bar code allows a wide variety of companies to track inventory movement from the retail outlet through the distribution center and back through manufacturing. With point-of-sale scanners, retailers capture consumer demand information accurately and cheaply and provide it throughout the supply web on a real-time basis at reasonable cost.

The logistics providers have also leveraged information technology to enhance their supply management capability. Drivers with handheld scanners and built-in data ports report back on deliveries at each stop. Further up the supply web, global positioning satellite systems track the movement of trucks, trains, and ships with pinpoint accuracy, allowing additional real-time control.

Even more dramatically, the Internet is fundamentally redefining the concept of a supply web. Jeffrey Rayport and John Sviokla of the Harvard Business School describe the concept of the "virtual value chain." They note, "With an integrated information underlay in place, companies can begin to perform value-adding activities more efficiently and effectively through and with information." Their emerging vision of the "marketspace" suggests fundamentally different supply web challenges, with many activities shifting from the physical realm to the virtual one.[4]

The degree of information exchange through the supply web was captured in a recent survey sponsored by *Strategy & Business*. The findings, shown in Exhibit 6.4, are drawn from a sample of companies across a wide range of industries. Clearly, many forms of information are now shared electronically with major suppliers. It is just as obvious, though, that many companies have not implemented these leading-edge techniques—at least not yet.

The confluence of the three trends portends further evolution in supply management. Fortunately, the age-old principles still apply, even if many of the answers are now different.

Principles for Effective Integration

Traditionally, effective supply web integration occurs when companies and their suppliers work jointly and apply a few simple principles. The principles are time-tested and apply despite the new paradigms in supply web management.

Structure the Supply Web Strategically

Though many organizations separate accountability for inbound and outbound management of the flow of materials, effective integration of a complex supply web requires a much broader point of view. Rather than having separate purchasing, materials management, and distribution functions, Chrysler has placed end-to-end accountability in a single function. The Procurement and Supply group manages the purchase and flow of materials from suppliers through the factories and out to the dealers.

Coupling such an end-to-end view with tiering and specialization among suppliers highlights the need to take a strategic view of structuring the supply web. A wide variety of options exist for configuring a company's extended enterprise of suppliers and distributors. Defining the optimal role for each party requires a detailed understanding of transportation and distribution economics. Both SUPERVALU and Kraft

Exhibit 6.4 Information Technology Throughout the Supply Web

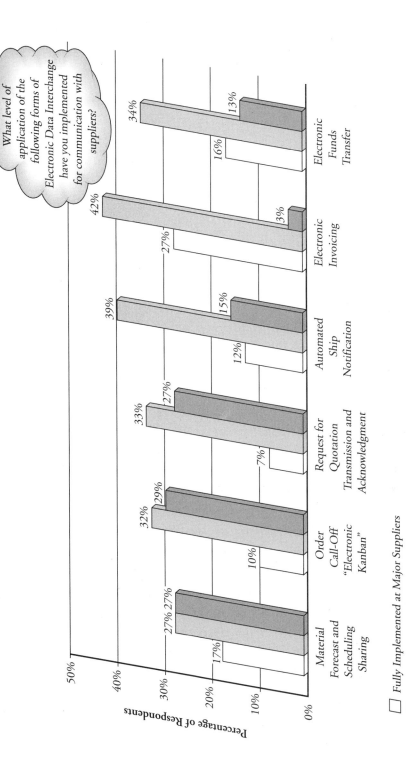

What level of application of the following forms of Electronic Data Interchange have you implemented for communication with suppliers?

Percentage of Respondents

□ Fully Implemented at Major Suppliers
▨ Used at Some Suppliers
▩ Not Used

Material Forecast and Scheduling Sharing — 17%, 27%, 27%
Order Call-Off "Electronic Kanban" — 10%, 32%, 29%
Request for Quotation Transmission and Acknowledgment — 7%, 33%, 27%
Automated Ship Notification — 12%, 39%, 15%
Electronic Invoicing — 27%, 42%, 3%
Electronic Funds Transfer — 16%, 34%, 13%

Source: Strategy & Business survey.

have extensive distribution networks that cover the country, for example. Deciding which company's distribution network will best serve a particular end customer requires a knowledge of each company's distribution costs.

Furthermore, changes in flow patterns can upset the overall economics of each player, forcing a reconfiguration of the networks. In the 1980s, Sears, Roebuck & Co. and General Electric Company struggled over how to distribute appliances to Sears's retail outlets. Sears wanted to use its own distribution network, which would allow the company to capture the scale economies afforded by the high volume of appliances. GE recognized that losing all of its Sears volume would undermine some of the scale advantages GE needed to serve many of its smaller customers. Ultimately, working jointly on the issues, the two companies found a satisfactory compromise solution.

Finally, configuring the supply web with a strategic view restrains the tendency to focus only on cost. Exhibit 6.5 illustrates the idea that a low-cost distribution network can be quite different from one designed for lead-time responsiveness. Marshall L. Fisher of the Wharton school advises, "Before devising a supply chain, consider the nature of the demand for your products," because "functional products require an efficient process; innovative products, a responsive process."[5]

Employ Differentiated Supply Policies

Differentiated supply policies offer one of the most effective means for improving performance along the supply web; unfortunately, such policies are exceedingly rare. In any supply web, certain products or product configurations cost more or take longer to produce than others. Typically, however, most customers try to impose common standards, such as delivery lead times, upon the supplier. Such efforts tend to drive suppliers to mediocrity, as they try to negotiate lead times that are long enough to support the full range of products for the full range of customer facilities.

Effective supply web integration requires customers and suppliers to agree on joint supply policies that reflect the true economics of the

Exhibit 6.5   Distribution and Lead-Time Trade-Offs

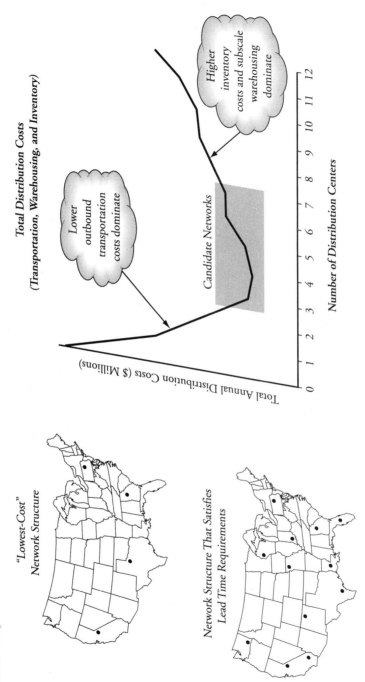

Source: Booz-Allen client case example.

network and drive the appropriate behavior by both parties. Exhibit 6.6 illustrates one form of differentiated supply policy. The policy reflects the economics of the supplier's national distribution center, located in Chattanooga, Tennessee. The supplier maintains a high level of safety stock for "A" products and can make shipments to the customer's Atlanta distribution center in a single day, though it requires more travel time to Newark or Chicago. The supplier holds less safety stock for "B" items and accordingly promises a lower fill rate. "C" items are held for picking during the night shift, from a stock that includes still less of a safety cushion; accordingly, the supplier requires an extra day of lead time and promises a lower fill rate. Finally, the "D" items—special or custom products—are not held in the supplier's distribution center but must be produced to order from the factory, requiring two weeks rather than a matter of days like the rest of the products.

Exhibit 6.6   Differentiated Supply Policy Example

Customer Distribution Centers

Products		Atlanta	Newark	Chicago
	A	98% Fill with One-Day Lead Time	98% Fill with Two-Day Lead Time	98% Fill with Three-Day Lead Time
	B	95% Fill with One-Day Lead Time	95% Fill with Two-Day Lead Time	95% Fill with Three-Day Lead Time
	C	90% Fill with Two-Day Lead Time	90% Fill with Three-Day Lead Time	90% Fill with Four-Day Lead Time
	D	90% Fill with Two-Week Lead Time	90% Fill with Two-Week Lead Time	90% Fill with Two-Week Lead Time

Even in pricing, where differentiated structures are common, policies have often reflected the results of confrontational negotiations rather than collaborative efforts to reflect the true economics of the supply web. Exhibit 6.7 shows one company's calculation of the significant difference between an order-size discount structure and the true cost to serve. Ultimately, the company began explicitly setting separate discounts for customer pickups to reflect the true cost differential of each option.

Apply Consensus-Based, Cross-Functional Planning

The different functional groups involved in the supply web have different priorities and sometimes conflicting objectives. For example, sales typically focuses on maximizing revenue and worries more about a lost sale than excess inventory. Manufacturing focuses on operational efficiency, which includes holding minimal inventory. Such conflicts can lead to gaming by each function: sales pads the forecast, expecting that manufacturing will produce to a more conservative plan. Unless these conflicts are resolved, the supply web can be whipsawed between extremes, with cost increasing and customer service suffering.

Tactical planning meetings provide the means for resolving the conflicts, thereby avoiding gaming and whipsawing. Most companies applying this principle hold monthly cross-functional meetings to develop a consensus view of the sales forecast, appropriate inventory targets, and the resulting manufacturing plan. Cost models that capture the true cost of options—such as line rate changes in manufacturing—facilitate decision making during the meeting. A well-run tactical planning meeting produces a common plan supported by all groups.

Tactical planning meetings to "close the loop" have long been advocated for effective materials requirements planning. With tiering of the supply base and greater dependence on suppliers, leading companies have recognized the value of extending tactical planning to encompass suppliers. Exhibit 6.8, drawn from the retail industry, illustrates how such a process can work—and the benefits achievable. The retailer's merchandising and marketing functions each provided information to the buyer, who made a preliminary, experience-based forecast. In parallel,

Exhibit 6.7 Cost-to-Serve Economics

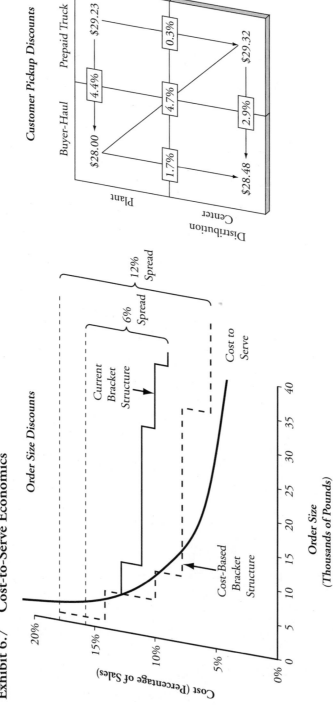

Source: Consumer goods company case example.

Exhibit 6.8 Joint Planning in Retail Industry

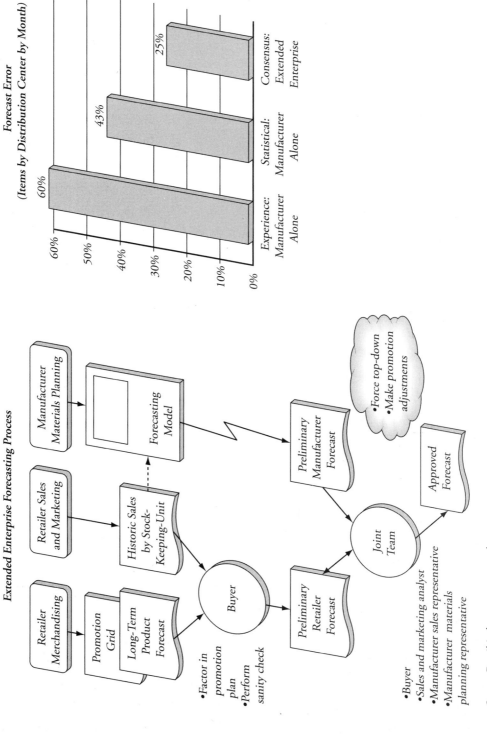

Extended Enterprise Forecasting Process

Forecast Error
(Items by Distribution Center by Month)

- 60% — Experience: Manufacturer Alone
- 43% — Statistical: Manufacturer Alone
- 25% — Consensus: Extended Enterprise

Manufacturer Materials Planning

Retailer Sales and Marketing

Retailer Merchandising

Forecasting Model

Promotion Grid

Long-Term Product Forecast

Historic Sales by Stock-Keeping-Unit

Buyer

- Factor in promotion plan
- Perform sanity check

Preliminary Manufacturer Forecast

Preliminary Retailer Forecast

- Force top-down
- Make promotion adjustments

Joint Team

Approved Forecast

- Buyer
- Sales and marketing analyst
- Manufacturer sales representative
- Manufacturer materials planning representative

Source: Retail industry case example.

the manufacturer developed a statistical forecast using a common database of historical sales provided by the retailer. The two preliminary forecasts were reconciled in a joint planning meeting, with dramatic results. Viewed from the manufacturer's perspective, forecast errors dropped from 60 percent for an average month to only 25 percent.

Plan Against Forecasts, Let Orders Drive Movement

Common forecasts allow each node in the supply web to plan resources in a consistent manner, dampening the Forrester effect. But despite their good intentions, most experienced practitioners realize that the following three "laws" of forecasting make the process inherently difficult:

1. Long-term forecasts are less accurate than near-term ones.
2. Aggregate forecasts are more accurate than line-item forecasts.
3. All forecasts are wrong.

Shorter lead times throughout the supply web allow shorter-term forecasts to drive plans, thereby dampening the effect of the first law. Product standardization and manufacturing postponement tactics allow aggregate forecasts to suffice over a broader range of products, offsetting the impact of the second law. Unfortunately, the immutability of the third law drives many to agree with Samuel Goldwyn, the motion-picture mogul, who once admonished, "Never make forecasts, especially about the future."

In supply web management, Goldwyn's advice is not the solution. Instead, well-run supply webs accept the fact that forecasts are merely plans—plans that will inevitably be wrong. Rather than relying on constant replanning to remove the errors, effective supply webs respond to the reality represented by orders. Forecasts establish the level of resources—production capacity, labor, and raw materials—required for a given time period. But the resources are deployed most effectively when the web responds to the "pull" of real orders rather than the "push" of the plan.

Admittedly, poor forecasts result in inappropriate resources, either too much or too little, which constrains the supply web from responding to the real orders cost-effectively. But blindly following a poor plan that is not in tune with the reality of orders produces worse results. Keeping forecasts separate from orders ensures that the best, most current information drives the supply line.

Rely on Simple Tools and Analytic Techniques

Much of the academic literature in supply web management involves complex optimization models or arcane derivations of safety stock calculations. Most companies operate at the other extreme, using experience-based inventory targets and forecasts. Alternatively, companies that have invested in leading-edge information technology tools often find themselves relinquishing critical tactical decisions to black-box programs that spew forth recommended actions, which may not reflect business realities.

At an oil company operating in Alaska, for example, the computerized inventory control system recommended a dramatic increase in the inventory target for a particular production gas, one that was no longer used in normal operations. On investigation, the inventory analyst discovered that field operations had injected some of the obsolete material into the pipeline to free up storage space. The computer recorded the usage as an up-tick in demand and accordingly recommended raising the inventory target.

Avoiding analytic techniques isn't the solution; neither is relinquishing decision making to incomprehensible models. Exhibit 6.9 draws on some Booz·Allen client examples to highlight the impact that analytic techniques can have on performance in the supply web.

In practice, the most effective analytic tools are built on a solid statistical foundation but are simple enough for users to understand. For a major flooring manufacturer, a simple decision support tool facilitated inventory target setting by maintenance planners. The tool applied Poisson arrival patterns—appropriate to the infrequent demand pattern of spare parts—but was not presented as a black-box recommendation.

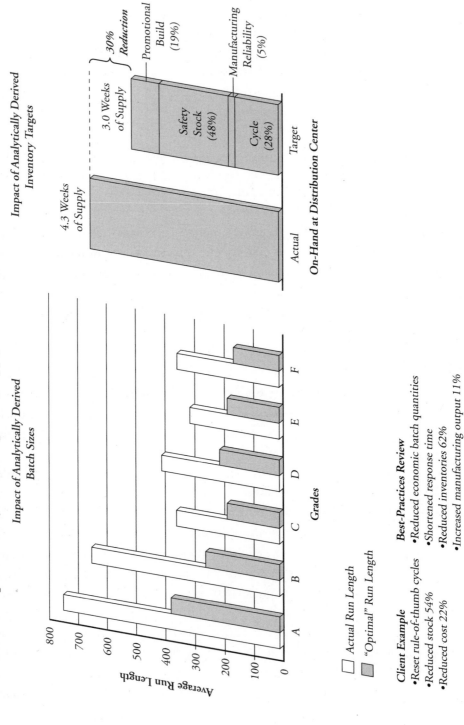

Exhibit 6.9   Impact of Analytic Techniques on Supply Web Performance

Instead, the tool calculated the impact of various stocking options for the maintenance planner, showing, for example, that a shift from an inventory target of two to three units increased the probability that the part would be in stock when needed from 99.1 percent to 99.5 percent. Without ever understanding the Poisson probability distribution, the maintenance planners soon learned the diminishing returns of safety stock in such an environment and accordingly began reducing it. At the same time, the planners ensured that the computer wouldn't drive illogical decisions, like stocking an odd number of items for a part that is always replaced in pairs.

Building the capability to effectively integrate the supply web on a day-to-day basis requires consistently applying these principles throughout the supply base as well as to the distribution or retail channels. The next section provides some practical advice for launching pilot programs to do this.

Supply Web Integration Pilot Programs

Because the principles of effective supply web integration apply upstream as well as downstream, pilot programs may be sponsored by customers looking to integrate suppliers—or by the suppliers trying to better integrate their customers. Whichever party provides the impetus for the pilot, a joint effort to integrate the flow of product should address the considerations highlighted for each of the following steps.

The first step is to select a clear area of focus for the pilot. Generally, a single facility, such as a manufacturing plant or a regional distribution center, defines a manageable initial scope. This allows the two companies to test selective changes without fundamentally redefining the entire supply network.

Second, conducting a baseline diagnostic provides a foundation for the improvement program. Without a baseline, setting reasonable improvement targets—or judging success—is not possible. The diagnostic should examine a wide range of performance indicators such as order lead times, inventory turns and coverage, and delivery reliability.

Selective benchmarking of best-in-class companies or competitors can sometimes prove useful, but be wary of "apples to oranges" comparisons.

Using findings from the diagnostic, the next step is to set appropriate objectives that reflect the strategic priorities of this portion of the supply web. These objectives should be few and focused on responsiveness or efficiency, not spread across the two. Diagnostics typically reveal opportunities for improved performance along both dimensions, but the most critical priority should be targeted. For example, a supply web pilot for a computer company should focus on improved responsiveness and perhaps focus on lead-time reduction and delivery reliability. A more traditional manufacturer, such as a food company, may choose to focus on efficiency, with objectives such as lowering distribution costs and increasing inventory turns.

Finally, extrapolating the lessons learned from a pilot requires that the knowledge be documented and shared. A phased approach generally works best for rolling out new processes and techniques across other plants, distribution centers, or suppliers. Often ignored, but potentially more critical than capturing the ideas that worked, is documenting what failed in the pilot. This step provides the greatest leverage in capturing the value of the pilot but often receives inadequate attention and resources. The original team sometimes disbands and moves on to new challenges rather than shepherding the change through the organization, which is far less rewarding than the challenging, but manageable, effort of the pilot.

Conclusion

Exhibit 6.10 displays the results of a recent survey sponsored by *Strategy & Business* across a broad mix of companies. The findings underscore the fact that respondents expect the trend to more frequent deliveries to continue into the future. And few would suggest that the other two major supply web trends—tiering and the explosion of information—have fully run their courses either. Clearly, managing the supply web will remain an important area of focus in the coming years.

The question remains: Is your organization capable of effectively integrating the supply web as the future unfolds?

Exhibit 6.10   Integrating the Supply Web (Delivery Pattern Mix)

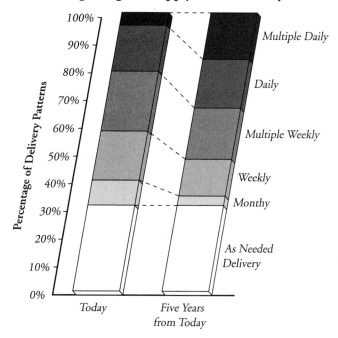

Chapter 7
Leveraging Supplier Innovation

Anything that won't sell, I don't want to invent. Its sale is proof of
utility and utility is success.
—THOMAS A. EDISON

Although the opportunities for improving customer-supplier integration of day-to-day product movement throughout the supply web have
not been exhausted, many companies are starting to focus on innovation initiatives to add value. Leveraging suppliers in innovation captures
increasing attention for a variety of reasons. First, 70 to 80 percent of
product cost is determined during the early phases of design, so capturing supplier design input up front can be critical in lowering the cost
of purchased materials.

Allowing suppliers to work concurrently at the subsystem level can
also speed up product development, which is increasingly critical in a
wide variety of industries. Finally, better supplier integration allows the
customer to focus on systems integration rather than component design and ultimately improves end-product quality.

Note: This chapter was based upon several *Strategy & Business* articles and a Viewpoint written in collaboration with C. V. Ramachandran of Booz·Allen & Hamilton's New York office
and Keith Voigt of Booz·Allen's Lima office.

A recent survey by the Procurement and Supply Chain Benchmarking Consortium at Michigan State University examined integration of suppliers in new-product and new-process development. Respondents quantified the impact on cost, quality, and time of their most and least successful supplier integration efforts. The results, presented in Exhibit 7.1, dramatically demonstrate the impact of successfully integrating suppliers in innovation.

Customers and suppliers can also work with each other across the entire spectrum of innovation activities, from the early phase of market understanding to the detailed phase of specific product design. For example, Marks & Spencer, the United Kingdom–based retailer, works with its suppliers to understand ever-changing customer tastes in apparel. Joint activities include discussing market experiences, suggesting fashions, and defining new technologies. The suppliers—garment mak-

Exhibit 7.1   Supplier Integration Effect

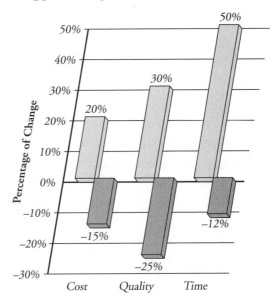

☐ *Most Successful Supplier Integration Efforts*
☐ *Least Successful Supplier Integration Efforts*

Source: Michigan State Global Procurement and Supply Chain Benchmarking Consortium.

ers, cloth suppliers, and even mills—work with Marks & Spencer's central design group and a color standards center to assess color, fabrics, and fashion trends. The benefit is a coherent, coordinated design brief for all clothing groups that can be applied by each division and its suppliers to develop and deliver specific garments.

Motorola works with equipment suppliers to ensure that robot technology for inserting components evolves in unison with the increasingly shrinking size of integrated circuits. As smaller chips allow further miniaturization of the end product, finer tolerances for placement of the components are required. By acknowledging these technology constraints and setting consistent priorities across the board, Motorola achieves consistent innovation with its suppliers.

In another example, Xerox recently determined that its internally focused product development process for lower-cost products targeted at the home-office market could be improved. The company responded by modifying its product development process, heavily emphasizing supplier involvement to reduce both resource requirements and cycle time.

Achieving such integration is not easy. It requires dramatic changes in the role of the suppliers and in the mindset of the people involved in product development. Furthermore, without thoughtful consideration of the suppliers' role, a shift to more integration can create more confusion, rather than simplifying and speeding up the development process. Finally, unless effective targets are set and the process effectively managed, the shift will neither fully leverage supplier capabilities nor extract full value for the company.

Key Innovation Concepts

Three key concepts are critical to effectively integrating suppliers in innovation: scope boundaries, technology planning, and target costing. Though this is not a comprehensive list, these three areas are garnering the most attention and are generating significant results when done well. This section explains each of the three concepts and provides examples.

Defining Scope Boundaries

To maximize suppliers' performance, a company must break down the end product into groups of components and functions. The company must then decide how to allocate these components and functions to the supply base. Some suppliers may be assigned a single component or a very narrow set of components. Others may be asked to produce a large number of components that function as a subsystem. We call the breadth of responsibility assigned to a given supplier its *scope boundary*. A narrow scope tends to focus the supplier on its own manufacturing and delivery process. Broad boundaries defined by functional performance specification, rather than by part tolerances, allow the supplier to create value through product innovation. Exhibit 7.2 provides a simple example of how scope boundaries affect the amount and type of value creation available to the company and the supplier. The example examines the possible evolution of a supplier of bolts.

In a traditional arm's-length relationship, a supplier has a very narrow scope. In this example, the bolt supplier does not understand the

Exhibit 7.2   Alternative Scope Boundaries

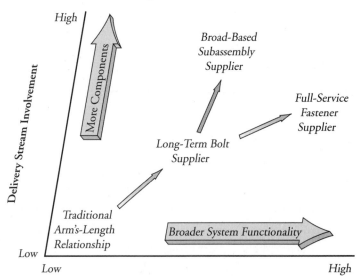

customer's needs beyond the design specifications. This is called a "make-to-print" arrangement. The only opportunity for the supplier to create value is by reduction of its internal manufacturing cost. As a result, opportunities for suppliers and customers to cooperate through tighter integration are lost. Fortunately, few companies are content to keep their key suppliers at arm's length.

With longer-term supplier relationships, new opportunities for value creation can be opened up. For example, the supplier may integrate its processes with those of the customer, as in just-in-time delivery and integrated quality assurance arrangements. Through such joint efforts, new cost reduction opportunities can be exploited in the shared value chain, not just in the supplier's portion of it. Additionally, in a closer relationship, the bolt supplier could begin to challenge the specifications, asking, "Why this tolerance?" or "Why should the bolt be plated?" Asking such questions, which ultimately lead to joint designs, is a vital initial step in increasing the level of value creation through supplier innovation.

Over time, the scope of the relationship with the supplier might broaden even more. For example, the supplier might be asked to provide a wider range of fasteners (such as Velcro or plastic clips) that have the same basic functionality as bolts. With this broader scope, the supplier can propose alternate product technologies to better meet the customer's need, without risking the loss of the customer's business. In such a broad relationship, the supplier is no longer motivated to suggest that a bolt is *always* the right solution. Rather, the supplier creates value by providing innovative solutions based on a deep understanding of the customer's needs.

In another instance, a supplier may be asked to provide subassemblies, not just components or parts. Here, the supplier can create value by making tradeoffs between the different components in the subassembly. By delivering larger modules to the customer, the supplier can minimize inventory and handling costs to save money. This approach, however, focuses more on the supplier's manufacturing capability than on innovation and customer understanding, which could be far more important.

Both approaches—the fastener provider's, which focuses the greatest opportunity on product innovation, and the subassembly producer's, which focuses on supply web integration—are logical options for broadening the supplier-customer relationship. However, each will tap a different set of opportunities and require a different set of supplier capabilities. The challenge is to select the option that provides the greatest opportunity for value creation.

When seeking the optimal supplier-customer relationship, few companies systematically define the tradeoffs that must be balanced in the process. Although the bolt supplier example looks fairly straightforward conceptually, in reality scope boundaries are more complicated. Leveraging suppliers in innovation presents the most complex issues in Balanced Sourcing.

Companies tend to encounter three major pitfalls in defining optimal scope boundaries:

1. Using historical boundary definitions rather than defining new boundaries that can create more value
2. Giving suppliers broader responsibilities but continuing to manage them too tightly
3. Developing overlapping boundaries between suppliers, or between the company and the suppliers, that result in suboptimal tradeoffs

The first pitfall, at worst, avoids change; at best, it simply allows change to happen without being actively managed. Even in this case, scope boundaries eventually change as suppliers find ways to deliver more value, but proactive competitors gain the advantage. A late follower merely restores parity. The second pitfall is common for companies trying to make the philosophical shift to broader boundaries. Unfortunately, the transition is difficult because it requires the often painful process of relinquishing traditional responsibilities to suppliers. The third pitfall is far more subtle and is only now beginning to menace some leading companies. Although they may have broadened the suppliers' scope boundaries, they now see conflicts and overlaps and are finding that defining optimal boundaries is a more complex task than they had anticipated. As the bolt example illustrates, even for a simple product, options abound.

Defining scope boundaries is complex because of the difficulty in quantifying value creation and in managing tradeoffs. Furthermore, the optimal boundaries are constantly shifting as new functionality is added to the end product and as new technologies provide innovative solutions. Nonetheless, understanding and optimizing the boundaries are critical first steps in capturing the full potential of the extended enterprise of suppliers.

Sharing Technology Plans

Sharing technology plans presents another difficult challenge in leveraging suppliers in innovation. Both sides are concerned about sharing proprietary information such as product introduction plans. Customers fear that their suppliers will leak the information to competitors. Suppliers fear that customers will "shop around" the suppliers' best ideas and designs to lower-cost producers who don't invest in innovation. Nonetheless, getting customer and supplier technology plans in sync curbs wasted effort and allows each to fully leverage the investments by the other. Two techniques are growing in popularity as means for sharing technology: supplier technology forums and technology road maps.

Technology forums allow a supplier to share new technology to encourage customer adoption. For example, Motorola holds an annual technical symposium for suppliers to introduce emerging technology to engineering and sourcing staff. Typically around 180 suppliers staff booths in a football-field-sized tent in a parking lot at Motorola's corporate campus. Black & Decker hosts a similar forum for its top 100 suppliers that it calls a Product Awareness Day. These exchanges often lead to new joint development efforts.

Technology road maps are gaining attention as a means of sharing customer plans with suppliers. Road maps explicitly plot the evolution of the customer's product plans to drive the supplier's technology plan. Accordingly, the plans are highly proprietary and are only shared with key long-term suppliers. Exhibit 7.3 shows a simplified example of a road map for occupant restraint technologies for an automotive company.

Exhibit 7.3   Occupant Restraint Technology Road Map

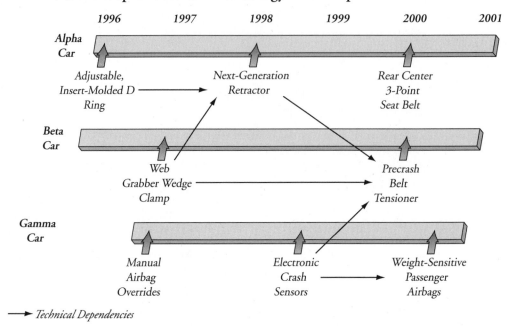

Technical Dependencies

Source: Adapted from U.S. vehicle manufacturer.

The example shows how new technologies map to the car company's new car program plans. It also shows technical dependencies to highlight how slippage in one area could affect the rollout of another technology in the future. What is not obvious, but just as important, is the fact that by excluding items, the road map also shows the technologies that are of no interest to the vehicle manufacturer. Such insight allows the supplier to either curb development efforts or enhance efforts to sell the concept.

Not surprisingly, IBM applies significant purchasing resources to managing technology development with suppliers. A group of over sixty technically oriented staff form the company's Technology & Qualification group, which reports to the chief procurement officer. These technologists are collocated with development teams and linked with IBM's worldwide commodity councils to provide the connection between long-term technology needs and commercial requirements. For example, the technologists provide guidance to the memory commodity team based on product road maps that show capacity, speed, and connectivity requirements. These expectations are aggregated across product lines and are shared with suppliers to help them prioritize their development efforts. In some cases, such as Intel microprocessors, the supplier drives the technology plan. IBM's challenge then becomes adapting its end-product plans to match Intel's plan.

The detail and content of technology sharing continue to evolve as customers and suppliers learn how to work together more closely. For example, Motorola leverages its total-cost modeling information to drive supplier technology efforts. Instead of "filtered information" describing its expectations, Motorola provides battery suppliers with end-consumer warranty data to focus the suppliers' technology plans.

Setting Target Costs

Target costing is not a new concept. One can easily imagine an early Roman artisan being asked, "Can you make me a shield for five denarii?" But in a world of unrelenting global competition, setting the right target for a given product has become absolutely critical.

Three very different approaches to target costing are employed today, often without any clear distinction:

1. Price-based targeting
2. Cost-based targeting
3. Value-based targeting

The first approach uses price-based competition, which is at the heart of the free enterprise system. In its simplest form, price-based targeting simply sets the target cost by comparing competitive offerings. Although it is a standard negotiating tactic in working with suppliers, many companies are also applying the technique proactively to their own products. These companies examine "what the market will bear" and subtract a desired margin to determine an appropriate target cost for a product. Products that do not meet the targets are canceled or sent back to product development to be redesigned to meet the cost target.[1]

Hewlett-Packard's entry into digital consumer photography provides an excellent example of price-based targeting of the end product. Although the digital system, which includes a camera, printer-scanner, and software, provides functionality not available in a film camera, the digital camera is priced to compete with traditional high-end cameras. Furthermore, Hewlett-Packard expects to eventually drive the cost down to the lowest possible competitive price point with a *disposable* digital camera.[2]

The second approach, cost-based targeting, has evolved substantially over the last few decades. In its least effective application, cost-plus contracts have been used by government agencies to ensure that contractors achieve an acceptable but not exorbitant profit margin. Unfortunately, this has often limited the motivation of suppliers to lower the total cost. Many large companies have developed a more modern version of the cost-plus mindset. These companies now demand open books from their suppliers to pierce the veil of price quotes.

For example, the automotive industry aggressively employs cost-based targeting. The large vehicle manufacturers have the buying clout to force their suppliers to share detailed cost information. Unfortunately, suppliers complain that many of the Western vehicle manufacturers misuse the information to squeeze margins, which often leads to an extra set of books that hides the profits. Japanese vehicle manufacturers demand the same cost information but generally use it differently. They use open books plus a detailed understanding of cost drivers to help suppliers eliminate waste, not simply to squeeze margins.

The third approach, value-based targeting, is the least understood technique and the most difficult to apply. Only a handful of companies do it well. Value-based targeting compares consumers' "wants" with their willingness to pay. When it is done well, this approach drives the design process by mapping the desired functionality back to the subsystems that create the functionality. Such a technique improves product development by ensuring that new designs are not simply innovative; more important, they create value the consumer recognizes and will pay for.

Swatch S.A. provides an excellent example of value-based targeting. In the original Swatch, major cost reductions were achieved by appropriately valuing the product's subsystems to change the level of functionality of the timepiece. For example, the original Swatch design employed a plastic casing, since the end product was priced low enough to be discarded when the battery died. The timepiece also had lower reliability and durability requirements, which allowed for less expensive mechanisms. The cost of the band was also significantly less, because Swatch used integrated plastic moldings rather than expensive, sewn-leather bands that required replacement. As a result, Swatch created a fundamentally new value proposition in the marketplace: a low-cost fashion accessory that also kept time. By developing an understanding of consumer tastes for fashionable products, Swatch has since moved its products to higher price-points while increasing sales.

All three target-costing techniques can ensure competitiveness in supplier pricing, but each one can be more effective in a given circumstance than the others. For example, price-based targeting can apply quite effectively to commodity products and services. Pricing of true commodities generally reflects supply-and-demand curves rather than bottom-up cost. Likewise, the price of a commodity like memory chips for personal computers does not vary as a result of changes in consumer value, but rather as a result of changes in competitive dynamics.

Cost-based targeting, supported by an understanding of cost drivers, can effectively drive improvement in supplier operations. Understanding cost drivers and doing comparative benchmarks can result in improvements such as reducing quality costs, improving equipment uptime, and lowering staffing levels. This technique is often applied effectively with make-to-print suppliers or suppliers of modules.

For its part, value-based targeting is unmatched for fostering the kind of major innovation expected from a supplier who serves as a "solutions provider." A solutions provider has the skills to take overall black-box responsibility for the specification, planning, execution, and performance of an entire system. Accordingly, such a supplier needs greater freedom. Appropriate value-based targets provide that freedom but ensure that the consumer will pay for the added value. The supplier must meet the challenge of applying its expertise creatively to develop a detailed design that meets the needs at the target cost.

The challenge is to maximize the suppliers' contributions. As the Gamma Watch case example later in this chapter illustrates, the targeting methodology is straightforward and logical, though admittedly not simple to apply to complex products. Even when it is applied with simplified assumptions, however, it provides a structure for the process of developing new products. It is an investment that will ultimately lead to better products, prices, and margins for both product manufacturers and their suppliers.

Pilot Project Methodology

This section describes ways to build the capability for leveraging suppliers in innovation through a specific product development pilot effort. Pilots demonstrate results while simultaneously refining a company's product development process. A pilot also offers the opportunity to overcome many of the problems that tend to inhibit efforts to integrate suppliers in innovation, including

- An unwillingness to take risks in establishing relationships
- Mismatches between the capabilities that are expected and those that are available
- Misunderstandings about how each organization really works
- Difficulty in assigning the profit pie fairly

Integrating suppliers in innovation usually requires a transfer to suppliers of broader roles, such as the design responsibility for subsystems instead of components. Relinquishing this control creates increased risk in the beginning and can be traumatic for a traditional organization. Often a "chicken and egg" problem emerges: businesses don't want to take the added risk until the supplier has fully proved itself, and suppliers can't demonstrate their capabilities until the customer provides the opportunity.

Mismatches between the capabilities expected and those available are another key factor—and the imbalance may be in either direction. In some instances, supplier capabilities simply do not meet customer needs, constraining the speed and effectiveness of efforts at innovation. More often, suppliers believe that they can deliver higher value than customers recognize. The most common supplier complaint is that the customers' engineers get into the component details and micro-manage innovation, though at the same time they are insisting that the suppliers take system responsibilities.

Frequently, customers and suppliers do not understand how to work effectively with each other's innovation groups. Confusion about acceptable innovation performance and responsibility occurs not because each organization undervalues integration, but because differences in their existing policies, procedures, and structures result in inconsistent levels of interaction.

Finally, it's difficult to clearly evaluate the individual contribution of each organization in creating value in innovation because much of the value comes from the synergy of collaboration. Even if the relative contributions are clearly understood, each company feels obligated to capture as much of the value creation as possible for its own shareholders. Hence, resolving financial arrangements can become frustrating. Though explicit up-front agreements for sharing savings move in the right direction, most schemes generally fall short of ensuring optimal collaboration.

Overcoming these barriers may seem easy: customers and suppliers simply need to trust one another and communicate more clearly. Unfortunately, the reality isn't that simple. To overcome the frustration and realize the tantalizing benefits, both sides need to prioritize the key issues and sort through several complex, interconnected decisions. The best way to do this is to incorporate a rigorous, iterative, pilot process that can be rolled out across development programs once it has been perfected. The pilot should force a fundamental rethinking of the level of responsibility of suppliers in both the design process and the ultimate product manufacture. One such pilot approach consists of the following six steps:

1. Select the project and form the team.
2. Set the specifications and confirm the targets.
3. Reexamine the subsystem boundaries.
4. Select the suppliers.
5. Launch the product design.
6. Document the new process.

Following are the key considerations for each step.

Step 1: Select the Project and Form the Team

The project selected for the pilot should be one in which the organization needs to make a step-function change to meet the market demands. The degree of change must be so great that the entire organization recognizes that incremental change will be inadequate and that the new design will require fundamental rethinking. Such an environment opens the company to new ideas, including a dramatic increase in the role of suppliers.

The product selected for the pilot should also be the base design for a large product family—potentially one with global scope. Working with a base design forces longer-term thinking about standardization and modularity. It also encourages potential suppliers to participate by providing a larger future volume base.

Successfully redesigning the product development process and the actual product simultaneously requires a highly motivated team. Team members must also be open-minded and capable of taking advice from nontraditional sources. However, the team should not be staffed completely with disciples of the concept of supplier integration; a few converted "doubting Thomases" provide huge credibility when rolling out the pilot to other areas.

Step 2: Set the Specifications and Confirm the Targets

Once the team has formed, it should confirm the specifications of the end product to meet a set of customer needs. This step can cover a lot of ground, depending on the industry, the specific project background, and even the team's composition. For a consumer product, a team may conduct basic market research to understand the wants and needs of the targeted consumer. Focus groups and broad-based surveys may provide insight into the consumer's key functional requirements and the price points for different levels of functionality. In other cases the "customer" may be an original-equipment manufacturer, such as a computer company or vehicle manufacturer.

Regardless of the degree of direct consumer input, the team must translate the customer's wants into product specifications. Techniques such as quality function deployment and competitive teardown analysis can be quite useful in setting the broad system specifications.

Setting a top-down, market-driven cost target for the end product is one of the most critical elements in this step. The target-costing methodology described in the Gamma Watch case example provides a structure for the targeting process. Since the cost target is ultimately allocated to the subsystems, the targeting process obviously must iterate with Step 3.

Step 3: Reexamine the Subsystem Boundaries

The definition of subsystems varies by industry: brakes for an automaker, the distillation process in an oil refinery, check processing in a bank. When defining boundaries across subsystems, customers should try to get beyond conventional thinking. The key is to understand how the boundaries can be configured to create value, especially by taking advantage of supplier capabilities. Suppliers who design multiple versions of a subsystem to meet different requirements can, for example, standardize the parts inside the subsystems to reduce total costs.

Furthermore, setting broader boundaries for suppliers offers the opportunity to "deintegrate" to reduce capital investment and increase flexibility. For example, Cisco Systems, the market leader of Internet equipment, employed roughly one thousand manufacturing employees to support more than $4 billion in sales in 1996, thanks to a highly deintegrated structure. Though the electronics industry is leading the shift to contract manufacturing, a number of industries are quickly following.

Defining interface requirements presents the key technical challenge in boundary setting. Allowing each supplier to innovate within a fixed envelope requires the company to have an extensive understanding of how the various subsystems will interact in the final assembly. A better understanding of interfaces provides greater freedom and independence for the suppliers. Unfortunately, the tendency when documenting interfaces is to define specifications that *minimize the impact* of interfaces based upon past experiences, rather than truly understanding the interactions. Such a tendency should be avoided, since the pendulum tends to swing back to a make-to-print mindset.

Step 4: Select the Suppliers

The need for innovation capabilities can vary across subsystems. In one subsystem, a significant understanding of market needs may be required, whereas in another, optimization of physical layout and designs during product development may be the critical capability.

After subsystem boundaries have been defined and capability requirements established, a company can turn to building the appropriate supply base for innovation. This requires the company to identify and select suppliers capable of driving innovation in each subsystem as well as across the subsystems. In some cases, a company may have to develop an appropriate supplier over time if an appropriate one is not currently available. A well thought out sourcing strategy will have already foreseen the need for more engineering-capable suppliers. In such cases the selection decision should focus on suppliers from an existing supply base who have the right capabilities for the particular project.

Step 5: Launch the Product Design

Once supplier selection is complete, it is critical for the company and its suppliers to work together to define specific roles and responsibilities. This requires a level of detail far greater than that of general capabilities. Who is responsible for each type of prototype development and the corresponding testing, for example? Without such clarity, miscommunication and wasted effort will inevitably result.

A clear understanding of, and commitment to, agreed-upon objectives must drive business and supplier behavior. On each side, management's responsibility is to build and maintain control mechanisms to achieve these goals, near term and long term. Processes must be put in place to track and report the performance of each party against the selected measures.

Step 6: Document the New Process

To extract the full benefit of the pilot, the team should document the key lessons learned. Though pilot programs typically operate with flexible processes and procedures, a well-functioning product development process must be well structured. Documenting the modified process guides future efforts and ensures that the inevitable mistakes of a pilot are not repeated in full implementation.

Just as important, the documented lessons must be communicated across the organization. The results of the pilot will be the best testimonial, but the firsthand experiences of the project team members and suppliers provide the real emotion needed to create new disciples. Ultimately, this information sharing should evolve from communication to more formal training to provide greater "how-to" insights, rather than relying on the typical war stories that elicit initial support. Finally, once communication and training are well under way, the new process can be explicitly rolled out across individual programs.

Conclusion

Increasingly, major companies are shifting product development responsibility to the supply base. However, the best companies know the difference between delegating and abrogating their responsibilities.

Chrysler President Tom Stallkamp's analogy from the movie industry illustrates his vision of how suppliers can be leveraged in the product development process. In the movie industry's emerging years, the motion picture companies controlled the entire value chain from the scriptwriters and set decorators to the directors, the actors, and the theaters the movies were shown in. To make a movie today, a complex extended enterprise of independent specialists must work together throughout the entire process.

Black & Decker even outsources the complete development of certain noncore products to suppliers but maintains expertise in the critical areas of consumer research, battery technology, and motor-based product designs. It simply leverages suppliers where it makes sense. Both Chrysler and Black & Decker leverage suppliers in innovation, but with well thought out limits and with active management. Both focus on ensuring the right balance in this capability, as well as the right overall balance in their supplier relationships.

Gamma Watch: A Case Example

Market research at the Gamma Watch Company identified a significant consumer segment that wanted a watch that was sporty, yet stylish. This group wanted a watch that had the functionality of a sports watch like the Timex Ironman series, but that was stylish enough to be worn on all occasions. The current offerings of premium sports watches by TAG Heuer and Rolex Watch Company were stylish enough for all occasions, but they were too expensive for the target market, which consisted of athletic men and women who were entry-level white-collar workers.

Ultimately, market research determined a retail price point of "under $100," which the design team translated to $97.50 per unit. Using a 40 percent markup in the channel resulted in a wholesale price target of $69.64. The company had the goal of a 17 percent return on sales and a 7.6 percent allocation for sales and general administration costs. These were subtracted from the wholesale price to yield a target cost of $52.50 for the design team. Exhibit A shows how the overall cost target was derived from the price-based retail target.

Focus groups held during the preliminary market research also examined the attributes the targeted consumers wanted in a "stylish sports watch for just under $100." The focus groups highlighted a wide variety of attributes, which were grouped into five functional needs:

1. "Comfort" meant that the watch should be light, slim, and comfortable.
2. "Stylishness" captured a set of attributes that indicated that the watch should avoid the appearance of a standard mass-produced product. Also, the watch should be appropriate for

Exhibit A   Market-Back Calculation of Target Cost

Overall Target Cost Calculation

Retail price (40% markup)	$97.50
Wholesale price	$69.64
Return on sales 17%	($11.84)
Sales, General, and Administration allocation	($5.30)
Target cost	$52.50

virtually any occasion, since the consumers expected it to be their primary (if not only) timepiece.

3. "Reliability" underscored the fact that the watch was a significant expenditure for these consumers and was expected to last.

4. "Simplicity" indicated that the watch should be easy to read, use, and wear.

5. "Functionality" denoted that, for the most part, only a lap timer was required beyond the basic functions of date and time to meet the needs of the athletic consumer. A few consumers said that waterproofing was desirable because they wanted to wear the watch when swimming and for water sports.

Exhibit B summarizes the primary attributes for each of the five functional needs.

Even with all that information, the design team needed more detail: it needed to know the relative importance of each of the functional areas. Since any design includes a set of tradeoffs, the

Exhibit B   Summary of Key Attributes

Functional Needs	*Attributes*
Comfort	▪ Not too heavy on the arm ▪ Feels smooth to the skin ▪ Not bulky
Stylishness	▪ Classy, but not flashy ▪ Looks elegant ▪ Brings out individual personality ▪ Stylish for almost any occasion
Reliability	▪ Always works ▪ Multiple-year battery life ▪ Will not scratch or lose finish
Simplicity	▪ Easy to use each function ▪ Easy to take off and on ▪ Easy to read (some indicated at night as well)
Functionality	▪ Needs basic functions of time and date ▪ Needs multilap stopwatch ▪ Some want waterproofing

Gamma Watch: A Case Example (continued)

team needed to understand the relative weighting of each factor in order to make the right decisions.

To quantify each attribute's importance, the team conducted a survey of consumers to rate the attributes that would be key to the decision to buy a "stylish sports watch for just under $100." Not surprisingly, the consumers ranked "stylishness" very high for that level of expenditure on a sports watch. Also, since this targeted price point was more than double the price of the primary competitive product (the Timex Ironman), the consumers ranked "reliability" very high as well.

The next most important functional need was "simplicity." The team noted that this factor had often been overlooked by higher-priced competitors, whose designs were not very user-friendly. Still important, but further down the list, was "functionality." This ranking was consistent with the focus group findings, which concluded that even though the consumers wanted to use the watch when they exercised, they really didn't need a lot of functions. In fact, many of the users of the popular Ironman had never figured out how to use some of its functionality.

The final functional need that made the cut for significance was "comfort." As shown in Exhibit C, the team converted the relative rankings to percentage scores and multiplied them by the overall target cost to set dollar values for each functional need.

Obviously, having a target of $6.83 for "comfort" did not provide enough guidance to the design team and the suppliers. To create meaningful targets, the designers used their understanding of how different parts of the watch contribute to the functional needs expressed by the consumers. This translation of the "voice

Exhibit C   Valuation of Functional Needs

Functional Needs	Importance, Percent	Value
Comfort	13	$6.83
Stylishness	29	$15.22
Reliability	24	$12.60
Simplicity	20	$10.50
Functionality	14	$7.35
Total	100	$52.50

of the consumer" into engineering requirements began with a breakdown of the major subsystems of the watch.

The first major subsystem was the watchband assembly, which included both the typical band plus the attachment screws and bar. The power supply was another major subsystem, consisting of the battery, coil block, and generating stator. The display subsystem included the key elements making up the face of the watch. The clock subsystem consisted of oscillator components to ensure reliable time tracking. The timer included the special functionality that made the watch a sports watch: the switches, lap counter, and memory functions. Exhibit D provides a breakdown of the five subsystems as agreed to by the design team.

Exhibit D   Subsystem Boundary Definition

Major Subsystems	*Typical Components Within Boundaries*
Watchband assembly	▪ Band ▪ Attachment screws and bar ▪ Length adjustment ▪ Clasp
Power supply	▪ Battery ▪ Coil block ▪ Coil block screw ▪ Generating stator
Display	▪ Hour, minute, and second hands ▪ Dial for time and stopwatch ▪ Day star ▪ Wheel for day and time correction ▪ Holding ring for dial
Clock	▪ Oscillator ▪ Oscillator weighting screw ▪ Oscillator weight bridge and screw ▪ Oscillator weight wheel ▪ Oscillator weight
Timer	▪ Counter ▪ Reset switch ▪ Start and stop switch ▪ Lap counter ▪ Memory

Gamma Watch: A Case Example (continued)

The next step—setting target costs at the subsystem level—
was among the more complex and critical ones facing the team.
The objective was to translate the cost targets for the functional
needs to the major subsystems. Once the targets were set at that
level, the team could work with suppliers to create the designs
that provided the right tradeoffs vis-à-vis cost and value.

The translation was performed by creating a matrix in which
the five major subsystems were listed in rows and the five sets of
functional needs were listed as column headings. (See Exhibit E.)
By comparing the primary functional needs and secondary attributes with the subsystems and components, the team allocated
the percentages of each need to the various subsystems. These
percentages were then multiplied by the cost targets for each of
the needs, as previously determined by their importance weight-
ings. The sum of these multiplications (that is, the addition of the
numbers by row) generated cost targets for each subsystem.

Next, tear-down analysis of the higher-end products offered by
TAG Heuer and Rolex were used to create a composite, "best-in-
class" subsystem design. This composite design was nearly 50
percent above the market-based price target. The team then
compared these subsystem cost estimates to the value-based
targets. This analysis showed that although the overall best-in-
class design was over the target by 50 percent, the cost gap at
the subsystem level ranged from 42 percent *under* to 156 percent

Exhibit E   Translation Table

	Comfort	Stylishness	Reliability	Simplicity	Functionality	Cost Targets
Functional Need Valuation	$6.83	$15.22	$12.60	$10.50	$7.35	$52.50
Band	23.2%	50.0%	5.0%	8.0%	25.0%	$12.50
Power system	32.0%		45.0%	1.0%		$ 7.96
Display	10.0%	50.0%	5.0%	80.0%	55.0%	$21.37
Clock	24.3%		35.0%	0.0%	0.0%	$ 6.07
Timer	10.5%		10.0%	11.0%	20.0%	$ 4.60
	100.0%	100.0%	100.0%	100.0%	100.0%	$52.50

over the target. Exhibit F shows the calculation of the gaps by subsystem.

The team also constructed a value graph, by plotting the targets against the tear-down cost estimates for each major subsystem. Exhibit G provides a clear visual focus on the appropriate areas of opportunity: the band and the power system.

Exhibit F   Initial Cost Gap Analysis

Subsystems	Tear-Down Cost	Value-Based Target	Cost Gap	Percentage Gap
Band	$32.00	$12.50	$19.50	156%
Power system	$16.00	$ 7.96	$ 8.04	101%
Display	$12.50	$21.37	$ (8.87)	(42%)
Clock	$ 9.50	$ 6.07	$ 3.43	57%
Timer	$ 8.25	$ 4.60	$ 3.65	79%
Totals	$78.25	$52.50	$25.75	49%

Exhibit G   Value Graph

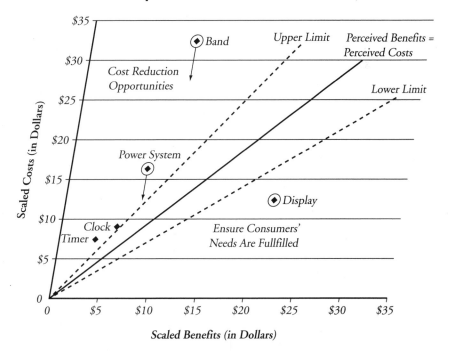

Gamma Watch: A Case Example (continued)

An internal subteam was asked to examine a wide range of new concepts for the band other than the gold-plated styles of the high-end competitors. The team discovered that gold plating was viewed as "too flashy" by the target consumer segment and not practical for true athletic use. The team visited a wide variety of suppliers, not just watchband makers, to get ideas. Ultimately, the team agreed on a design employing a cloth-covered nylon strap that was stylish enough for business wear and rugged enough for athletic use—and at a significant cost savings.

To address the power system cost gap, the team conducted a design competition among the key suppliers in the industry, including some nontraditional sources from emerging markets in Asia. Simultaneously, the team members examined the option of deleting some memory functions that required additional power but were not highly valued by the consumer. This option reduced the cost of the timer subsystem as well.

The value graph also persuaded the team to revisit the functionality provided by the displays of the competitive products. The team noted that neither product provided backlighting for nighttime use—a "want" by some, but not all, of the target consumer segment. Given the current favorable gap on the display front, the team set out to add the backlight functionality while still retaining some of the target "cushion" currently available. (See Exhibit H.)

Exhibit H   Final Cost Gap Analysis

Subsystems	Benefits Ranking	Value-Based Target	Tear-Down Cost	New Design Estimates	New Cost Gap	Percentage Gap
Band	23.8%	$12.50	$32.00	$11.88	$ (.62)	(5%)
Power system	15.2%	$ 7.96	$16.00	$ 8.26	$ .30	4%
Display	40.7%	$21.37	$12.50	$14.87	$(6.50)	(30%)
Clock	11.6%	$ 6.07	$ 9.50	$ 9.50	$ 3.43	57%
Timer	8.8%	$ 4.60	$ 8.25	$ 7.76	$ 3.16	69%
Totals	100.0%	$52.50	$78.25	$52.27	$ (.23)	—%

When the team reaggregated the new cost estimates, the design came in just under the overall cost target, while the individual subsystems now ranged from 30 percent under the value-based target to 69 percent over. The team assessed whether further efforts to drive the individual subsystem targets closer to the value-based targets would be warranted but concluded that the current design was appropriate to the target consumer market. The team agreed that value analysis efforts after product launch would focus on the gaps and would be incorporated into the next version of the product, which would also reflect evolving consumer desires.

Chapter 8
Evolving a Global Supply Base

Every man takes the limits of his own field of vision for the limits
of the world.
—ARTHUR SCHOPENHAUER

Many companies that are now facing maturing home markets see an
apparently limitless growth potential in emerging foreign markets.
Emerging economies often grow at 5 to 10 percent per year, compared
to the 2 to 4 percent rate common in more mature countries. Opportunities opened by improved communications and technology bring
world economies closer together every day. Shifting public policy and
regulatory attitudes continue to create more open markets throughout
the world. The result: industry after industry becomes global, with the
definition of *global* encompassing more and more countries.

The size of multinational companies reveals the extent to which
globalization is taking hold. In 1995, multinational companies were already generating foreign sales of $7 trillion.[1] Most European compa-
nies, for example, have more than half of both revenues and assets

Note: This chapter was developed in collaboration with the following Booz·Allen & Hamilton staff: Marco Kesteloo, Amsterdam; Michael Walsh, London; Keith Voigt, Lima; and
Marco Zurru, Milan. It also drew on a *Strategy & Business* article written in collaboration
with C. V. Ramachandran and Tonya Leary of Booz·Allen's New York office.

outside of their home countries in foreign operations. Even with U.S. and Japanese companies, whose operations are underpinned by larger domestic markets, the figures still tend to exceed 30 percent (see Exhibit 8.1).

McDonald's offers a telling example of global expansion. Its growth in the United States resulted from its ability to deliver exactly the same product quality at every location, through strategic suppliers and rigorous production and quality control. It became global, however, through its understanding of the needs of its non-U.S. customers and its ability to focus product characteristics—including price—on those needs. The brand gained such global appeal that it now operates restaurants in over 100 countries, and sales outside the United States have increased from 20 percent of the total in 1985 to nearly 50 percent today.

Exhibit 8.1   Globalization: Analysis of Global Top 100 Companies by Country

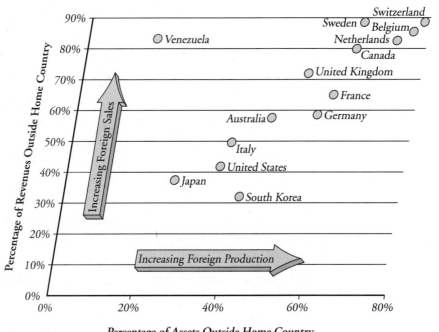

Source: United Nations, UNCTAD, Trade and Development Report, 1995.

Many purchasing organizations are being challenged to increase their level of global sourcing to support promising international growth and to leverage advantaged suppliers from around the world. Unfortunately, many companies enter new markets with their eyes focused intently on sales and profits, without giving adequate consideration to building the organizational capabilities needed for success.

Effective globalization of the supply base requires an organizational capability to understand the strategic imperatives and manage the inherent complexity of global sourcing.

The Strategic Imperatives

Global sourcing commonly refers to sourcing outside a company's traditional domestic markets. A company's desire to source globally may be motivated by two quite different strategic imperatives:

1. Suppliers outside the home market may offer superior technology or lower labor costs.
2. Global expansion into a new market often forces a company to establish a local supply base there.

A recent *Strategy & Business* survey showed that most companies are focusing on the first strategic imperative. The survey indicated that the primary factor in decisions to source outside of a home market is a desire to capture low labor cost. The second most important motivation is a need to access technology.

The strategic imperative to support global expansion by building a supply base to satisfy local content or offset requirements was of less importance to most respondents. The financially driven objectives of trade balance and tax savings—potentially important issues for a globally expanding firm—showed the lowest level of importance. (See Exhibit 8.2.)

The two different strategic imperatives influence a company's approach to global sourcing in a variety of ways. For example, companies focused on global expansion are more likely to have a local presence in the foreign country, which improves their ability to source globally. Such

Exhibit 8.2   Motivations for Sourcing Globally

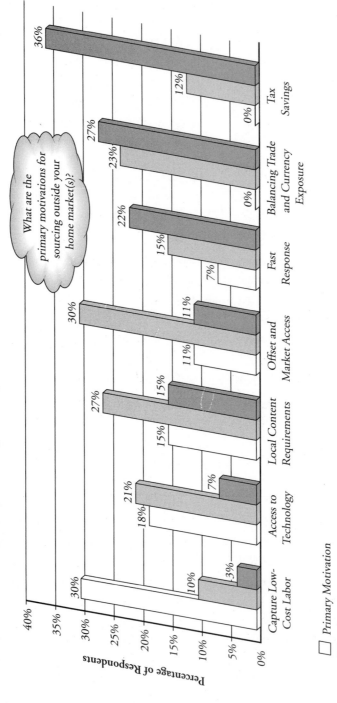

What are the primary motivations for sourcing outside your home market(s)?

Percentage of Respondents

Capture Low-Cost Labor: 30%, 10%, 3%
Access to Technology: 21%, 18%, 7%
Local Content Requirements: 15%, 15%, 27%
Offset and Market Access: 11%, 11%, 30%
Fast Response: 7%, 15%, 22%
Balancing Trade and Currency Exposure: 0%, 23%, 27%
Tax Savings: 0%, 12%, 36%

☐ Primary Motivation
▨ Important
▩ Unimportant

Source: *Strategy & Business* survey.

companies usually employ buyers who are native to the country, eliminating a potential language barrier with suppliers. These companies can also take a longer-term view of supplier development. Companies that are expanding globally, however, usually have more complicated strategic objectives than ensuring the lowest total delivered cost. They must also develop better government relations and balance trade and export targets.

The most important difference between the two imperatives is their effect on the commodities selected for global sourcing. A company focused on the second imperative, global expansion, seeks local suppliers for its bulkiest products, the ones that cannot be economically imported into the region. When the company is expanding into a growth market, the components it selects, such as large subassemblies, tend to have high labor content that captures the labor-cost advantages and reduces transportation costs. When it is expanding into mature markets, on the other hand, the company generally focuses on major systems that require technological sophistication, but not low labor costs.

Conversely, a company focused on the first imperative—global sourcing for import to its home markets—tends to concentrate on small, high-value components that can be shipped economically. This type of global importer looks to developing countries for components with advantageous labor costs in simple process technologies. In mature countries, this company would usually seek access to world-class technology expertise, but still in parts that can be shipped economically.

Globally expanding companies must also strive to optimize product development costs. Many companies try to capture scale advantages by amortizing product development costs over global volume, based on the converging expectations of customers around the world. Global sourcing decisions, nevertheless, must balance the scale advantages of using standard designs worldwide against the potential cost advantages of taking features out of designs to meet cost targets and local expectations.

Nike, which sources the full product rather than components, offers an interesting example of a company that captures lower labor cost while simultaneously building advanced technological capabilities in the supply base. Over the past two decades, Nike has developed an extensive supply base of approximately forty locations, predominantly in low-wage-rate countries throughout Asia. As a result, Nike achieves a landed cost in the United States for its Pegasus running shoe of about 25 percent of the retail price.[2]

Nike sources from an effective mix of lower- and higher-cost countries. Initially, much of its production was in South Korea and Taiwan, when those countries were considered low-cost. However, as those countries' wage rates increased, Nike developed new suppliers in even lower-cost countries, such as Indonesia and China. At the same time, Nike continued to increase the technological complexity of its product, adding features such as air cushion inserts and multicolored soles. Accordingly, the more sophisticated suppliers that have emerged in South Korea and Taiwan now produce these increasingly complicated products, while new suppliers in countries with lower wage rates produce the simpler, high-labor products.

The Complexity of Global Sourcing

Global sourcing has proved to be a challenge for many organizations. Four elements of complexity generally cause problems:

1. Language and cultural differences
2. Tariffs and customs costs
3. Currency variability
4. Supply web complexity

Language and Culture

Newcomers to global sourcing must never underestimate the challenges presented by language and the cultural barriers that can arise in a new foreign market. Although English is the most common language of business throughout the world, fluency cannot be assumed.

A major European aerospace company recently examined the Russian aerospace supply base and found it impossible to conduct even the written communication in English, though the company experienced no problems with potential suppliers in the former Communist-bloc countries of Central and Eastern Europe. Even when written communication poses no challenge, language can still be a barrier for companies that rely exclusively on English. For example, most global executives have experienced the frustration of having other participants in a cross-national meeting break into a "private" conversation in their native language.

Even where language barriers are minimal, significant cultural barriers may still exist. For example, non-Japanese business executives traveling in Japan quickly learn basic customs like exchanging business cards and small gifts. But many still fall into the subtle trap of addressing the bulk of their remarks to the individual who is most fluent in their language instead of to the most senior member of the Japanese team, which would be the more culturally appropriate behavior. Even the most experienced foreign buyers struggle in negotiations in the consensus-driven cultures of Asia, where harmony is generally considered more important than frankness and "yes" often means "I understand," not "I agree."

Tariffs and Customs

Tariffs introduce additional complexity in global sourcing. As shown in Exhibit 8.3, tariff rates vary significantly by country. Of even greater complexity is the variation by commodity or product classification within a country. Generally, nations impose higher tariffs on high-level assemblies or on critical industries to encourage—or protect—local production. As a result, even minor differences in a product's classification can have an order-of-magnitude effect on the tariff rate.

Currency Variability

The ability to properly assess currency risk can make a currency trader wealthy, but the need to assess currency risk often leaves a traditional buyer in a state of confusion or fear. Typically, the best tactic is not to try to outguess the currency traders, but rather to lock in currency exposure with forward contracts and hedging. Too many companies that should have focused on their core businesses have lost money speculating on currency.

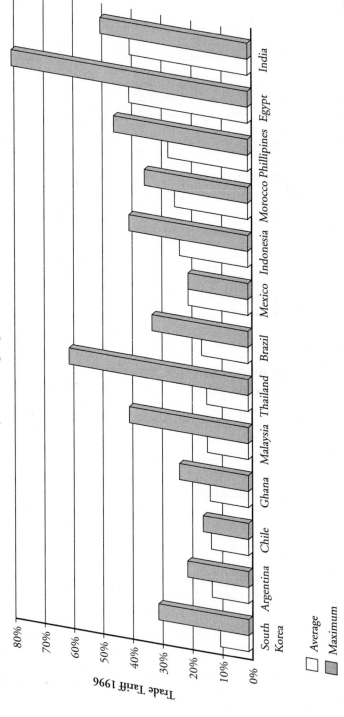

Exhibit 8.3   Trade Tariffs in Selected New and Emerging Markets

Trade Tariff 1996

Average
Maximum

Source: The Economist, "A Survey of India," February 22, 1997.

Responding quickly to currency fluctuations, however, can prove advantageous. For example, one global manufacturer tripled its sourcing in Italy as the lira fell against the German deutsche mark but then quickly reduced the sourcing as the lira grew stronger (see Exhibit 8.4). Such rapid sourcing shifts provide a real—though often temporary—advantage as long as switching costs are relatively low.

Supply Web Complexity

The complexity of a company's supply web is a major tactical challenge in global sourcing. Logistics costs are usually higher for imported materials, because transportation distances are generally greater. Companies should compare not only the transportation costs across the various modes (for example, rail, truck, air, or sea freight), but the inventory and expediting costs as well.

In addition, global sourcing often involves intermediaries, such as foreign distributors, brokers, freight forwarders, and customs clearing

Exhibit 8.4   Exchange Rate Effect on Sourcing Commitment (European Automotive Example)

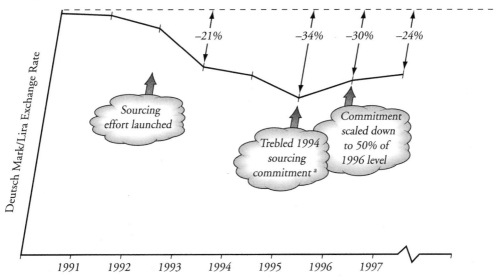

^aLetters of intent agreed.

agents, whose fees, though generally small individually, can be significant in the aggregate. This wide variety of intermediaries separating the customer from the supplier adds not only cost but also uncertainty to the supply chain. The multiplier effect of this uncertainty can make a global supply chain quite difficult to manage.

Simply tracking a shipment through each link in the supply chain can be time-consuming. For example, a typical truck journey from Romania to Germany covering less than 2,000 kilometers requires at least three border crossings and usually takes between 90 and 120 hours. Also, relying on the logistics provider to guarantee reliable deliveries is not always an option in emerging markets. Too often, the logistics providers themselves are still attempting to develop their own new infrastructure.

Building the Organizational Capability: A Case Study

The following case study offers some real-life insights into the practical response to global sourcing imperatives and shows how challenges can be met. It describes an automotive manufacturer's efforts to evolve an optimal global supply base with a particular focus on building a presence in Central Europe.

The disguised case examines the company's approach to segmenting commodities on a global basis, creating a global view of planned actions, targeting a region, screening suppliers, prioritizing suppliers for results, and building an organization to sustain the momentum.

Commodity Segmentation

Expanding sales in emerging markets provided the initial impetus for the company to build a global sourcing capability. Sales forecasts showed relatively flat growth in the mature markets but double-digit numbers in the developing regions. Such growth provided volume levels that justified fully integrated assembly plants rather than the typical "screwdriver factories" that assemble a small volume of cars from kits shipped from the domestic plants of major auto companies.

Negotiations with national governments for tax rebates and invest-ment incentives led to the normal complementary commitment to local content and even export sales. Independent "home teams" in each re-gion negotiated the deals, with purchasing typically left owning the tar-get but having no clear sense of how it could or should be achieved. Purchasing sensed the opportunity potential of such expansion as well: low-labor-cost suppliers in an emerging region have the potential to be-come global suppliers, generating major savings.

Though the company developed global commodity plans that sought out the best supplier for a particular commodity regardless of national origin, the plans tended to focus on suppliers in the mature re-gions: the United States, Western Europe, and Japan. Furthermore, since the commodity plans were developed independently to optimize at a commodity level, currency balancing and export agreements were achieved only by chance, or by "tasking" each product team to meet tar-gets independently.

Recognizing the need to make tradeoffs overall rather than product by product, the company created a segmentation model to identify which commodities would best meet different strategic imperatives. The segmentation scheme captured the total cost economics of manufac-turing as well as design.

The first segmentation of commodities, shown on the left side of Exhibit 8.5, focused on two manufacturing issues: scale and trans-portation cost. Commodities found in the top left-hand corner of the matrix were excellent candidates for global sourcing from a single sup-plier that would serve the company's worldwide needs. The commodi-ties in the bottom right-hand corner were the best candidates for local sourcing to support global expansion.

The chart on the right introduced the additional issue of whether to employ a single global design or use local specifications. The com-pany identified four tactics to optimize the tradeoff between design stan-dardization and local value engineering:

1. Where product development costs are high and the value of cus-tomized local designs is low, carryover designs identical to the origi-nal design for the mature market are used in the emerging markets.

Exhibit 8.5   Global Commodity Segmentation

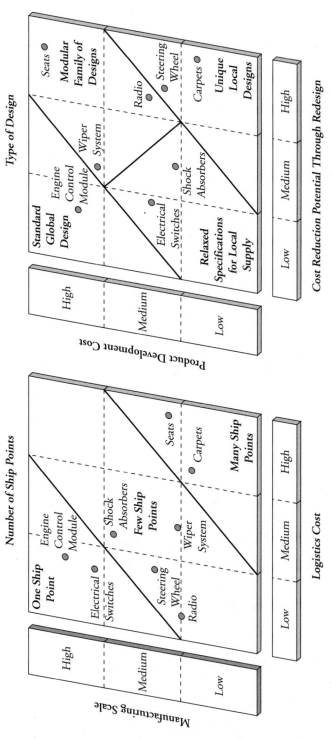

Source: Disguised automotive company example.

2. At the opposite extreme, where the cost-saving potential of customized designs is huge, the company creates new designs that meet local customers' needs.
3. Where the benefit of a new design is relatively low and the product development costs are also low, the company uses the original design with relaxed specifications to match the capabilities of the local supply base.
4. In the most critical area, where local design offers significant opportunity but the product development costs are high, the company has the original supplier develop a range of products using modular designs that allow local customization with lower overall development costs.

Bringing the two segmentation schemes together provided the strategic direction. For example, the company concluded that carpet should be manufactured in the same geographic locale as the assembly plants, because the manufacturing scale is only moderate and the transportation cost is extremely high. Given that new tooling would be required anyway, the incremental product development cost to localize the design was relatively low. On the other hand, the company determined that engine control modules should conform to a standard global design and be shipped globally, because transportation cost was relatively low and product development cost was quite high.

Creating a Global View

Though the segmentation framework provided directional guidance in creating commodity plans, it could not ensure that future targets would be met. Ever-changing demand forecasts, decade-long planning horizons, and the inherent complexity of the product presented an overwhelming challenge to tracking—much less understanding—the implications of decisions to evolve a global supply base.

Developing a comprehensive decision support tool to provide visibility to current and future decisions was the first step toward managing the evolution. The decision support tool used long-term forecasts by country of sale and country of manufacture, plus a table of the major vehicle subsystems, to provide "what-if" scenarios for different sourcing decisions. Despite the underlying complexity of the computations, the model presented the results in easy-to-understand visual displays. Exhibit 8.6 provides a simplified representation of the output, using bar charts to show imports, exports, and balance of trade by region or country.

Simply examining the current state, or even alternative scenarios, didn't drive change, because decisions were made in such myriad ways. One option would have been to centralize decision-making authority to overrule commodity strategies and program-level sourcing decisions. Such an approach, however, would have been at odds with the company's principle of empowering employees and teams. In light of the principle, enabling decision making required a new process, dubbed "global source planning." The new process provided information, highlighted issues, and challenged—but didn't mandate—the decision makers to help achieve such strategic imperatives as currency balancing.

Exhibit 8.6   Sample Display from Global Source Planning Decision Support Tool

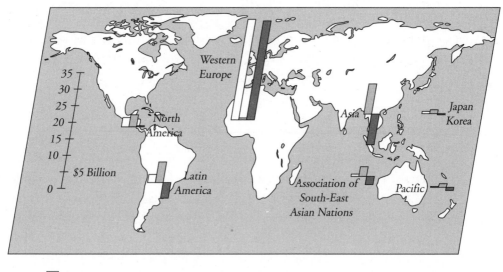

Given the uncertainty of the forecasts and the long-term nature of the planning, not every shortfall had to be addressed. But the participants at least understood where the shortfall risks were highest. By doing so, they broke the historic pattern of reacting to imbalances and instead began proactively planning to address them.

Selecting a Region

The source planning process provided insight into the strategic imperative of supporting global expansion. But the company also saw the opportunity to access low-cost suppliers in other regions. The opening of Central and Eastern Europe, coupled with the company's extensive manufacturing base in Western Europe, drove a decision to target the region for a major shift in sourcing.

To test the opportunity potential, a small team developed a business case for re-sourcing from Western to Central Europe. A key element of the case was the labor-cost gap between regions of up to 95 percent (see Exhibit 8.7). Interestingly, even though the percentage of increase in Central European wages was growing far faster than in

Exhibit 8.7   Labor-Cost Comparison

	Fully Loaded Average Industrial Monthy Wages		
	1992 ($)	1995 ($)	3 year △ ($)
Germany	4,400	4,612	212
Italy	2,622	2,499	(123)
United Kingdom	2,177	2,124	(53)
Spain	2,075	2,262	187
Czech Republic	300	420	120
Hungary	300	430	130
Poland	290	456	166
Slovakia	260	348	88
Romania	120	183	63

Source: Data adapted from the European Bank for Reconstruction and Development.

Germany, the absolute gap between the two was still increasing because of the huge difference in the baseline.

Further analysis examined currency exchange rate fluctuations to determine the speed at which the total gap would close. At a macroeconomic level, the analysis indicated that the gap was sustainable for many years. More important, the team emphasized that microeconomics would be just as important: even though wage and currency differentials would shrink, the Central European suppliers had far more opportunity to improve labor productivity, while Western European suppliers had begun to reach the point of diminishing returns in labor-saving capital investments.

Despite the macroeconomic analysis, many within the company doubted the potential, arguing that flashlights would be needed to search for suppliers in such an undeveloped region. Really moving the needle on Central European sourcing required proving that the region contained an adequate base of capable suppliers.

Screening the Supply Base

To find a qualified set of potential suppliers, the unavailability and inaccessibility of information in the targeted countries had to be overcome. Unfortunately, few countries have the sophisticated information infrastructure on which Western buyers depend, but fortunately, most Central European countries have organizations that play a "chamber of commerce" role in supplying information about their country's businesses.

In this case, limited information was coupled with the challenge of doing business in multiple languages. But the company combed published information in six different countries to identify several thousand potential suppliers for a set of relevant commodities. As shown in Exhibit 8.8, this very large group of potential suppliers was narrowed to a "long list" of several hundred suppliers that appeared to warrant further consideration. This smaller group received a written survey requesting information on a variety of topics such as quality certifications, Western European customers, capacity availability, and process technology.

Somewhat fewer than half of the narrowed group of supplier candidates responded to the survey. Based on their responses, potential sup-

Exhibit 8.8   Supplier Identification and Screening

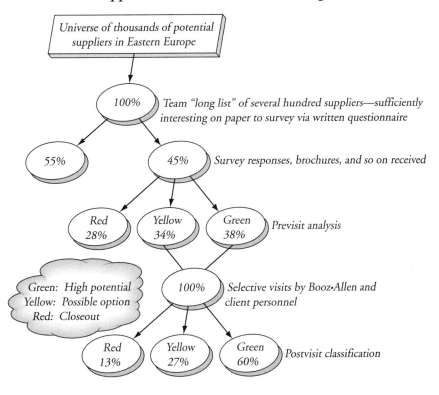

Universe of thousands of potential suppliers in Eastern Europe

100% Team "long list" of several hundred suppliers—sufficiently interesting on paper to survey via written questionnaire

55%

45% Survey responses, brochures, and so on received

Red 28%   Yellow 34%   Green 38% Previsit analysis

Green: High potential
Yellow: Possible option
Red: Closeout

100% Selective visits by Booz·Allen and client personnel

Red 13%   Yellow 27%   Green 60% Postvisit classification

pliers were sorted into three categories: green, for those with high potential; yellow, for those seen as possible suppliers; and red, for those who could be immediately dropped from consideration.

During site visits with suppliers in the green and yellow categories, the visiting team conducted basic quality audits and interviewed management representatives to assess each supplier's people and processes. After the site visits, the team concluded that about 13 percent of those visited were not capable of meeting the client's requirements. Yet 60 percent of the suppliers visited were now classified as green, based on the additional information garnered through the site visits. Despite the internal skepticism—and without using flashlights—the project team uncovered nearly one hundred capable Central European suppliers.

Prioritizing Suppliers

The company desired long-term, cooperative relations with these new suppliers but also wanted to drive near-term and long-term cost improvements. Spreading the buy across many suppliers would help capture near-term benefits quickly, but it might limit the ability to build the appropriate relationship. Also, some of the greatest cost savings potential resided in suppliers that needed the most help to become fully functioning supply partners. Prioritizing on a select set of suppliers offered the answer. The segmentation presented in Exhibit 8.9 classified the potential suppliers by company ownership and supply chain positioning (that is, direct source versus tiered source).

Concluding that the fastest savings would come through existing supplier relationships, the company launched an ongoing business review process with its most important suppliers to discuss opportunities. The meetings provided a forum for the company to advertise its com-

Exhibit 8.9   Central Europe Supply-Base Segmentation

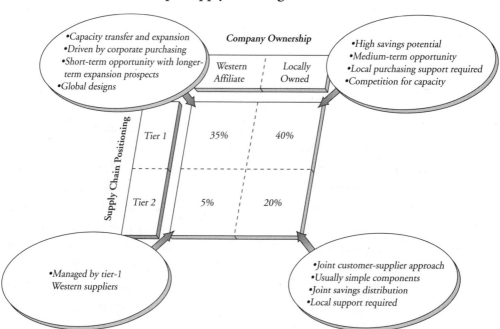

mitment to sourcing in lower-cost regions and to display its depth of understanding of the indigenous foreign supply base. Suppliers with Central European affiliations were challenged to immediately shift production and share the savings.

Using the knowledge garnered in researching the region, the company also encouraged its traditional suppliers to source basic components—for instance, wiring harnesses—from the region. Ultimately, sharing the results of the competitiveness assessment process with suppliers one-on-one led to mutually satisfactory low-cost sourcing and supply solutions.

To sustain the initial wave of savings, the company also pursued longer-term approaches focused on specific commodity strategies. It selected several less-developed suppliers that lacked one or more well-developed capabilities in technology, quality, or product development and committed to support them through a structured improvement program. By transferring knowledge of best practices to the chosen suppliers, the company helped many of them to make enormous operational performance improvements in as little as three to six months.

Building a Local Presence

Commitments to supplier development required company employees to spend significant amounts of time in the region. Initially many of them could make business trips into the region as needed. But the company recognized that building a local presence would be more cost-effective long term. Also, intermediaries such as consultants, who may prove very effective initially, are not necessary once adequate momentum for the re-sourcing program has been achieved.

The company invested in regional offices and hired native resources to minimize the cultural and language issues and, at the same time, to simplify supply chain management. The new employees were integrated into the project-based fieldwork and indoctrinated into the company culture through visits back to the Western European operations.

The regional purchasing offices were asked to play three key roles. First, they provided a physical presence for managing the flow of paperwork and materials in the new market. Second, they had local knowledge of the evolving supplier capabilities in the region, eliminating the need for every buyer in the home market to develop such skills. Finally, the offices provided local resources to train and develop the suppliers, thus avoiding a constant shuttling of employees from the Western European operations.

This pilot effort in Central Europe demonstrated, above all, that the key element in successfully implementing global sourcing is having a good understanding of the market, the economic environment, and the supply-base structure of the target region. Such knowledge is necessary not only for successful direct re-sourcing initiatives but also to ensure that existing suppliers see re-sourcing as a credible option, thereby giving the customer a more persuasive argument in driving change.

Conclusion

The Central Europe automotive case study provides a realistic view of the enormous challenges inherent in global sourcing. Whether a company is driven by the desire to expand into global markets or the need to achieve the lowest cost, the hurdles to overcome are many.

All of the hurdles can add cost, increase risk, or both. As a result, many companies find the benefits of global sourcing less rewarding— or at least far harder to achieve—than expected. Furthermore, ineffective global sourcing can work to the detriment of a company's global expansion efforts. An inability to build and then manage a local supply base can lead to failure of the entire business in a new market.

However, many companies that are willing to invest in evolving a global supply base can and will be successful. It is not easy, but it can be done. In fact, the companies that can overcome the steep learning curve will enjoy a tremendous advantage as the world economies continue to integrate, while others struggle to find quality partners that can be developed and integrated into their global extended enterprise.

Section Three

Balanced Sourcing Case Studies

Change is the law of life. And those who look only to the past or present are certain to miss the future.
—JOHN F. KENNEDY

Throughout this book, we have illustrated the practical application of Balanced Sourcing capabilities through short examples of purchasing practices extracted from real-life experiences in a variety of industries. In Section Three, we take a more in-depth look at the purchasing experiences of four very different companies, each of which demonstrates a varying mix of the six Balanced Sourcing capabilities.

Please note that these case examples are not intended to provide a rigorous analytic assessment of the purchasing capabilities of the subject companies. Rather they are anecdotal in nature, based on interviews with professionals in each of the companies, who tell their company's stories in their own words.

The case studies represent a wide range of industries, each company with its own corporate culture, marketplace dynamics, and purchasing requirements. The distinct differences among them are apparent, not only in the challenges they face in managing their purchasing processes but even at the most superficial level—the first impression a visitor gets of the physical environments within which each company operates.

Florida Power & Light's headquarters, sitting over an artificially created lake, is complete with a rooftop heliport and a private employee health club. The building reflects the company's origins as a highly regulated public utility, when competition was something for others to worry about and returns were based on a fixed percentage of assets. It belies the company's ongoing transformation into an organizationally lean, customer-oriented, and highly competitive global energy services provider.

SUPERVALU, one of the nation's leading wholesale grocery distributors, presents a modern, eye-pleasing facade to the public at its Minneapolis headquarters. Inside it's strictly business, with every inch of available space divided into cubicles filled with earnest staff, each intently focused on making sure that every truckload shipped delivers maximum value not only to SUPERVALU, but to its suppliers and retail grocery customers as well.

Honda of America presents a perfect picture of efficiency and orderliness. Its philosophical underpinnings are readily apparent at every turn, even down to the identical clothing—an egalitarian white jumpsuit—worn by each employee from the executive suite to the assembly line. The message is clear: every individual is respected, collaboration is expected, and energy is to be focused not on superficial trappings but on the details of the business at hand.

Cisco Systems, the Internetworking phenomenon, sprawls across acres of Northern California real estate in a constant state of new construction that parallels the company's incredible rate of growth. The staff are casually dressed, yet the atmosphere is anything but laid-back, with conference rooms constantly filled with meeting after meeting, all focused, no doubt, on the next new product and how to get it to market faster.

That these companies differ so dramatically from each other and yet have all progressed significantly along the Balanced Sourcing continuum argues strongly that Balanced Sourcing is not industry-specific. The six capabilities shown in Exhibit 1.2 apply across the board, though some are more strategically significant to one company than another according to the nature of the company's business and its marketplace.

This breadth of examples is no coincidence. The point is that the marked differences among these companies should convince individual readers that Balanced Sourcing can work in their own organizations as well.

Chapter 9
Florida Power & Light Company

Adopt the new philosophy. We are in a new economic age.
Western management must awaken to the challenge, must learn
their responsibilities, and take on leadership for change.
— W. EDWARDS DEMING

Any case study of Florida Power & Light Company would be incomplete without first telling the story of the company's rigorous journey to become the first non-Japanese company ever to win the highly sought after Deming Prize. At Florida Power & Light, quality—as demonstrated through the company's focus on multifunctional problem solving, fact-based analysis, and a deep commitment to exemplary customer service—is a part of the fabric of the enterprise.

But the quality process at Florida Power & Light is also an ever-evolving one reflected in a dramatic change in the company's vision and its organizational structure. The story of the evolution of the utility's purchasing practices offers insight into the many changes that have occurred within the company. As such, the story teaches a variety of lessons about the development of the skills and capabilities inherent in Balanced Sourcing.

Quality and the Evolution of an Organization

Florida Power & Light is one of the largest and fastest-growing electric utilities in the United States. Its service area covers half of the state of Florida, ranging from near Jacksonville on the east coast through central Florida and along the west coast, and it numbers more than eleven thousand employees. The company is also demonstrating its strength through its financial performance, with 1997 earnings of $608 million on approximately $6.1 billion in revenues.

The road to the company's current level of success and prosperity coincides with the evolution of its focus on quality. Retracing Florida Power & Light's steps reveals a three-stage transformation that offers some informative insights into both the opportunities and the challenges that a quality-focused organization encounters.

Stage 1: Laying the Foundation

The first of the three stages began in the early 1980s when electric power generation was mostly oil-based and its cost fluctuated at the mercy of world markets. At that time the rate of increase in the consumer price for power exceeded the rate of increase in inflation, and the level of customer dissatisfaction had followed a corresponding upward curve.

To its credit, Florida Power & Light recognized that it had to improve its public image through better customer service, and in 1981 the first quality improvement teams were formed. As quality consciousness continued to evolve, Florida Power & Light engaged counselors from the Union of Japanese Scientists and Engineers, the organization credited with bringing W. Edwards Deming to the attention of Japanese companies in the late 1950s and 1960s. Japan's Kansai Electric Power Company, the winner of the 1984 Deming Prize, agreed to provide informal mentoring support, and in 1985, Florida Power & Light implemented its first company-wide quality improvement program.

Stage 2: Intensification and Recognition

The second stage in the quality evolution story, which took place roughly between 1986 and 1989, was a period of intensified focus on quality. Florida Power & Light began using advanced statistical methods to diagnose problems and control processes. It initiated a rigorous seven-step methodology for problem solving and quality improvement to be used throughout the company at every level. And two new quality support initiatives began.

The first initiative, called Policy Deployment, focused employees on the highest priorities for improvement, so the greatest efforts would be invested where the greatest return could be expected. The second initiative, Quality in Daily Work, helped employees to develop a continuous improvement mindset focused on their customers, both external and internal, and on finding ways to serve them better.

In 1986, Florida Power & Light entered into a more formal relationship with Kansai, actually importing Japanese staff for consultation and education. Inspired by Kansai's performance and the Deming Prize achievement, Florida Power & Light took a bold step and decided to challenge for the prize too. In summer of 1989, after almost a full year of staff work to accelerate the pace of improvements and to document each step, a two-week on-site examination was conducted by quality experts from the Union of Japanese Scientists and Engineers. The result? Florida Power & Light became the first non-Japanese company to win the Deming Prize.

Stage 3: Applying the Lessons Learned

By any accounting, the decade-long quality improvement effort garnered impressive results:

- Unplanned outages at fossil fuel power plants were substantially reduced.
- Transmission outages declined.
- Service unavailability was cut almost in half.
- Personnel safety dramatically improved.

On the flip side, the quality process had begun to take on a life of its own, often producing consequences that were inconsistent with the company's ultimate quality objectives. Although it is true that Florida Power & Light employees took great pride in the Deming Prize, there was a widespread feeling that the quality program had become mechanical and inflexible, too paper-oriented, and bureaucratic and that it sometimes even created its own barriers to real improvement.

Jim Peterson, Director of Employee Selection, Performance, and Rewards, sums up the situation bluntly: "In 1990 we were a cost-plus, lethargic utility. Fat and happy. We had quality, but at a cost. The balance wasn't there. Our chairman said, 'Stop the music. We have to change.' It took that bold move to set the right tone for the entire organization to move forward."

That chairman was Jim Broadhead, who had assumed the top position in 1990 and who brought to Florida Power & Light the leadership and determination to take a soul-searching reexamination—and ultimately a redirection and reorganization—of the company and its mission. Says Broadhead, "Florida Power & Light at that time was simply doing the same things better, without considering whether the things it was doing were actually required for success." He immediately launched a far-reaching, course-altering effort to redefine Florida Power & Light's vision and strategy.

Using multidisciplinary employee teams to make recommendations, the company significantly reshaped its approach to quality by refocusing, streamlining, and enhancing the entire process. The results were impressive:

1. Many formal management reviews in the quality process were eliminated.
2. No longer would there be a single prescribed quality methodology; the focus would shift to results rather than process.
3. The responsibility for quality would be dispersed throughout the organization.

Employee communications stressed that these changes were intended to strengthen quality by encouraging employee innovation and creativity.

The Effects of Regulatory Change

In 1992, at the same time that Broadhead was reshaping Florida Power & Light internally, federal legislation passed that essentially deregulated the generation sector of the industry to encourage competition in the wholesale market. The law also required utilities to allow others to have access to their transmission lines for wholesale transactions at the same prices the utilities charged their own internal customers.

Compounding the situation was the very real threat that federal legislation would likely be passed that would require every state to give all customers, including individuals at the retail level, the right to choose their electricity supplier by the year 2000. A new era in electric power generation and distribution had begun, marked not only by intensified competition in the wholesale sector but also by the future prospect of intense competition in the retail sector.

Under Broadhead's leadership, the company recognized that being the low-cost provider of electric service would be the key factor for future success in a competitive market. Ironically, through the late 1980s, Florida Power & Light had been the highest-cost major electric utility in its region, with management clearly underestimating the speed of the oncoming competitive environment and the impact it would have. The reawakened Florida Power & Light now realized that it had to shift its corporate structure and strategy from the regulated mindset to one more appropriate for a company doing business in a highly competitive industry.

A New Vision and Strategy

Employing the multidisciplinary approach to problem solving that the company had clearly mastered, diverse employee teams began to identify, analyze, and assess the future challenges Florida Power & Light would face and what its needs would be in such areas as technology, regulation, customer demand, and competitive pressure.

A new corporate vision emerged: "Florida Power & Light will be the preferred provider of safe, reliable, and cost-effective products and services that satisfy the electricity-related needs of all customer segments." To realize this new vision, the company focused its attention and efforts on four primary areas of its business-planning and strategy processes:

1. Strong customer orientation
2. Continuing commitment to quality
3. Cost-effective operations
4. Speed, simplicity, and flexibility

It also became obvious that a new organizational structure was needed to support the vision and to accomplish the company's goals. Again, multidisciplinary teams were formed to reconfigure the entire organization from the top levels of management down. The results were dramatic.

First, the previously dense layers of management were cut in half, flattening the organizational structure and eliminating many levels of bureaucracy; and second, the size of the company's workforce, cut by about 30 percent in the original restructuring in 1992, was ultimately reduced by 44 percent by 1996.

Along with the restructuring came a major shift in Florida Power & Light's business processes and corporate culture. Policies and procedures were streamlined to enable faster, more strategic decision making, and much greater emphasis was placed on fostering employee innovation and creativity by encouraging unfettered thinking and multifunctional problem solving.

The effects of the complete organizational transformation on the company's performance have been measurable and significant. Its operations and maintenance costs were 30 percent lower in 1997 than they were in 1990, down from 1.82 cents per kilowatt-hour in 1990 to 1.27 cents in 1997. The prices charged to customers dropped almost 11 percent between 1985 and 1998, while the competition's prices increased.

The outcomes of the transformation are clearly visible in other aspects of the company's performance as well. Quality has continued to improve since the company won the Deming Prize. For example, in 1989 the Nuclear Regulatory Commission had rated Florida Power & Light's Turkey Point facility one of the worst in the country; it now ranks among the best. Power availability set all-time record levels in 1996, and customer satisfaction levels are higher than ever.

Many of the effects of Florida Power & Light's transformation are obvious to even the most casual outside observer. Others are more deeply rooted inside the company, though extremely significant to the company's realization of its vision. A prime example is Florida Power & Light's major strides forward in its approach to and execution of its purchasing process.

Transformation of the Purchasing Process

Through the 1980s, the purchasing function at Florida Power & Light had been highly centralized. According to Ben Fowke, the company's former Director of Corporate Procurement, "We were very consistent with the 1980s environment—lots of paperwork, lots of controls without any value added. We were spending 80 percent of our transaction time on 20 percent of the dollars spent."

Purchasing was characterized by little or no integrated cross-functional planning. As a result, the number of items purchased had proliferated excessively, resulting in an inventory turnover level far below that of the industry's top performers. Purchasing was also overstaffed and tremendously layered with multiple handoffs and fragmented accountabilities, all of which compounded the unacceptably high material and inventory costs. In addition, long processing times for requisitions and purchase orders made execution extremely inefficient.

Recognizing the opportunities for cost reductions and greater efficiency in purchasing, the company decentralized the procurement function by locating purchasing experts within each of the company's business units. At the same time, it formed the Procurement Strategy Board, based on a recommendation made by Booz·Allen consultants, which signaled that purchasing had been raised to a strategic level within the organization.

The Board, composed of key procurement managers from each of the company's business units, was responsible for setting core procurement policies and practices, with an emphasis on systems to reduce transactions and their associated costs. Yet each business unit retained the flexibility to customize the core policies and practices to meet its own individual needs.

The real value of the Procurement Strategy Board is that it develops and encourages the use of common purchasing processes and systems across the company. Secondarily, it seeks out new ways to leverage the buy across the business units. Fowke explains, "The big benefit of the Procurement Strategy Board is the sharing of information and best practices. We can challenge each other to higher levels." One of those best practices is commodity planning.

Commodity Planning

In 1991, Florida Power & Light's internal processes both contributed to and reflected inefficiency in procurement practices. Procurement lacked the required knowledge of its suppliers and the industry's economics and processes. Consequently, there was no reliable way to measure the competitiveness of suppliers' price quotes or to challenge them to improve. In general, the company's suppliers avoided price competition among themselves, preferring instead to share the orders.

Also contributing to the inefficiency was the lack of access by engineering to price and cost information when making design choices and evaluating products and suppliers. The Vendor Quality Program then in place recognized suppliers who instituted quality programs but failed to measure what those programs cost or the degree to which they actually improved quality. This combination of factors led to suboptimal price, performance, and quality decisions, as well as to disadvantaged supplier relationships and unjustifiable price premiums.

In one case, a star company in the Supplier Excellence Program quoted prices that were more than 20 percent higher than those of other suppliers, yet it refused to lower its prices, claiming that it was a "quality" vendor, despite the fact that at least one competitor had equally effective process quality and production capability. In another instance, more than half of the purchases for a particular commodity had been awarded over time to a single long-time supplier. An evaluation showed, however, that this supplier made little or no investment in manufacturing or in research and development. It also had poor process and product quality and was financially unhealthy and noncompetitive.

In 1991, with the help of consultants from Booz·Allen, Florida Power & Light began to address these shortcomings and problems with a rigorous examination of its sourcing decisions, through a strategic approach to commodity planning. A new operating philosophy emerged that defined new supply chain goals and sourcing strategies. It provides a classic example of applying the principles of strategic sourcing, as presented in Chapter Four.

The new operating philosophy was straightforward in concept. Be customer-driven. Improve cost-effectiveness. Be flexible and make decisions faster. Empower operating units. Focus on self-improvement. Living by that philosophy, however, would require a rethinking and retooling of the entire procurement process.

Florida Power & Light came to understand that a sourcing strategy entailed far more than a decision about which supplier to use. John Chism, Director of Corporate Real Estate and a leader in the change program, explains: "One of the keys to our success was intensive training on commodity planning and buying. And a big part of that was developing a widespread understanding that 60 percent of the effort is finding the correct specifications, 30 percent is finding the right vendor, and the remaining 10 percent is negotiating. Previously we were doing just the opposite. Our awareness and mindset are now in the right proportions."

The story of how purchasing has evolved at Florida Power & Light is amplified by the following examples of a number of different systems and commodity strategies the company has used over the past few years.

Leveraging Technology to Streamline Purchasing

To free up time for commodity planning, the Procurement Strategy Board began looking at ways to transform Florida Power & Light's procurement system. The old system was time-consuming and slow. With its high volume of transactions, administrative processing was very costly. This system—the Procurement Management Information System—was a legacy system and not year-2000-compliant. Florida Power & Light found itself facing the necessity of finding a new way to manage the way it purchased, especially in the area of the high-volume, low-dollar categories of materials.

The Board's response was to move quickly to replace the old system. The result was the Procurement and Receipt Information System, or PARIS, which was completely customized for Florida Power & Light at a relatively low cost compared to many of the all-encompassing packaged systems. The objectives set for developing PARIS were to

- Cut transaction costs
- Eliminate paper transactions
- Reduce keystroking
- Increase the use of bar coding and Electronic Data Interchange (EDI)
- Decrease inventories
- Allow quick payment to leverage discounts

The system that emerged met all those objectives and now allows for real-time interaction among all the parties involved in a purchasing transaction—the buyer, the supplier, and the storage facility. Now all high-volume, low-cost materials come in through the PARIS system. And because the orders are placed all the way through fulfillment, the only paper involved is the packing slip.

Bill Magrogan, manager of IM Development and Architecture, reflects on the lessons learned in developing the new procurement system: "You can't underestimate the difficulty involved in cross-functional system development. There was a lot of software out there and a lot of people had their own ideas about what was best. It's also important to consider the challenge of getting your suppliers enabled on EDI. Some are there, but many aren't.

"But the effort," he says, "has been worth it. We're much better off now than in 1991. We've had significant inventory reductions. Fewer people are doing the transactions and with greater efficiency. We've really leveraged electronic technology like EDI and bar coding. It's all helped us accomplish many things we couldn't have done before on an ad hoc basis."

High-Volume, Low-Cost Materials

Concurrent with the development of the new system, a Florida Power & Light commodity team implemented a strategy to rationalize the supply base for common consumables. Prior to the restructuring of the purchasing process, Florida Power & Light stocked approximately 184,000 items at any one time, compared to the industry average of around 152,000. These were mostly items that were bought in large volumes but that had relatively low dollar values, and they were purchased from as many as 700 different suppliers.

Recognizing the opportunity for achieving significant cost savings by leveraging its buying power, the company set out to reduce the number of suppliers for these basic consumables to the lowest number possible. Thanks to the broader mindset of strategic sourcing, the company quickly realized that the biggest savings would come from standardization and lower transaction cost. It focused its efforts, therefore, on the thousands of low-dollar, high-volume purchases for items such as safety equipment, abrasives, tools, and chemicals. Mark Waronicki, Supplier Manager, acknowledges that the effort was not about price alone. It required the company to create and maintain a delicate balance between cooperating with the chosen suppliers and sustaining competition among them to deliver the best price and service levels.

Florida Power & Light began the process by setting criteria for the vendors who would be invited to submit bids for supplying the low-dollar, high-volume items, seeking those who could provide the widest variety of items at minimum dollar levels. Prequalification questionnaires were sent to fifty vendors selected on the basis of the company's assessment of who could actually accomplish what would be required. Based on the returned questionnaires, the field was narrowed to thirty suppliers deemed eligible to receive the "big bid package" encompassing the bulk of the items in question.

Twenty-five of those invited to participate actually returned the completed bids, which were then scored on a weighted system that took into account not just price, but also the vendor's financial stability, transportation capabilities, past performance, EDI and bar coding capabilities, and perceived commitment to developing a long-term relationship. Again, though it was using a competitive bidding approach for screening the candidates, Florida Power & Light recognized that reductions in acquisition costs through improved supply web integration would produce the greatest savings over the long term.

About the negotiating process, Waronicki reports, "We did some commodity plans and price negotiations. I had to learn the vendors' cost drivers and help them find ways to reduce their costs so they could pass [the savings] along to us. For example, a supplier's marketing and internal administrative costs are part of the product cost to us. So I worked with them to help reduce their marketing costs associated with my items and to find ways to save on administrative activities like order processing and payments." Another example of balancing cooperation and competition.

Waronicki says that the numbers tell the success story of this initiative. "We reduced our suppliers of high-volume, low-dollar items from 375 to 7. We locked in contracts that were 5 percent lower than the previous annual buy. We reduced inventory levels by more than 50 percent, from $9 million to $4 million. And on-time delivery performance has risen from around 75 percent to nearly 95 percent for most of our suppliers now."

He adds, "Of those vendors who didn't make the cut, many were excellent suppliers. But because they didn't meet one or more of our essential criteria, they didn't get the bid. For some suppliers the loss was a significant part of their business, which added some emotional content to the process. But the business success is there and, in fact, some of the suppliers we cut have actually improved their own processes, and we may be able to bring them back some time in the future."

The success of the PARIS system is particularly evident in the buy on the high-volume, low-dollar materials, in part because of the supplier reduction effort, which emphasized vendors' capability to conduct purchasing transactions electronically. A good example is that of the area of office supplies. Any secretary within the organization can now order office supplies directly from the designated vendor from a desktop PC by simply selecting from the on-line Florida Power & Light catalog of supplies.

Distribution Lift Truck Maintenance

In 1992, Florida Power & Light's distribution resources management unit formed a multidisciplinary team to try to find ways to reduce the cost of maintenance and repair on its lift truck fleet, the vehicles used for materials handling. Although the team was not officially designated as a commodity-planning team, its cross-functional composition and the processes it used to approach its task mirrored those of a well-disciplined commodity team, underscoring the fact that sourcing strategy development is an organizational capability, not just a purchasing task.

Using data from a recent study of how 350 gas and electric utilities managed their lift truck fleets, the team benchmarked Florida Power & Light's fleet maintenance and repair costs against those of the industry. The results were eye-opening. Florida Power & Light was spending more than twice the industry average. With 251 trucks in its fleet, the company calculated that it could save hundreds of thousands of dollars if it could achieve just the industry average.

To get to the root causes of the problems, the team analyzed the entire maintenance and repair function, taking into account factors like the quality and cost of parts, the quality and cost of labor, and maintenance and repair's management processes. Among the important findings included:

- The decentralized management structure, the lack of systems to track costs by vehicle, and the large number of vehicles contributed to management inefficiencies.
- The extremely wide range of vehicle types hampered efficient and effective preventive and scheduled maintenance.
- The mechanics employed by external vendors of maintenance and repair services were less technically qualified in terms of

certification than the industry standard for in-house mechanics and technicians.

- The shop rates and parts costs charged by the service vendors were higher than industry averages; this was attributable to their high profit margins, taxes, and overhead.
- Maintenance and repair costs per engine hour varied dramatically by make and fuel type.

The most significant result of the analysis was the discovery that 92 percent of the maintenance and repair cost differential between Florida Power & Light and the industry average was attributable to sourcing-related decisions.

To solve the problems and regain as much of the industry cost differential as possible, the team committed itself to replicating the industry's best practices in fleet maintenance and repair. The major changes and results included

- Reducing outsourcing of maintenance and repair to large vendors and dealers and relying more on in-house capabilities and small repair shops, which resulted in a 56 percent improvement in annual maintenance and repair costs
- Shifting from the preventive maintenance model to predictive maintenance, including a computerized reliability maintenance system, which resulted in improved reliability and fewer unscheduled repairs
- Reducing the size of the lift truck fleet by 20 percent, which lowered the annual maintenance costs by at least $100,000
- Standardizing lift truck makes and models by reducing the number of manufacturers from seventeen to four, which also helped to standardize policies and processes such as predictive maintenance
- Developing a total quality control model to improve overall fleet reliability and optimize operating and capital costs

The team's disciplined, structured approach is consistent with Florida Power & Light's continuing evolution toward the Balanced Sourcing model. The dramatic results in cost savings and improved reliability make a strong case for multidisciplinary teams, cost modeling, rigorous analysis, and the development of a deep understanding of supplier and industry dynamics.

Cost Modeling for Transportation

The deregulation of the transportation industry in the early 1990s presented many opportunities to electric utilities like Florida Power & Light; the company spends approximately $350 million per year on materials that are subject to transportation. The challenge was to identify the opportunities and determine how to leverage them to the company's maximum advantage.

Prior to deregulation, transportation cost was fixed regardless of who provided or managed it. Deregulation said, "Let the marketplace determine the cost of transportation." This new environment was an opportunity for the purchasing agent to unbundle a major element of cost by breaking out delivery from material. To leverage this opportunity, Florida Power & Light had to negotiate very attractive freight rates with transportation providers. To do that, it had to know the actual transportation cost of material delivered by the supplier for comparison with what a transportation company contracted by Florida Power & Light would charge. Says Bill Rue, Manager of Transportation, "This required collecting a great deal of information: what you're buying, who the suppliers are, the origin of the material, the traffic lanes. Then we had to share that information with the freight companies so they could understand our transportation costs completely and offer the best rates." As part of the analysis process, Florida Power & Light benchmarked the rates it was offered by the transportation companies and found that they were in about the ninetieth percentile industry-wide. This meant that it was most often advantageous for Florida Power & Light to take possession of material at the source of supply and then manage and pay for the transportation directly. With this information in hand, the company set as its target to have half of all inbound shipments brought in by its designated carriers. A conservative estimate put the savings in freight costs at about 20 percent. Since the average cost attributable to freight for Florida Power & Light was about 5 percent, the transportation costs on the company's $350 million annual buy amounted to about $18 million, which would translate to approximately $3 million a year in savings.

Florida Power & Light knew that realizing those savings would require a good management information system. Purchasing agents would have to know freight costs in real time in order to negotiate effectively with suppliers. The company looked for a packaged software program, but those available only focused on the transportation side—getting goods into the market—not on analyzing costs from the buyer's perspective. So once again Florida Power & Light decided to develop its own system, the Transportation Information Management System. This system allows purchasers to automatically compare transportation costs offered by selected carriers for all materials along dimensions such as the type of carrier (surface or air), the urgency of delivery (overnight, two-day air, or deferred), the size of the shipment, and its origin. Once all the parameters of the delivery have been defined, the system compares the prospective carriers on a least-cost to highest-cost basis.

Florida Power & Light has found that for orders of less than $25,000, it's usually not advantageous to purchase and manage its own transportation. But, notes Rue, "On higher orders, especially approaching $1 million, the time spent analyzing costs is well worth the effort." He also notes another key factor in achieving cost reductions in transportation: focusing on building relationships with a limited number of carriers. "You have to make the transportation buy large enough for the carriers to be interested in negotiating favorable rates. That's why we went from twenty carriers down to six. That made our business a lot more attractive to all the carriers."

Rue acknowledges that the new system posed some potential problems, especially in transaction processing. But he points to improvements in the procurement system software as the answer: "Although 'going collect' has increased the administrative workload—transactions went from 500 to 36,000—the PARIS system has streamlined our ability to pay freight bills quickly. In fact, we've been able to handle the tremendously increased administrative burden while reducing the processing staff by one person."

Rue reflects on the broader strategic thinking that has become a way of life in purchasing: "This is only the first step. There are many more opportunities out there. But it will require us to again rethink some of our disciplines and work more closely together. We may have to think more in terms of logistics. All the elements are so inter-related—transportation, warehousing, inventory management, information systems—that they can't be managed separately. There's much on the horizon, particularly from the buying perspective, so it's very important to remember that what benefits your supplier doesn't necessarily benefit you."

Turbines: An Example of Innovation

Turbines are a major expense item for any electric utility, in initial capital cost as well as in ongoing operations and maintenance. Florida Power & Light's Combustion Turbine Manager David Stephens spends about $15 million a year on gas turbines alone. "My goal," he says, "is to drive out costs. The typical mindset for most commodity managers is tactical, for example, to budget for a three-year cycle. But I budget for the commodity's life cycle. I'll pay double for something that lasts three times as long. What I go for is the least dollar per service-hour. Everything gets reduced to that."

He cites as an example his search for an alternate, lower-cost source for combustion turbine liners. Stephens figured that he could build the component for about one-sixth of the cost of buying it. So he conducted a detailed tear-down of the component to get engineering data and physical information, then tested ways to make it better. Even with a one-time outsourced engineering cost and a one-time tooling cost, he was still able to custom-build the components for $6,000 each instead of paying $36,000 to the traditional original-equipment manufacturer. "Florida Power & Light has purchased enough of these combustion turbine liners to afford amortization of the tooling costs," he says. "This was an especially good 'build our own' target. We know machine and tool shops. We know the best alloys. We estimated our cost to build, and it was far less than we were paying the manufacturer."

Another example reinforces the old adage about necessity being the mother of invention. Florida Power & Light uses small gas turbines for handling peak-service requirements. The turbines it had been using were at the end of their useful life, requiring frequent repairs and replacement of the compressor blades. Unfortunately, the turbine manufacturer only made replacement parts when the demand was great enough. Not having a reliable source of supply was a significant problem.

Stephens once more determined that Florida Power & Light could make its own replacement parts. And again, he didn't have to engineer the part; he just took it to the machine shop and reverse-engineered it. "I'm not making parts to sell to someone else," he adds. "We only make about six of our own parts right now. But on compressor blades alone, we save about $250,000 per year."

Building his own components isn't necessarily Stephens's first solution to a challenge. He firmly believes in building mutually beneficial relationships with suppliers to meet his goal of minimizing life-cycle costs. "I work with the manufacturers to try to show them how to present their deal. It's not just price; it's life-cycle and maintenance costs as well. If I say to a supplier that I can build this component for one-fourth the price and then throw it away, it makes the supplier think. It's like razor blades. The manufacturers will practically give me the machine and then make their money on the replacement parts."

Preparing for the Future

For Florida Power & Light, deregulation will continue to be a major force in the organization's evolution. The company's revitalized vision and mission should serve it well. All signs point to Florida Power & Light becoming even more market-driven and cost-focused. Purchasing will continue to assume a greater, more pivotal role in driving out costs to ensure that Florida Power & Light can be the low-cost provider the market demands. As the company broadens its market with new alliances, like those it has recently forged with other power companies in South America and the United Kingdom, it will be able to transfer the purchasing capabilities and skills it has developed domestically to the global enterprise.

This broadening scope reflects Florida Power & Light's new awareness of its role in the expanding marketplace. Says Paul Evanson, President, "We're no longer a local electric utility company. We're a national energy services enterprise."

Chapter 10
SUPERVALU

Management's job is to see the company not as it is . . . but as it can become.
—JOHN W. TEETS

Minneapolis-based SUPERVALU is one of the nation's leading food distribution and retail companies, posting more than $17 billion in annual sales in recent years. With a workforce of approximately 48,000, SUPERVALU serves 4,300 food stores in forty-eight states including 324 of its own retail food stores and an additional 700 Save A Lot stores.

Like most other large grocery wholesalers, SUPERVALU for many years focused on making money through anticipatory or forward buying. Simply put, that means buying large quantities of product cheaply or "on deal" and selling them later at premium or "nondeal" prices. While it was the accepted and traditional practice in the industry, anticipatory buying was in fact a highly inefficient practice, resulting in excessively large inventories, double handling costs, and idle supplier capacity. Furthermore, the complex accounting and pricing required to support these practices added cost and created considerable dissatisfaction and distrust between SUPERVALU and its retailers and suppliers.

George Chirtea, Vice President for Merchandising, says, "The old system worked fine as long as we could get the deep discount and the forward buy. But 30 percent of our gross profit was at risk. And we recognized that the new way vendors were going to market would eventually destroy the old system and our ability to make money. We couldn't stay in business without making some major changes."

The Consequences

SUPERVALU had long been concerned about changes occurring in the industry and the way business would be conducted in the future. Many of the industry's larger retail customers had opted for systems of self-distribution. And smaller retail customers, forced to bear higher costs, were consequently losing market share to more efficient operators. It was a lose-lose-lose situation. Wholesalers were being squeezed from both ends. Vendors were having trouble recognizing any added value from wholesalers. And retailers were looking for ways to sidestep them. In addition, with no information sharing and little or no mutual understanding of one another's cost drivers, high levels of distrust had arisen between wholesales and their suppliers and retailers.

Says Jim Hayes, SUPERVALU's Director of Procurement and Inventory Logistics, in assessing the situation in retrospect, "A major barrier was getting over the lack of trust and adversarial relationships that had built up over the years. We've learned the hard way that you have to be up-front, frank, and honest. The facts, the costs, all the relevant pieces of information have to be communicated accurately and openly."

A Time for Change

In 1993, SUPERVALU CEO Mike Wright launched a corporation-wide initiative to evaluate the company's strategy and direction and to determine the feasibility of redefining and revitalizing the wholesale business. A detailed analysis of SUPERVALU's wholesaling business had confirmed what many felt was self-evident: traditional wholesaling was in dire straits. But Wright also saw that emerging changes in the whole-

sale industry offered tremendous potential opportunities, if SUPER-
VALU could act quickly and decisively.

Wright acknowledges that the firm could have operated under the
status quo for several years. But he adds, "As the industry changed, we
would have had to do things to improve our profitability that could
have impacted negatively on customers."[1] Instead, Wright seized the opportunities of the day and redefined and revitalized SUPERVALU with
sweeping changes that included

- Completely reorganizing the corporate structure and developing
  new pricing and distribution systems
- Giving independent retailers more meaningful services to allow
  them to compete with chains
- Creating incentives for retailers to lower costs
- Developing a highly structured, mutually beneficial program for working and communicating more closely and effectively with suppliers

The ADVANTAGE Solution

In April 1995, Wright introduced SUPERVALU's ADVANTAGE program, redefining the company's role in the supply chain and affecting
dramatically and permanently the way food is distributed nationally.
Bernie Grutsch, Director of Buying Systems and Inventory Control for
the company, puts it in a very practical perspective: "Because of the thin
margins in our industry, the ability to purchase well is a tremendous advantage. Sourcing the product and managing the channel efficiently give
us a competitive advantage."

Commenting on the ADVANTAGE program, Wright said, "It's a
new business system, not a tweaking of what we have been doing all
these years. It is a fresh look at how we provide food to our customers."
Indeed, the ADVANTAGE program represented a sea change in SU-
PERVALU's approach to the entire supply chain with its goals of

- Buying and delivering goods at the least cost
- Rewarding efficient operating and delivery choices by retailers,
  increasing their cost advantage

- Offering retailer marketing programs and services to foster sustainable growth and stronger competitive positions
- Ensuring the mutual success of suppliers and retailers through improved or new logistics and support processes and collaborative relationships
- Offering consumers the best value for their dollar through restructured logistics and pricing

Through ADVANTAGE, SUPERVALU was determined to create sales, distribution, and administrative efficiencies for itself and its suppliers by

- Focusing on least-cost distribution methods that eliminated practices that added excess costs for both SUPERVALU and the manufacturer
- Changing to activity-based sell (ABS) pricing
- Offering menu pricing, which reflected the efficiencies SUPERVALU could achieve by working collaboratively with suppliers
- Developing new product flow options that would leverage SUPERVALU's distribution network

Least-Cost Distribution

The goal of least-cost distribution is to eliminate excessive handling of goods and to reduce inventory at every step in the chain, ultimately achieving the lowest landed cost for the retailer. In order to realize this goal, SUPERVALU created a new multitiered distribution system designed to reduce overall distribution and logistics costs, including inventory, handling, and transportation expenses, within both SUPERVALU's and the suppliers' distribution operations.

The implementation of the system included development of three regional or "upstream" distribution centers to support existing or "downstream" facilities. These upstream distribution centers have three essential features:

1. A replenishment crossdock designed to meet replenishment requirements for downstream locations, with the potential for direct store delivery
2. Consolidation of slow-moving grocery items for downstream distribution centers
3. Consolidation of the previously separate general merchandise and health, beauty, and cosmetics lines

In order to take the fullest advantage of this new multitiered distribution system, SUPERVALU also developed a sophisticated flow-path planning capability that takes into account vendor pricing opportunities, plant locations, vendor distribution center locations, and product availability, to determine the least-cost path for delivering the goods to their intended destination. A more detailed discussion of this leveraging of information technology appears later in this chapter.

Activity-Based Sell Pricing

Probably the most visible change made under the ADVANTAGE program was the adoption of ABS pricing. ABS has four basic goals:

1. To change from subsidy-based pricing, SUPERVALU's traditional method, to a cost-to-serve-based system
2. To reward retailers for efficient operations and delivery choices through further cost advantages
3. To allow SUPERVALU to maintain acceptable gross profit levels
4. To support supplier goals by passing through all allowances

Bernie Grutsch, SUPERVALU's Director of Buying Systems and Inventory Control, explains ABS pricing in no-nonsense terms: "With ABS pricing, we make our margin in fees. In the old system, we'd make a huge margin one time and nothing the next, which really created mistrust among vendors and retailers because our margins were kept secret.

"The idea of ABS is to sell at cost and to charge fees for our services. It's a pure system. Regardless of what incentives the manufacturer gives

The Cost-to-Serve Mentality

The transition to the cost-to-serve mentality at SUPERVALU was a major departure from traditional practice. Instead of being inconsistent and undisclosed, SUPERVALU's margins are now preset: the cost to serve, an activity-costing (accounting) model that determines the cost of providing products and services to each retail customer based on that customer's activity level. In 1995, SUPERVALU conducted a test of the ABS model with retailers in its Denver market. In aggregate, the total of all store groups realized a decrease in landed cost from the old to the new model.

Exhibit A presents a cost comparison between the old and new systems for a single item. As shown, ABS attempts to separate the cost of product from the cost to serve the retailer. Dead net sell is determined by subtracting forward buy, performance allowances, cash discounts, vendor rebates, and net backhaul from the average inventory cost. Cost-to-serve fees include operating fees as well as freight fees.

In this example, the ABS landed cost is lower than the old cost in spite of increased fees. Although this example resulted in a lower landed cost to the retailer, the ABS landed cost can be higher than, lower than, or equal to the old cost. Under any scenario, however, it will reflect the cost SUPERVALU incurs to serve the retailer.

Denver retailers reacted positively to the ABS pilot program. Retailers were able to see exactly what areas were driving their expenses and could therefore manage their expenses more effectively to reduce the landed cost of goods.

Exhibit A   Cost Comparison of SUPERVALU Pricing Systems

	Old Pricing System	*Activity-Based Sell*
List price	$25.00	$23.25
Less: Manufacturer's allowances and rebates	1.25	2.00
Net price	23.75	21.25
Plus: Operating fee	.50	2.00
Freight	.40	.40
Total Cost	$24.65	$23.65

us—better backhaul, home office rebates, whatever—we pass the savings on through to the retailer. It says to the vendor: regardless of how you lower the price, we'll pass it through."

Grutsch admits that getting all the players on board with ABS pricing will take some time and effort, but he is convinced it's worth it. "So much of the early resistance has been old-culture thinking, which says, 'If we can get some money out of doing this or that, let's split it.' The challenge is getting people to recognize the benefits of putting the cost advantage back into the channel."

Menu Pricing

To achieve SUPERVALU's goal of being the low-cost provider, the company asked its supplier partners to offer menu pricing, which reflected efficiencies that create cost savings for suppliers, such as Electronic Data Interchange (EDI), advance orders, full pallets versus layers versus cases, and plant pickup.

SUPERVALU views meaningful menu pricing as a logical unbundling of these various services that allows the efficiencies of each to be accurately calculated and creates incentives for these services to be provided. The benefits of these efficiencies are in turn passed along to the grocery stores. This is in line with SUPERVALU's long-term objective "to reflect and pass through efficiencies of the new business systems to retailers."

SUPERVALU developed its Vendor Benefits Program as an umbrella system for categorizing and evaluating the three major areas for manufacturer cost savings: fully integrated EDI, more efficient buying, and improved distribution. To demonstrate the savings potential, SUPERVALU created a fictitious prototype company that was actually a composite of its five top vendors. At the highest level of output, the total overall savings resulting from applying the ADVANTAGE model amounted to $6.3 million, or approximately $0.38 per case. In an industry where a few cents per case can provide a competitive edge, such savings are significant.

How these numbers were achieved can be better understood by looking at each of the three major areas of manufacturer cost savings:

1. *Fully integrated EDI* accounts for approximately 20 percent of the total savings opportunities. With EDI, the time a manufacturer spends on processing a purchase order or a change order is greatly reduced. There are fewer customer service interactions and sales calls. The cost to generate an invoice is reduced from as much as twenty-five dollars per invoice to approximately three dollars per invoice, and the cost to process a payment to SUPERVALU is also lowered.

2. *More efficient buying* resulted in approximately 20 percent of the total savings, which were realized by reducing the manufacturer's inventory (by eliminating inefficient forward buying), reducing the supplier's manufacturing costs, and reducing SUPERVALU's inventory.

3. *Improved distribution* generated the remaining approximately 60 percent of the total savings. Improved distribution techniques included picking up goods directly from the plant when possible, which eliminates inventory at the manufacturer's mixing warehouse and results in fresher product at retail and lower handling costs for unloading, putting away, and selecting at the mixing warehouses. There was also an increase in full-pallet ordering, which results in less handling and more efficient distribution.

Says Bernie Grutsch, "We want a menu price that reflects the flow-path efficiencies. More and more manufacturers are looking at this. The industry's catching on."

Supplier Cooperation and Trust

Jim Hayes, Director of Procurement and Inventory Logistics, acknowledges that overcoming the years of dissatisfaction and distrust on the part of the vendors was not an easy task. SUPERVALU decided that the best way to start would be with a pilot program with selected vendors. "We chose the vendors we wanted for the pilot based on the size of the opportunity, the volume, our past relationship, and, frankly, on the degree to which we thought they were likely to participate," Hayes says.

The vendor benefits model SUPERVALU had developed proved instrumental in opening the dialogue. Hayes adds, "We brought both parties to the table with cross-functional teams on both sides. We knew we had to overcome a basic lack of trust and our historic adversarial relationship. But we demonstrated early on that we were willing to share our information and that helped put the vendors at ease. We'd start out by stating our assumptions about a particular aspect of cost. Then the vendors would correct them and make them more accurate. At the end we'd worked together, shared information, and defined the opportunities in each of the target areas. We then assessed the degree of difficulty of achieving each and prioritized them by ease of realization. We presented recommendations to executive management on both sides and got the OK to go ahead and make the opportunities reality."

Bernie Grutsch was also closely involved in the pilot testing of the Vendor Benefits Program. "Early on there was a lot of skepticism," he says. "We wanted to show the vendors their quantifiable advantages in working with us. But it was difficult at first to get them to give us the numbers. I suspect they thought we wanted to keep part of the savings, rather than pass them along to retail. We were able to demonstrate that we shared the same goals through our pricing system. Teaching them ABS pricing was one of the first big forward steps. Once they saw that, they were much more likely to come to the table. All of the vendors who went through the model with us came back and offered really good marketing or participation programs."

The Technology Key: Flow-Path Planning

As SUPERVALU's vendors continued to expand the range of distribution choices and menu-pricing programs, the number of procurement options facing SUPERVALU became bewildering. To purchase any given product, SUPERVALU had to consider the cost implications of multiple factors:

- Where to source the products, from a mixing warehouse or the manufacturing plant
- Whether or not to use a crossdock, and if so, whether to break bulk there

- What quantity to order each time and how often, taking into consideration any minimum-order quantities and shelf-life constraints
- How much safety stock to hold for each stock-keeping-unit to support desired service levels
- Whether or not to backhaul

The situation was made even more complex by the fact that decisions had to be made uniquely for dozens of vendors, each supplying thousands of SKUs, to any number of SUPERVALU's thirty-one distribution centers. The decisions were further complicated by product shelf-life constraints, customer service considerations, and various cost tradeoffs. Exhibit 10.1 shows just some of the many cost elements that had to be considered.

The complexity of the problem argued for an extremely detailed cost model with a fairly high degree of precision. Yet it had to be easily understood by buyers and distribution center managers who would use it in day-to-day operations, or they would never accept it.

SUPERVALU's answer was to develop a highly advanced, automated flow-path planning capability that would balance the need for precision against the need for simplicity. No one thought the task would

Exhibit 10.1 Cost Elements Affecting Total Landed Cost

Cost Category	Major Cost Data or Component
Cost of goods	• Bracket pricing • Discounts for sourcing from vendor plants and bypassing mixing warehouses
Transportation	• Full-truck versus less-than-truck-load transportation costs • Backhaul allowance benefits • Destination freight pricing
Product handling	• Receiving and handling costs at distribution centers • Crossdock handling costs (with and without bulk-breaking operations)
Inventory	• Cycle stock • Safety stock required to support desired customer service

be easy. Skeptics thought it couldn't be done at all. Yet within five months of the start of the project, SUPERVALU's internal team, assisted by Booz·Allen consultants, had completed programming on a desktop PC model. They accomplished the monumental task because they set four clear objectives:

1. Focus only on the most critical cost elements.
2. Use mathematical shortcuts to get 90 percent of the answer with just 10 percent of the complexity.
3. Build the model using an in-house skunk works on a desktop PC.
4. Create model outputs that communicate the results in a simple and user-friendly fashion.

One decision that helped to keep the model quick and easy to use was to run it one vendor at a time, rather than trying to optimize product flows for all the vendors simultaneously. This greatly simplified the data requirements as well as shortening the run time. Another time-saving tradeoff was to avoid running the model in real time for dynamic purchasing decision making. Instead, the model analyzes different data "snapshots" to simulate changes in business such as seasonality and promotions.

Optimizing product flows for a given vendor begins with entering a considerable amount of data, including SKU details; vendor information like manufacturing locations, distribution policies, and pricing patterns; demand data; and cost information. The model then calculates and compares the costs across different flow paths. Using a proprietary heuristic, it determines the best combination of SKUs to be ordered from each source, as well as the order quantity and order frequency for each SKU, to minimize the total distribution costs while maintaining service requirements.

This approach to purchasing proved to be a major mindset change for SUPERVALU. Buyers, long accustomed to looking only at price, now had to focus on achieving the lowest total landed cost. Furthermore, they had to rely on a model that often produced answers that were counterintuitive. For example, conventional wisdom says that it is almost always better to have less inventory. Yet in some cases, the model determined that it was more cost-effective to buy directly from the plant, even when it meant significant increases in inventory.

The example in Exhibit 10.2 compares different distribution routes for sourcing dry beans. The tabular data offer the user an insight into why a certain flow path is best for a given product family. In this example, the lowest-cost alternative is to source the products directly from the plant, using the crossdock. The additional costs of crossdock handling and transportation are more than offset by the reduction in inventory-carrying costs that would be incurred without using the crossdock. Note, however, that although using the plant to crossdock to distribution center routing is best for dry beans, for another product—soup, for instance—it may be less costly to source both products directly from the plant, bypassing the crossdock.

Since the distribution cost model was built, it has already been used to analyze a number of large vendors. Identifying the opportunities was just the beginning of the process. Communicating, getting the appropriate buy-in, and implementing the "right answer" has been the more challenging step. Although the training process has been slow, SUPERVALU has been successful in capturing immediate savings by implementing the results of the model. SUPERVALU also uses the model to conduct sensitivity analysis and identify potential opportunities, then leverage that knowledge to negotiate new programs with the vendors.

SUPERVALU's flow-path model is an extremely successful example of how extended enterprise sourcing processes can be optimized to take total cost out of the system. Predicts SUPERVALU's George Chirtea, "We believe our PC-based flow-path planning program will save us eight to ten million dollars this year alone."

Conclusion

In the context of the overall Balanced Sourcing model presented in this book, SUPERVALU has made significant strides in developing many of the required capabilities. SUPERVALU has clearly focused on integrating the supply web, with suppliers as well as with its retail customers.

Exhibit 10.2 Example of Cost Comparison for Different Product Routes (Item Group: Dry Beans)

Cost Components	MW→DC Cost per Case	P→DC Cost per Case	P→DC Savings	P→XD→DC Cost per Case	P→XD→DC Savings	MW→XD→DC Cost per Case	MW→XD→DC Savings
Product cost	5.602	5.362	0.240	5.362	0.240	5.602	—
Inventory carrying cost	0.043	0.116	(0.073	0.087	(0.044)	0.043	—
Backhaul savings	0.047	—	(0.047)	—	(0.047)	0.047	—
DC handling	0.312	0.312	—	0.312	—	0.312	—
DC receiving	0.034	0.034	—	0.034	—	0.034	—
XD handling	—	—	—	0.013	(0.013)	0.013	(0.013)
Transportation cost	—	—	—	0.010	(0.010)	0.010	(0.010)
Total	5.943	5.823	0.120	5.817	0.126	5.966	(0.023)
Frequency (days)	1.655	73.232		37.355		0.319	

Note: MW = mixing warehouse; P = plant; DC = distribution center; XD = crossdock.

The ADVANTAGE program has fundamentally redefined how the wholesale grocery supply chain should operate and how companies along the chain will be rewarded.

SUPERVALU's ability to model costs accurately and effectively for ABS pricing has been critical in driving the change. Furthermore, through open and honest dialogue with its suppliers and retailers, SUPERVALU has built strong, sustainable relationships, regaining the trust and cooperation that was previously lacking. The whole ADVANTAGE business model employs a collaborative, win-win philosophy.

SUPERVALU, like other leading companies in our research, has also shown a willingness to invest in information technology—most notably with its development of the flow-path planning system to determine the least-cost method of distribution. These decision tools have helped the company to restructure its supply web and, by focusing on creating incentives, to reduce costs throughout the entire network.

George Chirtea acknowledges that SUPERVALU has changed dramatically in its approach to purchasing. He sums up the capabilities that SUPERVALU has developed to allow it to overcome the monumental challenges it faced just a few years ago and to continue to grow not only in purchasing capabilities but also in terms of its organizational culture. "Our people have a leading-edge mentality," he says. "They're smart, challenging, and interested in innovation. And the company as a whole has chutzpah. We have the courage to step out to the edge, the way Mike Wright did when he reorganized a $17 billion company in just six months. He did it right and that's why we've been able to maintain our position in the industry and to grow." He also adds, "We were willing to pay for change. And the cost was well worth it."

Chapter 11
Honda of America

A desk is a dangerous place from which to view the world.
—John Le Carré

At first glance, what Honda of America does to develop its products, sustain its supply base, and manage its purchasing function seems little different from what most other carmakers do. But the results that Honda achieves are often remarkably superior. In 1996, for example, Honda exported more automobiles from North America than any other manufacturer for the third straight year. That same year, the Honda Accord outsold all other cars among retail customers in the United States, setting an all-time sales record. And for the past eighteen years, the company has ranked number one in owner loyalty, according to R. L. Polk & Co.

So what makes Honda different? Dave Nelson, formerly Honda of America's Senior Vice President and the only non-Japanese on the company's board, answers simply: "Everything starts with our philosophy." And he's not just paying lip service to some lacquered plaque on the wall. What he says is true: the basic philosophy on which Soichiro Honda founded the company more than forty years ago has survived and thrived, informing and guiding every decision and action at every level in the company.

Ask Larry Jutte, Plant Manager at Honda's Anna, Ohio, engine plant, who can quote the Honda philosophy chapter and verse: "How do we get better results? It all goes back to our basic philosophy. Focusing on the customer. Being creative. Respecting fresh ideas. Enjoying your work. Understanding that change is good."

Turning Philosophy into Action

For evidence of how deeply Honda's people have integrated the founder's philosophy, look no further than *Cornerstones,* the basic bible of purchasing at Honda. The entire first chapter is devoted to explaining the Honda philosophy and the remainder to translating the overall philosophy into workable ideas for the purchasing function.

The articulation of the Honda philosophy began in 1954 when Mr. Honda set forth his concept of the "challenging spirit" in the company principle: "Maintaining an international viewpoint, we are dedicated to supplying products of the highest efficiency yet at a reasonable price for worldwide customer satisfaction." Based on this principle, Honda pursues consistent customer satisfaction by developing a self-reliant presence in each of its major markets, localizing sales, production, development, and operations consistent with each location's customers, expectations, and abilities.

Although Honda localizes by understanding and blending into the surrounding environment's culture, the company's management policy remains the same regardless of location. As the *Cornerstones* document confirms, the backbone of the challenging spirit articulated by Mr. Honda is the company's respect for humanity, which is reinforced by the Honda management policy:

• Proceed always with ambition and youthfulness.
• Respect sound theory, develop fresh ideas, and make the most effective use of them.
• Enjoy your work and always brighten your working atmosphere.
• Strive constantly for a harmonious flow of work.
• Be ever mindful of the value of research and endeavor.

Philosophy of Threes

Two of the high-profile elements of the Honda philosophy come in sets of three: the Three Joys and the Three Realities.

The Three Joys. The philosophy is that each person who comes in contact with the company—customer, employee, or supplier—should enjoy the experience. Customers who purchase a Honda product should enjoy the satisfaction of ownership. The dealer who sells Honda products should enjoy the process of bringing satisfaction to the customer. Honda, which produces the product that brings joy to both the customer and the dealer, should derive equal joy from the production.

The Three Realities. Also often referred to by the Japanese phrase *sangen shugi,* the Three Realities are actual place, actual part, actual situation. This philosophy, simply stated, means "going to the actual spot" where the action is taking place, such as at the supplier's plant to address a quality problem. Being in touch with all the realities of the situation contributes to a more complete understanding and better decision making.

Such statements may sound too simplistic to the skeptical outsider, but Dave Nelson strongly defends their practical applicability: "Some people might think we're too philosophical. The practical side is that our philosophy is our long-range plan. We all know where we're going."

A closer look at Honda's purchasing function and its business practices provides a clear understanding of how the company and its people translate philosophical thinking into concrete action.

Achieving the Balance

Honda of America's approach to purchasing stacks up well when compared to our Balanced Sourcing model. All six capabilities—at varying degrees of development—have been incorporated into day-to-day purchasing practices. Three of the six, however, stand out as very highly developed: modeling total cost, building and sustaining supplier relationships, and leveraging supplier innovation.

An examination of how Honda has mastered these three capabilities shows clearly the company's philosophical underpinnings:

- The high expectations Honda sets for itself and its suppliers
- The willingness to apply whatever resources are necessary to get the job done
- The commitment to cooperation and collaboration
- The unrelenting attention to detail

Modeling Total Cost

Honda's attention to cost modeling starts with high expectations in cost management. Dave Nelson provides an interesting example: "Imagine someone saying to purchasing three years ago, 'We have to take 30 percent of the costs out of the 1998 Accord.' It did not seem possible."

Recalling how purchasing responded to the challenge by digging into the cost details, John Miller, Purchasing Senior Manager at Honda's East Liberty, Ohio, plant, explains: "We determined the selling price up-front. Then we deducted our profit, and the result was what the cost should be. Then we broke out all those costs by component—chassis, engine, and so on—and set targets for each area and each part. We cut up the pie and then dissected each of the pieces."

Despite the intense focus on cost, John Cope, Purchasing Senior Manager at the Marysville, Ohio, plant, is careful to emphasize Honda's overarching customer satisfaction philosophy: "We build a quality car so we can maintain high levels of customer loyalty as well as good resale value. So when we talk about cost reductions, we don't mean just lopping 30 percent off the top. We knew that to add the features we wanted in the 1998 model and to reach our goal of keeping the price about the same, we had to add value, not inflate the price of the car."

Consistent with setting such high expectations, Honda's meticulously detailed cost-modeling process demands discipline and rigor from both the company's purchasing staff and its suppliers. Says Miller, "We actually take the time to break down all the cost components ourselves."

"We want to know what the suppliers' cost structure should be," says Charles Baker, Chief Engineer for Honda Research and Development Americas. "We analyze their manufacturing processes to determine what their cost is so we can estimate what our cost should be. Sometimes we understand the vendors' cost structure even better than they do. Then we can calculate what a world-class supplier's cost would be and that's our target."

Honda's philosophy of frank, open communication, cooperation, and collaboration with suppliers extends even to sharing cost-modeling data. "We show our suppliers our logic in coming up with the cost, and they show us theirs," says Miller. The cooperative approach ensures that targets are achievable—and world-class. According to Rick Mayo, Purchasing Manager at Marysville, "The initial cost gives us a place to start negotiating the factors that contribute to cost. We have an idea of how it's got to be done, but the supplier may have a new or unique technology we don't know about."

If cost negotiations stagnate, Honda will go so far as to send in its engineers to help the supplier find a way to meet the cost target and yet maintain acceptable margins. And what if Honda's target is off the mark? "We'll change it," says Dave Nelson. "The worst thing we could do would be not to admit a mistake."

Honda's cost-modeling process extends well beyond simply determining the cost of a part or component. It's an integrated process that takes into consideration every factor that contributes to the total cost. Rick Mayo explains: "We know all the components of cost. In the past, sales, manufacturing, purchasing, and design didn't work all that closely together. But we've learned over time that to keep the customer our central focus, all areas must be closely coordinated."

According to Rick Mayo, Honda's meticulous cost-modeling process, with its broad-based perspective, stems directly from the company's philosophy of *sangen shugi*—the actual place, the actual part, the actual situation. "It's another thing that makes our purchasing function unique. We're located on the plant sites and in touch with manufacturing every day. We see the problems. We understand the issues. We know what the cost implications are."

"If we're going to make a change in a car, we have to go into the plant and get them to sign off on it," adds John Miller. "If we didn't, we might think we could save a million dollars on parts costs and then end up with two million in downtime for manufacturing."

Honda has been able to develop its methodical, precise cost-modeling capability over time in large part because of its willingness to apply the resources required to get the job done right. Early on, Honda's central "cost research" group—two dozen or so buyers with specialized commodity expertise—would work in collaboration with their suppliers to develop sophisticated cost models. Over the past decade, that expertise has been translated into cost tables that practically anyone can use to quickly and easily identify the key cost elements of a part. Now, rather than being a specialized individual skill, cost modeling has evolved into an organizational capability deployed throughout the company.

Building and Sustaining Supplier Relationships

Honda of America has developed a network of more than 400 supplier companies throughout North America, including 180 in Ohio alone. True to Honda's philosophy of "purchase where you produce," these companies supply more than 80 percent of the parts and materials for the automobiles, motorcycles, engines, and components the company manufactures. And Honda is intent on making sure that every supplier is totally in sync with the company's philosophy.

Ironically, many of Honda's supplier development programs and activities—supplier awards programs or supplier incentives, for example—appear very similar to those found at most other automobile manufacturers. But former Senior Vice President Dave Nelson says the difference is in how much time, money, and effort Honda invests in building and sustaining its supplier relationships. "When we select suppliers, we expect to be with them for years," he says. "Other companies don't put the appropriate amount of resources against supplier development, so their programs aren't as well received. To score big with suppliers you have to win their hearts."

And scoring big is precisely what Honda aims for in its supplier development program. Witness the high expectations it sets for productivity improvement. "When we go in to help a supplier, we set an overall goal of 100 percent improvement in productivity—parts per worker per hour," explains Nelson. That "help" comes in the form of a thoroughly charted thirteen-week program designed and led by Honda staff members.

"We first try to identify a way to make a big impact," Nelson continues, "like doing a major cleanup, buying lights, putting in special floor mats, whatever it takes." (This, of course, is a natural extension of the philosophical tenet of "brightening the workplace.") "The supplier's associates start to see improvements right away. In almost every case, without prompting, everyone in the factory starts asking, 'When are you going to start improving my area?' They call it Honda-land. And everyone's smiling."

Nelson says that the thirteen-week program also focuses on involving the suppliers' associates directly in the process. "We try to take some of their first ideas and put them into place immediately, so they see them in action right away. Then they start trying to make the program a success because it's their program."

In one example of supplier development, Honda applied its BP process[1] at Tower Automotive, an important supplier of stamped parts and welded assemblies. Honda helped Tower redesign the work cell for making a B pillar, the stamped metal part between the front and back doors connecting the roof to the floor pan. Honda proposed using fixed-position welding stations, with simple pick-and-place robots moving the parts between stations, rather than having a sophisticated welding robot move around the part. The new cell design doubled production output from 63 to 125 parts per hour. And because the fixed position of the welding gun reduced wear and tear on the welding tips, their useful life was extended from 50,000 to 250,000 welds.[2]

Consistent with Honda's attention to detail and its focus on performance measurement, it uses a comprehensive program evaluation at the end of such efforts. "We always like to collect data," says Nelson. "We use them to set new goals and measure future success. Early on in supplier relationships, we can get 100 percent productivity improvements. But even in the more difficult projects, we've found we can get at least 50 percent. When you think about it, 50 percent improvement is excellent."

The BP development process reflects Honda's methodical, institutionalized approach to continuously improving its suppliers. But the company also demonstrates a ready willingness to commit significant resources toward ad hoc problem solving when needed.

Larry Jutte, the Anna, Ohio, Plant Manager, makes a homespun analogy to illustrate Honda's commitment to supplier development. "If there's the possibility of a severe issue, we'll dispatch any resource to help a supplier in any way we can. It's almost like the farming communities around here. If a barn burns down the whole community comes together. No one asks, 'Will you pay me or feed me?' Everyone just comes together. That's the way we work. We never have discussions about how we'll get paid back. It simply never comes up in discussion."

For example, one well-qualified supplier unexpectedly started to have quality and delivery problems. Honda dispatched an inside expert to assess the situation. The problem? To meet Honda's parts requirement, the supplier had been forced to nearly double its workforce over a very short time frame. Unfortunately, the supplier lacked the advanced management capabilities required for the larger operation. In response, Honda physically relocated four staff members to live and work with the supplier for ten months to help the supplier restructure and build the company's capability to meet Honda's need.

Dave Nelson is quick to point out that even though the cost to Honda was substantial, the company's motives for helping this supplier were hardly altruistic. "Of course we didn't charge him for what we did. But it was also self-serving. There was plenty of benefit to be gained on both sides by making sure we kept this supplier for the long term." Suppliers see and appreciate the long-term commitment demonstrated by Honda, which increases their willingness to make investments for Honda.

Honda's approach to building and sustaining supplier relationships extends well beyond productivity improvement programs and on-the-spot problem solving. A cooperative, collaborative relationship, by definition, is a two-way street requiring clearly expressed and understood expectations, performance measurement, attention to detail, and ongoing communication.

Larry Jutte illustrates with another homespun analogy: "Once suppliers are part of the family, discussions are open and honest about expectations for the relationship. For example, if I only talk to my son or daughter once a year about being good, I won't get a good response. But constant communication and feedback ensure that my children are taking the right course.

"It's the same with suppliers. You can't just write a memo once a year. You must have ongoing communication with clear targets for productivity, delivery, and quality. We monitor these three very closely. Nothing is ambiguous. You can't work toward the same end if there's no clear definition of what we're working toward.

"My attitude with suppliers is 'Give me the opportunity to say you're doing good.' It's just as important to reward good performance as it is to recognize and correct poor performance. It's not an attitude of 'I'm watching over you because I don't trust you.' It's simply a matter of working together expediently. We get to our targets more quickly if we monitor our control points and discuss our performance openly."

Leveraging Supplier Innovation

To leverage the capabilities and technology of its suppliers in research and development programs, Honda has developed a process called Design In, which focuses directly on early supplier involvement. Honda will "invite" guest designers—as many as 100 at a time—from their outside supplier organizations to actually locate within Honda's facilities and work side by side with resident engineers, designers, and technologists in the very early stages of a new project.

Charles Baker believes that this process is critical to ensuring that Honda will successfully integrate the best thinking and the latest technology into its new products. He says, "Our focus on building cooperative relationships requires getting the outside designers' input at the very beginning of a project, while we're still in the planning phase for the vehicle. By involving these suppliers early on, we can pick up their latest technology to make sure we're integrating it into our vehicle."

On major strategic systems, where the technology is evolving and the cost implications are large, Honda develops technology road maps and shares them with suppliers. Says Baker, "We use the technology road map to show our critical suppliers the direction we're going in and to ask them to help us. We set high expectations for focused and targeted project management. And because our development schedule is very compressed, we expect suppliers to make their latest technology available to us and to keep up with us to get the final product to market." Reaffirming Honda's central focus on the customer, Baker says, "We're very much a product organization, focused on making the product better for the customers. We work best with suppliers who view product development as a strategic process—suppliers who can target and develop technology and apply it in sync with us."

Honda has also had great success in leveraging its suppliers in removing cost during new product development. The dramatic cost reduction goal for the 1998 Accord offers a good example of Honda's focus on collaboration in leveraging suppliers in innovation. Dave Nelson recalls, "The first thing we did was compile a big list of every possible way we could remove costs from the 1998 Accord; most of them, in fact, came from our suppliers' work with purchasing and engineering. We studied each idea, prioritized them according to their likelihood of success, and then just started focusing our work on developing them."

Most of the cost-cutting efforts centered around the design aspects of the new model. Suppliers played a major role here too. "We took competitors' cars apart," says John Miller, "and then asked our suppliers to tell us about their components and parts: what's better, what's worse, what's costly, what's not. We did this in the U.S. and in Japan over the span of two years."

By the time the 1994 model hit the market, Honda had already determined what the 1998 model was going to be, its cost, and its price. Says Nelson, "Since the front end of the process took place about two and a half years before product launch, about 10 percent of these savings on the 1998 Accord splashed over into the 1996 Civic. And it showed in our profitability."

Honda's success in setting high expectations for its suppliers and then working cooperatively to help the suppliers meet them has earned the company's purchasing function national respect and recognition. Says *Purchasing Magazine:* "Kudos to Honda for its supplier development! Together purchasing and its suppliers work to reduce costs, improve quality, and develop technology—a system that has earned Honda the Medal of Professional Excellence."

Investing in People

It's true that Honda has developed the full set of the six Balanced Sourcing capabilities—three to quite advanced levels. But the fact remains that the nature of what Honda does in terms of cost modeling, supplier development, and leveraging supplier innovation really doesn't differ greatly from what other successful companies do. So why does Honda get better results?

The first answer on any Honda executive's list of "whys" would probably be "people." But is it reasonable to assume that Honda gets the best of the available crop of associates and all other companies settle for the rest? A more rational explanation is that Honda's people are no more exceptional than other companies'; Honda simply expects more from them. And it invests in them to make sure that they perform to its high expectations. "To move up in this company," says John Miller, "you're expected to have well-rounded knowledge and experience. And Honda is good at rounding people out. They don't always keep you in an area where you're an expert. They want you to be challenged. A little uncomfortable. So you'll have to stretch to reach even higher levels of performance."

Respect for the individual and a de-emphasis on hierarchical differences among Honda workers—everyone from the executive suite to the production line wears identical white uniforms, parks in the same parking lots, and eats in the same cafeterias—also contribute to a highly motivated, involved workforce. "I'm given a lot of respect every day at Honda," says Elizabeth Geboy, who works at the East Liberty (Ohio) Auto Plant. "I'm listened to when I give a suggestion or an idea. That's the basis for respect."

Larry Jutte cites Honda's atmosphere of open communication as one of the primary reasons that every individual has the confidence to step forward and contribute. "Anybody can make a suggestion about changing anything. There's a strong undercurrent of making continuous improvement."

According to Darrell Hoy of the East Liberty Auto Plant, "Associates who work on the line every day are the experts in how we build our products. It's rewarding to see an idea implemented by the associate on the line and watch it have a very big impact in terms of reducing costs or improving quality."

But Larry Jutte points out that there's another side to contributing as an individual: "You really can't take sole ownership of an idea you had or protect something you did. You have to stay open to improvements on your own ideas too to bring out the best and build total team ownership. But it's still our people who bring forth some of our best new ideas. That's why we talk to them, listen to them, and funnel their ideas into improving equipment, processes, and systems."

Honda also invests its resources in making sure its people get the training and development opportunities they need to succeed, as it did with its initial "investment" of fifty seasoned experts who were sent from Japan to the United States to teach, advise, consult, and transfer their knowledge and skills to their American counterparts. Since Honda of America has developed its own cadre of experts, most of the original Japanese associates have returned to Japan or other Honda locations throughout the world.

And the company guards its investment in people closely. There's never been a layoff in the history of Honda of America.

Even staff who have chosen to leave Honda for another employer are highly valued. For example, those who have left the purchasing function are referred to as Honda "purchasing alumni" and efforts are made to remain in communication with them, to sustain amicable relationships, and possibly even to bring them back if the time and circumstances are right.

Conclusion

Dave Nelson has good reason to take pride in Honda of America's superior performance and is justifiably optimistic about the company's future. He's more guarded, however, in his assessment of other American companies' willingness and resolve to set aggressive improvement targets and to commit the resources necessary to achieve them.

"Most of our large companies in North America have the same capability that Honda has to take costs out," he says. "With the hundreds of billions of dollars' worth of purchases we all make, there's easily 25 to 30 percent cost to be taken out. That ought to be an incentive for anyone to recognize the opportunity, grab hold of it, and integrate it into their company. Many simply don't have the heart for this sort of thing."

As Honda's purchasing guidebook, *Cornerstones,* confirms, the concepts and ideas expressed in purchasing's underlying philosophy may seem like basic common sense, but attention to the basics and the challenging spirit is what sets Honda apart from other companies. Certainly, as a philosophy-led company, Honda stands apart from most U.S.-based companies. But the company's ability to turn that philosophy into action is where the difference meets the bottom line. It's the high expectations Honda sets for itself and its suppliers, its willingness to apply whatever resources are necessary to get the job done, its commitment to cooperation and collaboration, and its unrelenting attention to detail that have put Honda and its purchasing function among the very few who have fully embraced and applied the Balanced Sourcing model.

Chapter 12
Cisco Systems

Nothing endures but change.
— HERACLITUS

If there's one place in the universe where life actually is lived in "Internet years," the high-tech equivalent of "dog years," it's Cisco Systems. Witness the Internetworking wunderkind's phenomenal metamorphosis from an ad hoc solution to an academic communications problem into a Wall Street darling in little more than a decade. Or the fact that a dollar invested in Cisco in 1990 was worth $100 in 1997. Or the company's matter-of-course commitment to deliver highly sophisticated, customized Internet software and hardware solutions in a matter of weeks, not months or years.

Cisco literally feeds on change and challenge. And it obviously thrives and grows on the diet. Investors are certainly satisfied with their return. Cisco customers are amazed—and pleased—at how fast the company responds to marketplace demands for the Internet technology needed to keep pace with electronic communications and commerce. And Cisco's suppliers and strategic partners, though they are often called on to meet seemingly impossible deadlines and high quality standards, apparently would much rather profit than switch.

But how does Cisco do it? It has pushed complex, high-tech products out the door at breathtaking speed; integrated a baker's dozen of high-tech companies worth billions of dollars in only three years with astonishing ease; and asserted without the slightest hint of irony, as Tom Fallon, Vice President and Plant Manager, did, that the $6.5 billion company (FY 1997) could eventually be at $15 billion or more.

A little bit of history and a look at how Cisco is rewriting the industry's book on supply chain management and manufacturing offer some answers and insight, and perhaps a model for those with the horsepower, the skill, and the stomach to cross eight lanes of traffic at full throttle without looking in the rearview mirror.

Cisco in the Fast Lane

Cisco Systems was founded in 1984 by a couple of academics, a husband-and-wife team of computer scientists from Stanford University, who were frustrated by their inability to communicate electronically across their different computer platforms. Their solution formed the cornerstone of what has become Cisco's pioneering efforts in "Internetworking." Simply put, Internetworking is the capability to connect incompatible computer networks through a "multiprotocol router"—a highly specialized microcomputer that can process, "package," and send electronic communications (e-mail or any other type of digital data) from one computer platform to another.

Cisco shipped its first routers in 1986 and consistently doubled revenues annually in the early entrepreneurial years. After passing the $1 billion mark in 1994, Cisco's growth rate slackened a bit, to about 75 percent per year. In 1997, Cisco was the third largest company on the NASDAQ index and made the Fortune 500 list for the first time, ranking among the top five in return on revenues and return on assets. Only Microsoft and Intel matched that accomplishment.

Fortune called Cisco "one of the hottest stocks of the decade." The *New York Times* concurred, describing Cisco as the "leading maker of the networking gear that keeps the Internet running."

Cisco and How It Grew

For a very short while, the router business was enough to position Cisco at the forefront of Internet-solutions providers. But for the company to become the full-service provider it wanted to be, its executive leadership recognized that Cisco would have to do more than make and market routers. To expand its product offerings, it settled on a strategy of acquiring the technological capabilities and engineering expertise of compatible companies that could logically extend Cisco's product lines. In fiscal year 1998, Cisco will spend $800 million on research and development.

Acquisitions Made Easy

In August 1993, Cisco made its first acquisition: it purchased Crescendo Communications, a manufacturer of hubs—the devices that link small work groups in local networks—for $90 million. By the end of 1996, Cisco had acquired thirteen more companies, including Stratacom, a manufacturer of frame-relay devices and switches, with approximately $400 million in annual sales and 1,200 employees.

Although such acquisition strategies have proved problematic for others, Cisco has been able to integrate its acquired capabilities into its overall operations with minimal problems. Why? Because, according to Cisco, it primarily buys Silicon Valley firms, easily absorbing new products and people without the extraordinary hassles of relocating or managing remote companies. This, however, has not prevented Cisco from successfully integrating companies acquired outside the Valley.

Will the company's growth be sustainable? Look only to the company's 1996 annual report for what Cisco thinks about its future prospects: "While the past ten years have been marked by the extraordinary growth and proliferation of Internetworking around the world, the best is yet to come. The growth of the Internet and the evolution of the information age have created a market that will continue to expand rapidly. By any measure, networking is no longer the focus of a select few. From education to government, large organizations to small businesses to individual users, Internetworking technology is affecting everyone, everywhere."

Manufacturing Redefined

As Cisco continued along its path of rapid-paced success, a very tangible concern soon emerged: how could the company continue to expand its product offerings without investing extraordinary capital resources in more bricks and mortar? The solution was to rely more and more on external manufacturing supplier-partners to sustain the exponential growth in product complexity and market demand.

Says Linc Holland, Vice President, External Manufacturing and Logistics, of the company's continuing movement toward greater reliance on outside manufacturing partners, "It's the right solution for high technology. We shouldn't have a core competency in building [printed circuit] boards." Carl Redfield, Senior Vice President, Manufacturing and Logistics, concurs: "I want my people focusing on the intellectual portion, establishing the supply base, qualifying new suppliers and working with old suppliers, and developing better processes, not managing direct labor. We supply the intellect; they supply the labor."

Keeping Up with the Pace

Obviously, a company that moves at "Internet-year" speed requires a purchasing process that is flexible and dynamic. And that is precisely the description of purchasing at Cisco. Within a six-year period, purchasing has moved through four distinct phases of evolution, from a purely transactional approach to a much more closely integrated one.

But throughout the evolution of the way purchasing is executed, the basic purchasing strategy has remained essentially the same, reflecting Cisco's emphasis on partnering with value-added external suppliers. "We don't do make-or-buy decisions," says Pete Rukavina, Director of Supply Operations. "If we can buy it, we buy it." Tom Fallon adds, "If we can make it cheaper, we do. But even then, we look for suppliers who can match our costs. Strategically, we want to outsource."

Purchasing's Four Stages of Evolution

It's not unusual for a company's purchasing process to evolve as the company grows and refines its business strategies. But to go through four distinct stages of transformation in only six years seems extreme, until you remember that this is Cisco, where change is a cornerstone of the corporate culture. Something else noteworthy about Cisco purchasing's evolution is that the lessons learned are remembered and built upon in succeeding generations. As evolutionary theory would predict, Cisco has kept the best of what it has learned and developed new capabilities to adapt to its environment, albeit one it has created for itself.

Stage 1: Managing the Transactions

Cisco's first stage of purchasing transformation reflected the traditional, transactional approach—the "three bids in a cloud of dust" mindset. But such an arm's-length purchasing approach proved incompatible with the reality of Cisco's turn-on-a-dime, get-the-product-out-the-door culture. Because the company relies so heavily on outsourcing, suppliers have to be totally in sync with Cisco's goals and way of doing business. This requires a much tighter integration of the supply base, with both sides recognizing, and respecting, their mutual interdependence and shared commitment to one another's success.

"We engage our supply partners with the intent of a long-term relationship," says Tom Fallon. "Six years ago most of purchasing was done through competitive bidding, very transactionally oriented. But we've learned to be less transactional and more focused on building a strong, stable base of supply partners—companies that are compatible with our corporate culture and how we get our product to market."

Stage 2: Focusing on Cost

As Cisco developed that strong, stable supply base, the purchasing function moved into a second stage of evolution. To maintain solid supplier relationships, yet keep product development and manufacturing costs within acceptable boundaries, it began to look at the individual elements of its suppliers' cost structures in order to excise those that added little or no value to the transaction.

"As we matured, we went through a period where we became more focused on cost modeling," says Fallon. "We began detailing what people were actually charging us for, deciding what we wanted, and then dissecting the rest out, paying for only the services we want and only those we considered efficient." As an example, he cites technical sales support. "If we don't acquire the services, we cut them out. We do this especially for value-added suppliers like sheet metal assemblers, the kind who provide a lot of services."

This approach signaled a step in the right direction toward the Balanced Sourcing model. But as described in detail in Chapter Three, identifying the elements of cost is only the beginning of advanced modeling capabilities. Thoroughly understanding the drivers of the cost creates the most value. And as Cisco moved closer to this type of understanding, purchasing developed a much deeper understanding of the risk—and its associated cost—that suppliers were being asked to shoulder in partnering with Cisco. This is especially true when new products are constantly being developed and introduced, when forecasts are highly unreliable, and when having excess production capacity is often the only safeguard against falling short of meeting customer demand.

Stage 3: Sharing Risk

Cisco's purchasing function quickly learned the art of balancing known risk against potential reward. And this led to a shift in how it structured relationships with and set expectations for suppliers. With a 65 percent average gross margin on its products, a dramatic growth curve, and a short product life cycle, the profit implications to Cisco of a lost sale are huge. Because having the right parts and components at the right time is so critical to getting the product out quickly, Cisco recognized that sharing risks and rewards with the supply base was essential to ensure that it could meet its extremely aggressive product delivery goals.

"We understand risk and reward, and what we value," asserts Fallon. "And what we value most is time—the ability to execute new products and to change quickly. What's more important: perfect execution or driving down our suppliers' margins to the lowest possible level? We always say the value to us is in time and technology."

This is not to say that Cisco is oblivious to supplier margins. "We expect reasonable margins," says Fallon. "But we want our subcontractors to make a good return on assets. In some companies purchasing is very transactional, because suppliers don't know how long the relationships will last. But our suppliers know that we have the potential to grow rapidly, and they appreciate that. They also know we're going to protect them on the downside."

Concrete evidence of Cisco's broad commitment to protect its supplier relationships is found in what Mike Campi, Vice President, Global Supply Management, terms the willingness to "invest in its suppliers." When he speaks of this kind of investing, he doesn't mean that Cisco actually takes a financial position in the supplier company. He's referring to the fact that Cisco can use its ample cash assets to mitigate some of its suppliers' risks. "Our use of capital may be more forgiving than theirs," he says. "If ROA [return on assets] drives the financial reporting of our suppliers, maybe we'll establish very aggressive payment terms. That could give us a discount and help their cash flow at the same time. It takes the cost of capital out of their equation."

Stage 4: Transferring Knowledge

Sharing risk has become a key component in Cisco's approach to developing and sustaining good supplier relationships, one of Balanced Sourcing's essential capabilities. But Cisco pushes beyond the standard. "We've moved in purchasing now to a phase of knowledge and information technology transfer so we can add even more value," says Fallon. "We want our subcontractors to think like us and to use our tools without our having to shoulder the cost of acquiring people or capital assets."

Mike Campi further explains the how and why of Cisco's focus on transferring knowledge: "We stick closely with our selected suppliers to make sure they can fulfill our needs. Since there's no way they could develop all the necessary capabilities fast enough for us, we transfer intellectual capital, like electronic communication tools, so they can use our information. To get their capabilities up to pace, we're willing to make a real investment in human capital and information systems."

Tom Fallon says that over the life cycle of a product, the benefit of knowledge transfer in terms of cost, quality, and performance is readily apparent. In his words, "It's like intellectual property put into a package so suppliers can optimize their capital investment."

Balanced Sourcing at Cisco

The preceding short history of Cisco Systems and the tracing of the evolutionary path of purchasing have highlighted the emergence of the six Balanced Sourcing capabilities and the development of some to fairly sophisticated levels. The following discussion takes a more focused look at just how balanced the company's approach to purchasing has actually become.

Integrating the Supply Web

The fact that Cisco has maintained an extensive network of distributors comes as a surprise to many. Pete Rukavina explains that Cisco started out very distributor-oriented and that it's fairly unique in staying with distribution. Most companies, he says, phase out distributors near the billion-dollar level. Cisco's decision to stay with distribution has to do with the fact that it sells a wide variety of products built by many different subcontractors, but using many common components. Rather than manage the logistics of getting components and parts to the subcontractors, Cisco relies on a tight network of distributors with clearly defined roles.

"What we've done is to focus distributors on logistics and materials management," says Rukavina. "Think about it logistically. Distributors handle billions of dollars of parts and their ability to manage the transaction set and distribution is more efficient than if we tried to coordinate it with all the manufacturers and all the subcontractors."

Carl Redfield sees the three-way arrangement as an example of how Cisco has managed to integrate its supply network to everyone's advantage: "We're trying to reduce the handoffs in the supply chain. Our model allows Cisco, the distributors, and the subcontractors to all co-exist and not get paid until the product ships. It's a cost structure built around ROA. The quicker we get the final product out, the sooner we all get paid. The compensation has a return on assets built into it. The fewer assets employed, the faster the return moves through the chain. If a distributor supplies the material, it owns the material until the product ships. Having too many handoffs just adds unnecessary costs."

Linc Holland agrees: "I think using distributors was the right model. It's allowed us to execute to match the tremendous growth rates we've had. We're at the point now where we have a few sophisticated suppliers, the best in the world. Companies that can give us supply, flexibility, and price."

Building and Sustaining Supplier Relationships

The very nature of the way Cisco develops and manufactures its products demands excellent relationships with suppliers. Mike Campi acknowledges the pressure Cisco asserts on its suppliers: "I have a road map twenty-four months out. It's our blueprint. We want to know the suppliers who are qualified, those who can provide the technology we need, so I can execute against the business plan. We want terms and conditions that allow us to successfully meet customer needs. We have to ask for virtual lead times out of our partners, more efficiency in planning. They have to learn to live with inaccurate forecasts and deal with brutal lead times. We need supplier flexibility."

Because suppliers are expected to bear such a considerable burden and risk in the new product development process, Cisco pays particular attention to building a reasonable level of protection into the relationships. "At Cisco, there's a real ethical, moral support of suppliers," says Linc Holland. "We know we jerk our suppliers around from time to time and we appreciate the implications of that. So we do everything we can to stick with them longer than most companies would. If a supplier screws up, we say, 'Stuff happens.' If one product really goes south, we frantically look for another project to give the supplier so it's not too damaged. Many suppliers would say we're a good partner because of that."

Carl Redfield confirms the importance of Cisco's focus on knowledge transfer and risk sharing. "In our business the keys to survival are open and honest relationships with our suppliers. We share with suppliers all our knowledge regarding our business and they do they same." By doing so, he explains, Cisco and its suppliers "don't blow a project because we second-guess each other." He adds, "Many of our suppliers have profited greatly from their relationships with us, but they always know there could be a downside too." He maintains that in the vast majority of cases, however, Cisco's suppliers have "bet with us and won. They feel confident that if they work with us, share costs, and participate fully they can ride the life cycle of the product."

Despite its heavy emphasis on cooperation with suppliers, Cisco also tries to maintain the appropriate balance between cooperation and competitive pricing. "My concern," says Linc Holland, "is how to get competitive pricing and still have a cooperative relationship. I didn't want to have to establish a new relationship every time a new product came along." One solution to the cooperation-versus-competition dilemma revolves around the way Cisco has structured the relationship between itself, its parts distributors, and its manufacturing subcontractors. Although the distributors and subcontractors do not compete directly against each other, there is an overlap in what both groups supply to Cisco, and each would like to control as much of the value added as it can. Cisco uses this overlap to create an aggressive, yet healthy, price competition between suppliers and distributors. But because each group plays a unique role in Cisco's extended enterprise, distributors, which are centered around logistics, and subcontractors, which are focused on manufacturing, both feel that their relationships with Cisco are secure.

An outside observer might say that cooperation has not always worked to Cisco's advantage. And because Cisco's historical focus has always been on rapid product development and distribution, most of its purchasing management team would agree that the company has come away from supplier negotiations having "left money on the table."

"Of course we always ask suppliers to give us their best pricing, but we know there's probably someone out there who would give us better pricing," says Linc Holland. "In one instance, one trusted supplier was simply basing price on the previous year's history. So we reopened negotiations. We did benchmarks and found that the supplier wasn't competitive. When we told the supplier, we got a 20 percent reduction. I don't mind holding suppliers to world-class numbers, but I don't want to put them in a competitive bid situation every time either."

Leveraging Supplier Innovation

Consistent with the Balanced Sourcing model, Cisco puts a great deal of emphasis on getting its suppliers and external manufacturers involved very early in the new product development process. Linc Holland maintains that close collaboration, especially in high technology, is absolutely essential to controlling costs: "In our business, where pretty much all we're doing is final assembly and testing, there isn't much in the process we can change to pull the cost out. The key thing is to get the external manufacturer and our engineer in the same room early on. Sometimes we change the design to take cost out. Since the design guys don't worry about cost as much, I have to get manufacturing to the table very early so I can still deliver a product that can be manufactured at a competitive price."

Technology road maps are another tool Cisco uses to leverage its suppliers' innovation. "We share information and technology with our suppliers and they listen," says Tom Fallon. In periodic meetings with suppliers and subcontractors, Cisco typically will hold a technology road map session, "where we tell them where routing is moving or where switching is going and then encourage them to try to hammer out their own transformation to the new technology."

The road to innovation runs both ways. For example, at one point there was a worldwide shortage of memory chips. Suppliers had begun allocating specific quantities to their customers based on their previous year's usage. But with Cisco's growth rate, such a system certainly didn't mesh with the company's needs. Cisco approached a group of suppliers, explained on a technical level the modes Cisco was going to be using and what the memory requirements would be, and asked the suppliers to start thinking within those parameters. At the same time, Cisco also asked what technologies the suppliers were working on and expressed a willingness to shift direction, if that was what was required.

Says Fallon, "We wanted to know all the new and emerging technology; high-density flash was one of the emerging technologies at that time. We made arrangements for market share with several suppliers, so even in that allocated market we could encourage competition among them. As a result, we met our need for memory and quickly became the major user of the new technology."

The Future of Purchasing at Cisco

Not surprisingly, given its history, Cisco has focused on the Balanced Sourcing capabilities that directly feed into what Mike Campi calls the "raw execution engine": building and sustaining supplier relationships, leveraging supplier innovation, and integrating the supply web. But Campi also recognizes that to meet the ever-increasing demand for current products and to continue to aggressively expand its offerings—as well as to manage costs—Cisco must quickly improve its other capabilities as well. He says, "We've got to more effectively leverage other capabilities besides execution. Our customer focus won't change—delivering product fast. But we have to concentrate our efforts on other aspects of the supplier relationship as well. We have to keep our eye on execution, but we'll be looking much more closely at cost, globalization, supplier efficiency, and so on."

In the area of total-cost modeling, Campi says, "We need a better understanding of the cost drivers, particularly in contract manufacturing like printed circuit boards. We must understand what's behind direct cost, labor, and material markups. We need to know what suppliers need to be successful, and what we need to make margin."

Linc Holland puts a very pragmatic spin on Cisco's need to more fully develop its cost-modeling capability, especially in view of the company's extremely truncated product development time frames: "I can't wait until all the real costs are known to award the product contract to a supplier. I need the supplier early on in the product development process. Because I make my decision early, I need a good cost model to avoid having a supplier take advantage of me."

In the area of developing a global sourcing strategy, Cisco has only recently begun to seriously look at sourcing, manufacturing, and distribution capabilities beyond Silicon Valley. As Linc Holland quipped, "At Cisco, anything outside of San Jose is international. It's just the way we plan, control, and ship our product." But Holland also acknowledges that the company's increasing reliance on external manufacturing could lead to a more far-reaching sourcing strategy. And with the company's commitment to delivering complex, customized products literally within days of the order, the additional time it takes to fulfill orders outside the United States becomes a critical customer service factor. He says, "When total lead time on the entire order is only fourteen days, taking four days instead of two just to ship the order can have a significant impact on meeting a commitment to a customer."

Mike Campi appears confident that Cisco can build the full set of Balanced Sourcing skills with the same emphasis on speed that it puts on product development. And he thinks the key lies in more fully developing the skills and expertise of the company's purchasing professionals. His description of what needs to happen in the area of "developing our people" dovetails with the emergence of a more highly developed strategic sourcing capability. "We're still in our infancy in building people," he says. "The great news is that we have a very strong base of talent in the procurement area. It's a matter of taking the best of what we have and complementing it with skills that exist outside of Cisco. The future requires more emphasis on getting experts in key commodity areas.

"The current Silicon Valley focus is on business units, which forces people to be generalists. We want a vertical depth of knowledge in commodities so everyone understands that the core competencies for things like memory reside here. So the business units know that's where they go to get their needs satisfied.

"I distinguish between the buyer and the commodity expert. Over time the transactional stuff will be addressed by information systems. Commodities are driving the business relationship externally and the business decision internally. It's all about the ability to build a team with complementary skills. I want an organization where you can't distinguish the commodity teams from the engineering and execution elements. Engineers involving commodity guys. Asking questions like 'Who do we need to source with?' Searching for the most competitive way of making design decisions. Embedding commodity thinking deep inside the product development process.

"I want to know that when I benchmark, all the metrics will say I'm leveraging Cisco's procurement dollar better than anyone else in the industry."

Notes

Chapter One

1. Peter Drucker, *The Changing Face of the Executive* (London: Heinemann, 1982).

Chapter Two

1. Rainbow Chen of Booz·Allen's San Francisco office was instrumental in collecting and analyzing the survey results.

Chapter Four

1. Michael E. Porter, *Competitive Strategy: Techniques for Analyzing Industries and Competitors* (New York: Free Press, 1980).

Chapter Five

1. Jeffrey K. Liker, Rajan R. Kamath, S. Nazli Wasti, and Mitsuo Nagamachi, "Integrating Suppliers into Fast-Cycle Product Development," *Engineered in Japan: Japanese Technology-Management Practices,* chap. 7 (New York: Oxford University Press, 1995).
2. John McMillan, "Managing Suppliers: Incentive Systems in Japanese and U.S. Industry," *California Management Review* (Summer 1990), 38–55.
3. Kevin R. Fitzgerald, "Show Suppliers the Money!" *Purchasing Magazine* (Aug. 14, 1997), 40–47.

Chapter Six

1. Paul Anderson, Steve Griffiths, and Tim Laseter, "Strategic Sourcing: A Competitive Imperative," Booz·Allen & Hamilton Viewpoint (1993).
2. "The Extended Enterprise," *Purchasing* (Mar. 4, 1993).
3. Alex Taylor III, "The Auto Industry Meets the New Economy," *Fortune* (Sept. 5, 1994), 52–60.
4. Jeffrey R. Rayport and John J. Sviokla, "Exploiting the Virtual Value Chain," *Harvard Business Review* (Nov.–Dec. 1995), 75.
5. Marshall L. Fisher, "What Is the Right Supply Chain for Your Product?" *Harvard Business Review* (Mar.–Apr. 1997), 105–116.

Chapter Seven

1. Robin Cooper and W. Bruce Chew, "Control Tomorrow's Cost by Today's Design," *Harvard Business Review* (Jan.–Feb. 1996).
2. Lawrence M. Fisher, "How Hewlett-Packard Runs Its Printer Division," *Strategy & Business* (4th Quarter 1996), issue 5, 76–83.

Chapter Eight

1. United Nations, UNCTAD, Trade and Development Report, 1995.
2. Mark L. Clifford, Michael Shari, and Linda Himelstein, "Pangs of Conscience: Sweatshops Haunt U.S. Consumers," *Business Week* (July 29, 1996), 46.

Chapter Ten

1. *Progressive Grocer* (Jan. 1996).

Chapter Eleven

1. "BP" is internally described as "best practices" but formally stands for Best Position, Best Productivity, Best Product, Best Price, and Best Partner.
2. John Paul Macduffie and Susan Helper, "Creating Lean Suppliers: Diffusing Lean Production Through the Supply Chain," *California Management Review* (Summer 1997), 118–151.

The Author

Timothy M. Laseter is a vice president in the Operations Management Group of Booz·Allen & Hamilton Inc. He is one of the firm's leading practitioners and thought leaders addressing strategic issues in purchasing management. He has extensive experience with clients in the United States, Europe, and the Pacific Rim, covering a wide range of industries including aerospace, automotive, building products, consumer goods, communications, electronics, industrial equipment, natural resources, and textiles.

Mr. Laseter received his B.S. degree with high honors from the Georgia Institute of Technology in industrial management in 1980. In 1984 he received his M.B.A. degree from the Darden School at the University of Virginia, where he received the Faculty Award for Academic Excellence. He is currently pursuing a doctorate in operations management at the Darden School on a part-time basis. Mr. Laseter is a frequent contributor to *Strategy & Business* journal as well as *Purchasing* magazine.

Prior to joining Booz·Allen, Mr. Laseter was employed by Siecor Corporation, a manufacturer of fiber-optic cable for the communications industry. There, he advanced through a wide variety of manufacturing positions. Additionally, he is certified at the Fellow level by the American Production and Inventory Control Society and has been certified as a quality engineer by the American Society for Quality Control. Mr. Laseter was also a recipient of Booz·Allen & Hamilton's 1990 Professional Excellence Award.

Index

Booz·Allen & Hamilton

Booz·Allen & Hamilton is one of the world's leading international management and technology consulting firms, providing services in strategy, systems, operations, and technology to clients in more than seventy-five countries around the globe.

Founded in 1914, Booz·Allen & Hamilton pioneered the business of management consulting. Today, Booz·Allen has more than eight thousand employees in ninety offices on six continents and revenues of $1.4 billion. Its clients comprise a majority of the world's largest industrial and service corporations, as well as major institutions and government bodies around the world, including most U.S. federal departments and agencies.

Booz·Allen is a private corporation organized into two major business sectors: the Worldwide Commercial Business (WCB) and the Worldwide Technology Business (WTB). WCB clients are primarily major international corporations; WTB generally serves governmental clients both in the United States and abroad.

Booz·Allen helps senior management solve complex problems through its expertise in more than two dozen industries as well as information technology, operations management, and strategic leadership.

Consistent with its position as a business thought leader, Booz·Allen publishes the award-winning quarterly journal *Strategy & Business,* which reports on the latest developments in global management techniques, competitive tactics, and strategic thinking.

Booz·Allen & Hamilton is a founding cosponsor of the annual Global Business Book Awards. GBBA recognizes the most innovative contributions to business literature and promotes worldwide readership of business books.

For more information, please visit Booz·Allen's Web site at www.bah.com. Or contact the company at:

Booz·Allen & Hamilton
101 Park Ave.
New York, NY 10178
(212) 697-1900

This *Strategy & Business* book is an excellent business relationship-building tool. By giving this book to your clients, partners, and prospects, you can contribute to their knowledge in a business world where staying current is the only lasting competitive edge. Receive substantial quantity discounts when you place bulk orders. Let us personalize the books with your message.

For quantity discounts and customized orders, contact:

Bernadette Walter
Corporate Sales Manager
Jossey-Bass Publishers
350 Sansome Street
San Francisco, CA 94104–1342
phone: (415) 782–3122
fax: (415) 433–0499
e-mail: bwalter@jbp.com